INTERNET RICHES

INTERNET RICHES

THE SIMPLE MONEY-MAKING
SECRETS OF ONLINE MILLIONAIRES

SCOTT C. FOX

AMACOM AMERICAN MANAGEMENT ASSOCIATION

NEW YORK ▲ ATLANTA ▲ BRUSSELS ▲ CHICAGO ▲ MEXICO CITY
SAN FRANCISCO ▲ SHANGHAI ▲ TOKYO ▲ TORONTO ▲ WASHINGTON, D.C.

Special discounts on bulk quantities of AMACOM books are available to corporations, professional associations, and other organizations. For details, contact Special Sales Department, AMACOM, a division of American Management Association, 1601 Broadway, New York, NY 10019.
Tel.: 800-250-5308. Fax: 518-891-2372.
Website: www.amacombooks.org

This publication is designed to provide accurate and authoritative information in regard to the subject matter covered. It is sold with the understanding that the publisher is not engaged in rendering legal, accounting, or other professional service. If legal advice or other expert assistance is required, the services of a competent professional person should be sought.

Disclosure: Because of my years of work in the e-commerce business, I may have content, promotional, customer, consulting, or equity relationships with the companies mentioned in this book. I've tried hard to identify the best suppliers/vendors in each of these areas, but you must accept all liability and use your own independent judgment to evaluate their services and fit for your needs.

Library of Congress has catalogued the hardcover edition as follows:

Fox, Scott C.
  Internet riches : the simple money-making secrets of online millionaires / Scott C. Fox.
        p. cm.
  Includes index.
  ISBN 10: 0-8144-7356-3
  ISBN 13: 978-0-8144-7356-6
  1. New business enterprises. 2. Electronic commerce. 3. Internet. I. Title.

HD62.5.F695 2006
658.8'72—dc22

                                                                2006002361

Printing number
10 9 8 7 6

To my beautiful and talented wife,
Katherine, and my lovely daughters.
Your love helps make dreams come true.

To all those who dream of fulfilling
careers and financial freedom.
You are not alone and you deserve better.

CONTENTS

INTERNET RICHES

INTRODUCTION

WELCOME TO THE INTERNET
"GOLD RUSH," TAKE TWO!

CONTRARY TO popular wisdom and what the media tells you, the Internet is not "over." The years 2001–2004 were tough for Internet businesses, but the development of the digital economy is still only in the early innings of a nine-inning ball game.

Online sales are continuing to explode and could reach more than $300 billion in the United States alone by 2010.[1] This is more than 12 percent of overall retail U.S. sales from a new category of business that hardly existed ten years ago!

For entrepreneurs like you, numbers like this mean that new online business opportunities are actually increasing. That's because the Internet continues to change so many of the basic assumptions that you were taught about business as its technology gets easier to use and more widespread.

Whether you are a high school dropout or hold an advanced degree from a prestigious university, you are a product of the twentieth century's "industrial age" education system. This means that (like me) you were probably taught to see corporate employment as a more desirable path than taking the risks of starting your own business.

In fact, when surveyed, 58 percent of Americans say that they've dreamed of starting their own businesses, but almost half (49 percent) of them cite "insufficient financial resources" as their primary obstacle.[2]

My number-one "Internet Millionaire Secret" for you is that the Internet has significantly reduced the costs and even eliminated many of the risks of starting your own business. The arrival of e-business has changed the rules of business so dramatically that now is the best time in history for you to take charge of your life and start your own business.

You should read this book if you are one of the millions of people who want to:

▲ Change careers

▲ Exert more control over your career and lifestyle

▲ Experience the flexibility of being your own boss

▲ Explore the potential of working from home

▲ Pursue a creative business idea or two (or at least try to develop one)

Times Have Changed (in Your Favor!)

In the twentieth century, starting a business was risky and expensive, but the Internet has changed the equation. Unfortunately, the bad first impression left by the dot-com collapse of 2001 still dominates popular understanding, our education system, and media coverage of e-business. The opportunities to start profitable new e-businesses have never been better. Yet lately, when the media covers e-business at all, it's usually to scare you with stories about computer viruses or identity theft.

Think about how the Internet has continued to grow, improve, and penetrate your daily life in the years since the dot-bomb crash. Hasn't it made shopping more efficient, keeping in touch with friends easier through e-mail and instant messaging, and probably improved the productivity of the business where you work, too?

The result of this disconnect between popular perception of the Internet and its daily reality is that today few people realize that e-business now offers greater potential rewards with lower risks than any type of business at any time in history. Additionally, because the Internet directly reaches a larger audience of consumers than any medium in history, any e-business has the chance to generate enormous profits if it can convert just a small fraction of the online audience into customers.

Internet Riches is the first "how to" book to introduce you to e-business in an easy-to-understand way, complete with dozens of specific examples and interviews with "regular people" who have accomplished their dreams by building online businesses.

"How Can I Make Money from the Internet?"

There are millions of people like you asking this question today. They want more out of their careers and are intrigued by the self-employment opportunities offered by the Internet, but they don't know where to go for answers.

I wrote this book to help *you* answer that question. In it, I share with you the specific strategies that I've developed in order to help you improve your life and career. You'll see that the detailed, practical, current advice in this book—from me and dozens of top Web entrepreneurs—offers proven secrets of Internet success that can help you "reboot" your life and career. As a result, once you have read *Internet Riches,* you will be one of the few who has a personal action plan for Internet millionaire success.

I also promise that this book can help you find and start your own e-business, even if you don't know much about technology.

Yes, that's right, *no technology expertise required.* One of the principal reasons I wrote this book was to help the nontechnical audience (maybe that's you?) understand that the Internet has advanced to the point where it is more user-friendly than ever. With all the new web-based tools and services available today, even a nontechnical user can set up a worldwide Internet e-business for less than $25! In this book, I'll show you how.

Who Is Scott Fox?

I'm a highly successful e-business veteran and director of The Liminal Institute (www.LiminalInstitute.org), a California-based think tank dedicated to promotion of entrepreneurship. Based on my own success in e-business, I founded this organization because I believe that the secrets of prosperity offered by the new generation of Internet businesses deserve to be shared.

As a graduate student at Stanford University in the early 1990s, I was introduced to the Internet earlier than most people. In the subsequent decade, I've consistently been "ahead of the curve" and have gained a deep understanding of the great opportunities that the post-industrial economy is offering to today's generation of workers. With this book, I'm inviting you to share in my vision should you choose to open and operate an e-business.

E-business today offers average folks everywhere the biggest profit and personal growth opportunities of our lifetimes. I know this is true because of the many successful e-businesses I have helped build, from my wife's SweaterBabe.com venture to the e-retailing phenomenon loved by young brides nationwide (www.WeddingChannel.com) to the multimillion-dollar online businesses of celebrities like Bill O'Reilly (www. BillOReilly.com).

My expertise has previously only been available to top celebrities and venture capital-backed startups, but now I'm making the success I've enjoyed available to you through this book. Although it took me more than ten years to develop my techniques for e-business success, by reading this book you'll soon see that today, you can start a new online business and begin changing your life in just hours!

Release Your "Inner Entrepreneur"

I was born an entrepreneur but didn't realize it until well into my career. Our society, our education system, and my friends and family all consistently pushed me toward "steady jobs" rather than encouraging my dreams of personal and financial freedom. Yet when I landed prestigious and lucrative corporate jobs, I couldn't understand why I was unhappy.

Perhaps like you, I eventually realized that I had been fighting my "inner entrepreneur" for years. Again probably like you, it was fear that had been preventing me from pursuing the entrepreneurship that is in my blood. I had been taught my whole life that starting a business was a risky, dangerous financial decision that should best be avoided in favor of "safe" corporate employment.

Then, in 1991, I decided to change my life and pursue my own dreams, not those of big corporations. Today, I refer to myself as a "graduate of corporate America" instead of its employee. If you chose to buy this book, you're probably ready to release your inner entrepreneur, too. This book is dedicated to helping brave entrepreneurs like you to learn how to use my Internet Millionaire Secrets to build your own million-dollar business with minimal risk.

The E-Business Trend Is Your Friend

Since 1994 I have worked with dozens of startup e-commerce companies that have gone on to generate many millions of dollars in sales in a variety of industries. Every year I have found that it has gotten easier and cheaper to start an e-business: Online audiences have gotten larger and more familiar with online shopping. Online advertising and sales revenues have increased. Website-building tools have become cheaper and easier to use. Technical and content expertise has become more widely available and cheaper. And the software that runs websites has gotten more reliable, faster, cheaper, and more powerful, too.

In 1996, a company would have raised millions of dollars in venture capital to get started; today, that that same company can often bootstrap its way to success with minimal investment from its founders, especially if they follow the guidance in this book.

For example, in 1996 I founded my first company, which was a pioneer in e-commerce that targeted young music consumers. I started with six figures of my own money, added to that funding from supportive friends and family, and even received strategic investment from Intel Corporation and venture capital from a Seattle-based venture firm.

By contrast, in 2005 I partnered with a celebrity on a startup venture planning to offer interactive entertainment and online sales that were much more sophisticated than was even possible ten years ago. The amazing difference is that despite the 2005 venture being a much bigger company with a much broader reach and more sophisticated offerings than my first startup, the celebrity venture raised zero outside capital before launch! The partners each contributed a small amount for expenses, but many sophisticated technical, marketing, and merchandise services are now available purely on a pay-as-you-go basis. In addition, third-party providers are now so savvy and familiar with the profit potential of e-business that they offered services in exchange for participation.

This trend has the potential to benefit everyone who has ever wanted to be his (or her) own boss while reinforcing America's greatest competitive advantage: *entrepreneurship*.

YOUR HOBBIES CAN MAKE YOU RICH

By examining your local markets, the people you know, the inefficiencies you can identify in your day-to-day life, and your own special interests, I'll help you develop your own innovative e-business ideas. I'll show you that by examining your daily life, you have a built-in business development laboratory that this book will train you to exploit using the Internet. I can't guarantee you business success, but I know that this book can help you realize that the risks of entrepreneurship have been so greatly reduced by the Internet that you owe it to yourself and to your family to give e-business a shot.

Starting a business is still not easy, but the Internet does make it easier than ever before. Short of writing you a big check or somehow arranging for you to win the lottery, this is the best I can offer you: a wake-up call to participate in the e-business revolution!

SPECIFIC, PRACTICAL STRATEGIES

Internet Riches offers you specific, current guidance on how you can take advantage of the most powerful set of business-building tools ever available. It's not about get-rich-quick schemes or vague strategies for "envisioning abundance" or "positive thinking." To take advantage of these revolutionary business opportunities, you need to bring your own creativity and dedication to the party. Few businesses, online or offline, make it big overnight. You'll see from the many interviews with successful e-business entrepreneurs in this book that even with the Internet there's still "no such thing as a free lunch." But the Internet does offer you greater flexibility to choose your target markets, work hours, style, products and services, and resulting lifestyle than was ever available in corporate America. You'll see from the many successful e-business entrepreneurs profiled in this book that even moderate success at building an e-business can help you live a "millionaire lifestyle" on your own terms.

Defining a "Millionaire E-Business"

Here are three short examples of how you can build a million-dollar e-business:

▲ Selling $100,000 worth of products per month online equals $1.2 million of gross sales per year—*instant million-dollar e-business!*

▲ Selling $35,000 of products per month online equals $420,000 of gross sales per year—which means in 2.38 years you'll gross $1 million.

▲ Selling $5,000 per month online equals $60,000 of gross sales per year, or almost seventeen years to gross $1 million. However, you're still making $60,000 per year, probably doing something you like, being your own boss, and perhaps not even leaving the house! That's a pretty great "worst case," isn't it?

The point that I'm trying to make is that this book's "Millionaire Secrets" are as much about empowering you to take control of your life as they are about specifically making a million dollars.

This book is full of real-world examples of mom-and-pop entrepreneurs who have successfully started businesses part-time or on the side while working traditional jobs. Although not all are now millionaires, all of them have used clever but often simple ideas, hard work, and dedication to *live more like millionaires* by creating exciting new e-businesses that are detailed here in *Internet Riches*. While many of them gross (or even net) more than $1 million a year, there are also many who "only" make $50,000, $150,000, or $500,000 each year from their Internet businesses. If you follow this book's guidance and add some inspiration and hard work of your own, a few thousand extra dollars per month is within your reach. Take a minute and think about how your life would change with an extra $5,000 per month in your pocket.

What's just as important is that these entrepreneurs don't measure their success simply in financial terms, because their lives have been positively changed by becoming self-empowered entrepreneurs. In fact, most of them don't even track the hours they work because they have succeeded in making money doing something that they love. They have attained "Internet riches," even if they don't actually gross a million dollars per year.

This is because a properly designed and marketed e-business takes less time than a traditional job, allows you "flextime" to work when and where you want, and allows you to be your own boss, too. On top of all those benefits, you'll find a huge boost in self-esteem by starting a successful business of your own.

The Internet offers you more job mobility, more flexibility, and greater opportunity to make big money from a global audience than our parents' generation ever would have dreamed possible. If you have chosen to read this, then you are the target market for this information. The pool of opportunity is big and there's room for everyone!

What This Book Will Do for You

I wrote this book because I got tired of the vague or unrealistic "get rich" theories in most books. Instead, this book is full of practical steps you can take to replicate the real-life experiences of successful e-business entrepreneurs from all walks of life. In this book I'm going to share with you three categories of information:

1. The benefits of my more than a decade of experience at the cutting edge of the Internet revolution

2. The results of original, never-before-published research conducted for this book, specifically examining the critical success factors for e-commerce entrepreneurism

3. Interviews with top e-commerce entrepreneurs from all walks of life, with analysis of their real-life success stories. You'll learn about:

   ▲ How Matt makes six figures a year selling top-quality products without owning any inventory or even leaving his house in Spartanburg, South Carolina (TrafficMatt.com)

   ▲ How Genevieve, a recent college graduate, has built a nationwide company by simply creating a website that matches parents and babysitters (Sittercity.com)

   ▲ Sid, a former grocery-store meat department manager in a small Midwestern town, who built a major international web-based business around his favorite game: shooting pool (Seyberts.com)

▲ How a literary review webzine and blog (Bookslut.com) helped Jessa quit the job she hated to make a living instead by reading and writing about books she loves

▲ How a baby-boomer artist couple from rural Minnesota uses the Internet to sell their handmade bath toys to states and countries they've never even visited (Bathboats.com)

▲ How Katherine, a young mother, started her own part-time business selling knitting and crochet patterns online so she could be at home with her child—and now regularly has her designs published in top knitting and crochet magazines and books (SweaterBabe.com)

▲ Connie, a sixty-two-year-old grandmother, who applied her years of experience in the art show business to start a national art fair listings site (ArtFairCalendar.com)

▲ Kit, a retired healthcare executive, who profitably reinvented herself as the Web's leading authority on "foraging and enrichment toys" for pet parrots (BirdsJustWannaHaveFun.com)

▲ How 26-year-old Drew grew his hobby of posting funny articles and links online into a profitable website with more worldwide traffic (and advertising revenues) than many major names (FARK.com)

And much more!

Parts 1 and 2 explain the world of e-business and how you can develop your successful e-business strategy. Skip ahead to parts 3 and 4, though, if you are already online and solely interested in the technology and marketing strategy secrets for your e-business. Please feel free to skim along to find the information most relevant to your needs.

The focus of this book is to share with you specific, practical secrets to creating nontechnical, idea-driven e-businesses that the average person like you can still replicate today. Following the guidelines in this book— and the updates available at InternetMillionaireSecrets.com—could help you realize your dreams, too.

I hope that it helps you build the life you've always wanted.

FOR THE MOST UP-TO-THE-MINUTE INFORMATION
As the fastest-moving business medium in history, the Internet offers you huge opportunities, but it also means that things change constantly. Any of the businesses recommended here could have changed their products, services, or pricing just yesterday. Additionally, competitors may have introduced new services that leapfrog the recommendations made here.

Once again, the Internet provides the answer to this dilemma. If you visit **www.InternetMillionaireSecrets.com,** you'll be able to find all the latest updates on the vendors that I recommend in this text. Check in regularly and please sign up for the free e-mail newsletters, too. They'll help keep you informed about the latest, greatest Internet Millionaire Secrets.

Notes

1. Heather Clancy, "E-Tail Therapy," *Entrepreneur* (January 2005), p. 36; available at http://www.entrepreneur.com/article/0,4621,319052,00.html.

2. Center for Media Research "Research Brief," July 26, 2005, citing eBay survey.

PART ONE

THE UNLIMITED OPPORTUNITY
OF THE INTERNET

THE INTERNET BUSINESS REVOLUTION

STARTING YOUR own business on the Internet is by far the number-one business opportunity currently available to entrepreneurs. Far from being over, the Net offers you huge business potential today. Even non-technical users can set up, operate, and market their small businesses worldwide for less cost than ever before. Even better, these businesses can often be run from home with minimal overhead costs, allowing their owners unprecedented flexibility and lower risk than ever before.

But Isn't the Internet "Over"?

After all the hype in the 1990s and the subsequent dot-com crash, many people (and especially the media) soured on the Internet. However, many world-class investors will tell you that the best time to invest in something is when common wisdom is against it.

Now is *your* time to get better acquainted with the huge money-making opportunities you can create by operating an online business. The fact is that the Net still offers a huge opportunity to those with the tools and training to capitalize on it.

This book summarizes for you years of Internet business experience offered by me and the successful entrepreneurs (many of them millionaires) I've interviewed. It will give you the tools to create, develop, examine, and launch an online business just as though you already had years of experience doing it.

Here are just a few of the reasons why today's Internet offers unprecedented opportunities for entrepreneurs like you:

▲ With virtually no capital you can launch a business and reach customers with your product information and advertising.

▲ Because the Internet is global, you can reach a worldwide audience like never before, including people in places you've never been.

▲ Because the online marketplace reaches customers 24 hours and 7 days of every week, you can make money while you sleep.

▲ You can update your pitch, pricing, and product information quickly, easily, and cheaply without incurring printing or mailing costs.

▲ You can research product ideas and test them more cheaply and quickly than ever before.

▲ You can track your competition in the marketplace, because competitors, too, provide easily accessed and regularly updated product information and pricing on their websites.

▲ You can have inexpensive access to multimillion-dollar software to distribute your business worldwide, across the Internet without having to buy or maintain the computers.

▲ You can operate a business from your home and employ talented personnel remotely, without having to provide costly office space.

All of this adds up to great business opportunities with little capital required to get started.

For these many reasons, my sole recommendation is to focus on developing a business that you can operate through the Internet. It is 100-percent the best entrepreneurial opportunity available to you, even if you're not technologically sophisticated.

The Small-Business Advantage Online

In the online world, for the first time ever the "little guy" like you actually has advantages over the big corporations, Harvard MBAs, and technology wizards. Here are three reasons why:

1. *Lower costs mean higher profits for you.* Big companies must do things BIG—they have lots of employees making generic products that appeal to general audiences. Because you are smaller with less overhead and personnel costs to cover, you can afford to specialize your products to directly meet the needs of your target market. Specialty products usually mean higher profit margins, too.

In addition, because the Net allows small business owners like you to reach consumer audiences worldwide, you can find and serve niche market needs that the big corporations are not even aware of yet. You can also react more quickly than big companies (with their big, bureaucratic management structures) to update and refine your products to serve your audience better.

2. *Worldwide customer reach is yours through the Web.* The biggest difference between successful mega-corporations and small home-based businesses is often simply the size of the audience that they reach with their products. In other words, if you can get the word out widely enough, you can get your share of sales—even if your competitors are much bigger corporations.

The Internet lets you extend your customer reach inexpensively worldwide. Part 4 of this book, the marketing section, will show you specific "secrets" of how to do it cost effectively, too.

3. *Enterprise software is available for pennies per day.* Online you can often turn the tools of the large companies against them. Major corporations use "enterprise software" to run their businesses. These multi-million-dollar software packages are developed for big companies to help manage their large and complex business operations. While this may sound like an insurmountable obstacle to you, it is in fact great news! Why? Because to recoup some of their costs, many software providers today are offering consumer or small-business versions of their enterprise-grade software for mere dollars per month. On top of that, they are spending millions more in development costs to make the software as easy to use as possible in hopes of attracting entrepreneurs (like you) as new customers.

The wonderful thing about e-businesses is that they can be profitable at lower volumes than big companies and with less capital investment. The increased efficiency of a successful e-business (as compared to a traditional big business) also means that even sales of less than $1 million can be dramatically profitable for their owners.

That's because on the Internet, you can inexpensively combine specialized products (advantage 1) with the ability to reach a worldwide customer audience cheaply (advantage 2) and outsource your technology needs (advantage 3) with the low overhead costs of working out of your home. In other words, your fixed costs (e.g., office space, parking, equipment) can be much lower, and your variable costs (e.g., inventory, customer service help, and especially advertising) can also be lower, and more easily managed, limited to increasing in proportion to your growth.

My experience and research prove that e-commerce offers exactly this combination of low production costs with wide reach. Combine that with the many tax advantages of owning your own business and it means that small entrepreneurs actually have a competitive advantage versus big corporations when using the Internet. Taking advantage of this can make you rich or at least change your lifestyle so dramatically that you'll be able to live more like you're rich. Then, when you factor in the use of outsourced service providers (which I'll explain more about shortly), you can build a highly profitable online business cheaply—even if you know little about technology!

By owning your own successful e-business, you can make good money with a higher profit margin than bigger companies, plus enjoy your work more, set your own hours, and probably even work from home. Even an e-business that grosses "only" $100,000/year can change your life for the better and leave you feeling and living like a "millionaire" every day!

INTERNET MILLIONAIRE SECRET:
The Law of Large Numbers

An important secret that I want to share with you is called the Law of Large Numbers. It's how the big boys of banking make their money. I want you to learn about this technique because it can help you evaluate business opportunities and recognize their potential correctly.

I learned this principle on Wall Street, in my first job out of college. I was recruited by the blue-chip banking firm of J. P. Morgan & Company in New York City. This very highly respected, old-school bank spent a lot of time and money training its young bankers, and I still remember many of the lessons.

WHAT IS THE LAW OF LARGE NUMBERS?

It is a simple formula that says that:

[A Really Small Number] × [A Really Large Number]
= A Big Number!

This concept sums up the idea that if you can reach enough potential customers with a profitable business offer, you can make serious money even if only a very small percentage of them purchase it.

This Wall Street banker secret helps explain why the Internet can be the answer to your dreams of owning your own business. The Internet is the perfect example of this principle in action. Here's an example: If there are 100 million people online and you can just get one percent of them to consider your offer, then only one-tenth of those people to buy it, that means you sold 100,000 units of your product! If you charged $10 for your product that means you have created a million-dollar business just like that!

While these numbers are not necessarily realistic for every business, the concept remains true: A small profit potential multiplied by millions and millions and millions of potential customers can create serious revenues very quickly.

If you have a business that can reach all these people inexpensively, you can be extremely profitable without much cash investment. The Internet is perfect for this kind of approach and it is just one of the many reasons why Internet-based businesses are my sole focus.

Disintermediation

Another reason that the Internet is your best bet for a profitable new business is called *disintermediation*. Business was traditionally based on a "wholesale to distributor to retail store" supply chain with each link in the chain adding its own profit margin to the final retail price. This is what made distribution of physical goods to local consumers so expensive. Similarly, in the media world, broadcasting and publishing companies built huge businesses on aggregating information and entertainment from writers, entertainers, and production companies in order to resell it to you, the consumer.

The Internet has changed all that because it allows customers to shop online for goods without visiting retail stores. The entrepreneurs who operate these online stores can sell their goods and services at lower prices directly to customers because neither party has to pay a middleman or real-world store owner for its part of the distribution chain. Similarly, anybody with an opinion can write commentary and "blog" it, bypassing the media conglomerate.

Moreover, transaction-processing software, drop-shipping services, and online advertising have become so effective that distributor middlemen with local warehouses full of inventory and advertising agency middlemen are often no longer necessary. By using the Internet to eliminate distributors, wholesalers, salespeople, and store staff, you cut down your overhead costs, thus increasing your profit potential with every transaction. In business schools, they call cutting out the middleman "disintermediation."

Although it may be hard to believe that global economic forces would make a difference to an individual like you, you can simply look at the thousands of people who make their living operating an online eBay store to see what I mean. According to a July 26, 2005, Center for Media Research "Research Brief," there are more than 700,000 eBay store operators selling directly to online customers at great prices because many of them have "disintermediated" the middlemen from their business lines.

You can rest assured that all those entrepreneurs would not be spending their time online unless they were making money.

Similarly, you can turn your own expertise and interests into products for sale through the Internet in a more cost-effective manner than has ever before been possible. In fact, I'm going to show you how you can open an online business that reaches the whole world for only $25!

Why Even You Can Master the Internet

Now that you've agreed to listen to me about the excellent business opportunities on the Internet, I'm going to convince you that you, too, can learn the technology you need to build your own online business. Yes, *you!*

Although it's true that the Internet is a very sophisticated computer network, it's also true that every year it has gotten easier for newcomers to use. This is largely because many of the first people to go online were techies who came from software backgrounds. To make money in the new online marketplace, they chose to compete with one another by building better and easier-to-use software. Today, the technology companies that these techies built are trying hard to find new customers like you to pay for the expensive systems infrastructure they built during the technology boom of the 1990s. The result is that ten years later, Internet "newbies" and small-business owners like you now have access to millions of dollars of Internet technology, equipment, software, and expertise for little cost by using services on a "pay as you go" basis from a type of company called an application service provider (ASP).

> **INTERNET RICHES GLOSSARY**
>
> I've tried hard to make this book easy to read by thoroughly explaining any technical buzzwords and acronyms I use. If I've slipped up, I invite you to consult the glossary of e-business terms in the back of the book. There you'll find plain-English definitions of over a hundred important e-business and technology terms.

ASPs—The Key to Your Success

Building an online business is easier than ever because you can obtain your most important tools and services directly through the Internet in an ASP format. This means that you just pay a monthly fee while the company providing the service (the software "application") handles all of the technology support and maintenance.

I prefer and recommend such ASP services because they will allow you to build a great-looking Web business without having to know much about technology. (Of course, if you already know about technology you have even more options, but this book's focus is for the nontechnical entrepreneur.)

There are thousands of software companies, Web design firms, e-commerce companies, Web hosting facilities, and other related corporations competing with each other to offer easy-to-use software services designed specifically to help small-business owners work online. They make it easy for you to access all the services and technology that you need to beat the big corporations at their own game. You can build and operate a world-class business with little technical knowledge required. And those services are getting cheaper all the time.

Keep reading and I'll show you the secrets of taking advantage of these ASPs and much more! I will explain the most important of these services for you to get your e-business started. I'll also include specific recommendations of the best vendors and values in each service category for you.

STARTING YOUR E-BUSINESS
CAN YOU AFFORD NOT TO?

THE INTERNET has fundamentally changed the rules of business. Its worldwide reach, instant 24/7 communications capability, ease of updating, and low cost have all converged to create vast new market opportunities for those smart enough to capitalize on them.

Despite media coverage to the contrary, these e-business opportunities have been increasing every year. More people continue to join the online party from all over the world, and faster connection speeds allow increasingly compelling information and entertainment to be delivered inexpensively. In fact, according to Forrester Research, in the U.S. alone, online retail sales have rocketed to $172 billion per year and will nearly double to $329 billion by 2010.[1]

The advancement of the Internet has also induced rapid evolution in related fields that help make the Internet easier to use for both consumers and business owners. These developments include quicker shipping, faster credit card transaction-processing, 24/7 customer service, easier-to-use software, higher-quality online video, and much more. The combination of these improvements creates a fertile environment for the launch of new business ideas, some of which we are going to discuss.

In short, the advancement of the Internet and all of its related technologies and services means that now is the best time in history for individual entrepreneurs like you to launch their own businesses.

Why? *Because it is cheaper to launch a business today than ever before.*

Traditional businesses are stuck with many of the legacies of the industrial economy that you can avoid by starting an online business. These include expenses for store or office space (or both), employees, inventory, recurring printing and postage costs for marketing, and many more categories of overhead that e-businesses can avoid. By lowering or eliminating these costs, your online business can reach more customers than traditional businesses at lower cost. This means more profits for you.

As you can see in Figure 2–1, starting a business used to be a major financial undertaking. There was high risk associated with any new business venture because it required thousands of dollars just to get the business up and running. Investment in facilities, equipment, advertising, and employees quickly escalates traditional business startup costs into the tens or hundreds of thousands of dollars. And most of these costs were recurring, so the financial risk to the owner of the business was constant.

The size of this commitment also usually required entrepreneurs to quit their jobs to focus solely on the new venture.

Figure 2–1.

FIRST YEAR STARTUP COSTS COMPARED:
TRADITIONAL RETAIL BUSINESS VS. YOUR ONLINE BUSINESS

	Traditional Retail Business	Online Business
PC & Internet Access	$500–$1,000	$500–$1,000
Office Space & Parking	$5,000–$50,000 *(+ multiyear commitment)*	$0 (work from home)
Store Space Lease	$25,000–$100,000+ *(+ multiyear commitment)*	$0 (work from home)

Furnishing/Decoration	$1,000–$25,000+	$0 (work from home)
Signage	$100–$5,000+	$0 (work from home)
Insurance	$500–$5,000+	$0 (work from home)
Phone & Fax Lines	$1,000–$5,000+	$300 or less (if using Internet calling and e-mail instead)
Printing of Marketing Materials	$1,500–$15,000+	$0 (e-mail distribution of full-color marketing materials)
Marketing Postage	$1,500–$10,000+	$0 (with worldwide reach via e-mail and Web)
Employee Wages	Variable	10% to 50% less via Web
Shipping Costs	Variable	Paid by customers or eliminated by digital delivery
Credit Card Merchant Account	$600 set-up + sales percentage	$0 set up (plus sales percentage)
Website Costs	N/A	$100–$1,000
Advertising	$500–$100,000	Pay for performance only
TOTAL ESTIMATE:	**$35,000–$250,000+**	**<$1,000**

Today, however, you can start and run an online business for mere hundreds of dollars a year! This low cost (which every year declines even more) means that e-businesses are much more affordable to start—plus their owners don't have to quit their primary jobs until they are ready to do so.

E-Business Costs Continue to Decline

Let's be more specific: It's obvious that real-world businesses are much more expensive to operate than web-based ones. Did you know that even e-business costs have dropped dramatically in just the last few years? For example, Figure 2–2 shows how costs such as registering an e-business domain name or hosting a website have dropped between the late 1990s and 2003, and then further between 2003 and today. Impressive, right?

Figure 2–2.

HOW THE ANNUAL COSTS OF OPERATING AN E-BUSINESS WEBSITE ARE DECLINING OVER TIME

	1998 Costs (estimated)	2003 Costs (estimated)	2008 Costs (estimated)
Domain Registration	$40	$15	Included
Website Design	$1,000–$15,000	$150	$100
Website Hosting	$1,000–$6,000	$250	Included
Shopping Cart Software	$600–$6,000	$500	Included
Credit Card Merchant Account	$750–$1,500	$250	Not needed
E-Mail Marketing Tools	$500–$2,500	$300	$180
ONE-YEAR TOTAL	**$4,000–$30,000+**	**<$1,500**	**<$300!**

Today many Web services vendors offer package deals, too, that include many of the services detailed in Figure 2–2 for one low price. In Chapter 9, "Technology Secrets and Strategies Overview," I'll tell you about high-quality vendors offering packages that include most of these services for prices you won't believe!

Every year it gets cheaper to operate an online business. This decline in costs is unleashing a wave of creativity and business opportunity that I'd like you to join. If your preconceptions of computer and website costs are still stuck in 1999, now's the time to reconsider!

INTERNET MILLIONAIRE SECRET

The Amazing $25 Startup Budget

You can start a professional business online that includes all of these services for less than $25 per month. With costs this low, can you afford not to try pursuing your dream?

You're reading this book because you have a desire for positive change in your life. You may already have an idea or two about an e-business that appeals to you, or you may have nothing more than a desire to supplement your income or quit a job that you hate. Either way, you deserve a chance to participate in the e-business revolution.

The rest of this book will go into more detail about how to identify and exploit the best target market and product opportunities for your e-business idea. For now, though, I want to prove to you that you can afford to take the risk of starting your own venture.

Figure 2–3.

MONTHLY UP-FRONT COSTS FOR ONLINE SERVICES, WITH ONE-YEAR CONTRACTS

$7.95	**Website package, including:**
	▲ Domain name registration
	▲ Website design template
	▲ Website hosting
	▲ E-mail accounts
	▲ E-mail Autoresponder
$0.00	**Credit card processing capabilities**
	▲ Including shopping cart software
$15.00	**E-mailing list management software**
	▲ HTML design templates
$22.95	**TOTAL**

Figure 2–3 shows that you can get a credible, professional-looking website that even takes credit cards and tracks all of your customers for less than $25! (I am assuming that you already have a PC with reasonably

modern software, a decent Internet connection, and probably a phone line, too. If you didn't have those assets already in place, I doubt that you would have bought this book!) This small budget will allow you to get started without a major cash investment. I don't claim that it will provide the perfect solution for every situation, but it will provide anyone with the tools to get started online to test a new million-dollar business idea.

By using the services of outsourced service companies known as application service providers (ASPs), as I recommend throughout this book, you won't have to worry about technology support and maintenance either, since these services are included in their service fees, too! With no knowledge of HTML programming code, Adobe Photoshop graphics programs, or FTP (file transfer protocol) processes, you will be able to follow these recommendations to build a website as easily as you can type a letter into Microsoft Word. Press a few more buttons and your work will be visible on the web for customers worldwide to see.

Of course, the recurring monthly charges for these services can add up over time. But contrast this $25-a-month startup cost to the thousands or even hundreds of thousands of dollars that starting a real-world business can cost! The savings are truly remarkable. And, in some areas of e-business, such as publishing a "blog" or opening an online apparel store (using certain services I explain later), you can spend even less—all the way down to zero!—and still create a potentially profitable e-business with worldwide reach.

Of course, you could spend a lot more than this if you want to. And I need to warn you that your more techie friends probably won't believe this approach can work. Instead, they are likely to insist that you need a fully integrated e-commerce platform to succeed. Even then they will encourage you to upgrade your systems constantly. Well, your techie friends are wrong. The world has changed, and that change has been dramatically in favor of individual entrepreneurs like you.

Rethinking Startups

This is not theory. I'm talking about real services that are available online today to anybody who cares to sign up. Additionally, none of these service companies are small, fly-by-night operations that are likely to disappear.

As you'll see later, Yahoo, Network Solutions, iPowerWeb, Go Daddy, and the others that I recommend are all major corporations that you can rely on to meet the needs of your e-business today.

Because it is their business to service small business owners like you, these companies will also keep expanding their services as new technology becomes available (so you don't have to worry about upgrades, viruses, or new software).

The end result of this simple $25 spent can be a fully functional and professional-looking website, complete with credit card transaction processing, technical support, and maintenance, that can reach the entire global Internet audience for your goods and services. Because all the technology is outsourced, you have zero maintenance or technology issues. Instead, you can concentrate on making the great products, content, or services that will differentiate your million-dollar business.

The conclusion that you should draw from this analysis is that most of what you were taught about startup businesses is wrong. Although it used to be true that startups were very risky, this was primarily because of the financial and time commitments they demanded.

Today, however, you can see that you can launch a new business online for less than you might spend on dinner! All it takes is $25 a month to get started. Why not invest some time and this small amount of money in yourself and your future? You could (and probably do) spend more than that regularly on activities or products that are forgotten as soon as they're over.

Can you afford not to pursue your dream?

INTERNET MILLIONAIRE SECRET:
Understanding Moore's Law

Betting on the benefits provided by continuing advancements in computer processing power is how many technology investors, venture capital firms, and e-business entrepreneurs have made millions. Understanding this dynamic of the industry that powers the Internet can also help you make better decisions for your new e-business.

Gordon Moore, one of the founders of computer chip manufacturer Intel Corporation, summarized the expected growth pattern of these advances way back in 1965. He predicted that the number of transistors that could be included on a computer chip's integrated circuit (which determines its speed and power) would double every eighteen to twenty-four months.

This was a bold and visionary prediction back at the dawn of the computer age, but it has now largely held true for decades. Advances in production techniques have led to consistent, rapid drops in the prices of technical components.

Understanding "Moore's Law" is what leads the technology industry, and those who invest in it or rely on its products, to plan their businesses around continued improvements in performance accompanied by dramatic reductions in cost over time. This dynamic growth curve has powered the Internet revolution. It has powered advances in the availability of bandwidth, audience adoption of e-mail and Internet shopping, e-commerce software improvements, and all the technology pieces that converge to make e-business the hottest entrepreneurial growth area in history.

Understanding Moore's Law and its probable effect on the target markets your new e-business pursues can help even nontechnical folks identify how best to profit from the continuing advancement of technology and Internet penetration.

E-Business Models

To help you discover the best approach for you, I'd like to introduce you to a fancy MBA concept called a business model. A successful business model is a method of operation that allows you to source and offer the right products to the right audience at the right price.

E-business has evolved in three waves, each of which exploits a different type of business model:

Wave 1: Efficiency-based e-businesses

Wave 2: Product-based e-businesses

Wave 3: Niche-based e-businesses

In chapters 3, 4, and 5, we're going to walk through each of these "waves" together to learn about their business models. I'll explain how each one has made entrepreneurs into millionaires, interview the founders of leading companies in each area, and help you apply the lessons to your own situation.

Yes, I know that these three business models don't perfectly account for all the businesses online today. The beauty of the Internet is that it has unleashed far too much innovation to be summarized in just three categories. Bear with me, though, and you'll see that dividing up the world of e-business into these somewhat academic categories will help us discuss it more thoroughly together.

Notes

1. "US eCommerce Forecast: Online Retail Sales to Reach $329 Billion by 2010," Forrester Research press release, September 19, 2005.

3 THE INTERNET'S FIRST MILLIONAIRE WAVE— EFFICIENCY

THE FIRST OF the millionaire types we're going to discuss in detail is the Efficiency Millionaire. Efficiency Millionaires start million-dollar businesses based on helping people and businesses do things faster, easier, or in more entertaining ways.

The twentieth century saw more improvements in business efficiency than can be counted. Examples include Henry Ford's pioneering automobile assembly lines, which introduced mass production to industry worldwide; department stores and shopping malls that made it more efficient for people to shop by combining previously separate retailers under one roof; VCRs and their successors, TiVo-style digital video recorders (DVRs) that allow people to record and watch programs on their own schedules; and improvements in communications that advanced from postal mail to telephone calls to faxes to e-mail and instant messaging.

Each of these advancements in productivity created its own crop of Efficiency Millionaires, either directly from the inventions themselves, by building out the facilities needed to implement the efficiencies, or by taking advantage of the new efficiencies to improve the lives of customer audiences. By looking for things that don't work as well as they should in your daily life, you can identify million-dollar business opportunities, too.

Internet Efficiency

Of course, the biggest current contributor to improved efficiency is the Internet. By linking people worldwide in an inexpensive, round-the-clock communications network, the Internet has greatly increased the availability of information and the speed of business transactions. Additionally, sharing information via e-mail and Web pages is virtually free.

Efficiency Millionaire e-business models are based not on products but on trading information that helps sell products more efficiently. Their defining characteristic is that they carry no inventory themselves. Instead, these e-businesses use information about other people's products to create new efficiencies that create profit for themselves. Yahoo, eBay, and Expedia are all familiar examples of efficiency-based business models.

Online tools have made it much more affordable than was historically possible for solo entrepreneurs to start million-dollar companies. Trying to increase efficiencies in industrial or manufacturing businesses requires large capital investments in materials and engineering know-how. But redistributing information to improve efficiency via the Internet is effectively free. Because of this, the world's most recent crop of Efficiency Millionaires is composed mostly of Internet entrepreneurs.

For example, eBay alone has introduced tremendous new efficiencies in the markets for the sale of used goods. The simple idea of using the Internet to provide an online marketplace for garage-sale-type selling has brought thousands of new retailing opportunities into the economy and has made many people very rich.

The eBay phenomenon has helped millions of people create extra income on a part-time basis by making it more efficient for buyers and sellers to find one another. It is this redistribution of information that is the hallmark of Efficiency Millionaire businesses. Travel websites that offer online booking, search engines that help you find information, and even e-mail lists that trade jokes are all examples of new efficiencies introduced by the Internet that are making entrepreneurs like you rich.

Efficiency Millionaires

The traditional way to identify new business opportunities is to find the biggest market you can, then figure out what it needs that you can sell. Leading twentieth-century companies such as General Motors, PepsiCo, Wal-Mart, DuPont, or Nike all serve fundamental human needs on a worldwide basis by manufacturing and distributing physical goods.

More modern equivalents include some of the first generation of successful Internet companies, such as Priceline.com or Expedia (travel), Yahoo (search), or eBay (marketplace). Each of these firms started as a small venture that attempted to use the Internet to make a targeted market more efficient. They make money by making their chosen products or information easier to access or more affordable for their customers. All of these companies have grown to become huge corporations, but their approach to identifying and building new businesses based on Internet efficiency is still viable today for you.

As Sergio Zyman, the former chief marketing officer of The Coca-Cola Company puts it: "The companies that survive are the companies that improve the thing customers are doing already."

How do the entrepreneurs behind Efficiency Millionaire companies identify and choose to pursue their new business models? Here are some examples of successful companies that started with entrepreneurs dedicated to improving the efficiency of their target markets.

EFFICIENCY ENTREPRENEUR #1:
TIM GRAY, WEDDINGCHANNEL.COM

Although it was often confused with a cable TV channel dedicated to weddings (when I worked there in its early years), millions of people now know that WeddingChannel.com is an online bridal registry service.

Founded by Raj Dhaka and Tim Gray in 1997, WeddingChannel.com is a great example of how the Internet can collect widely dispersed information to make its customers' lives easier. The company helps brides, grooms, and wedding guests by collecting bridal gift registries from stores nationwide to make shopping for wedding gifts much easier.

The information collected is the wedding registry gift requests of hundreds of thousands of brides and grooms around the country. The company aggregates that data on its website so wedding guests can find and buy the requested bridal gifts online, without having to visit the stores. The efficiency this introduces into the normally complicated wedding gift process is such a great service that WeddingChannel.com has been used by more than one million about-to-be-married couples in recent years.

Cofounder Tim Gray was inspired to start the company because of the gift-giving difficulties he saw his own wedding guests having when he got married. In discussing business concepts with his friend Raj Dhaka, they realized that combining this consumer need with e-commerce technology could put the bridal registry process online for the first time.

Tim and Raj saw that the way people typically buy wedding gifts requires many steps: driving to a store, printing out a registry gift list, finding a product in the appropriate price range that has not already been purchased by another guest, buying it, and then carrying it or shipping it to the bride and groom. Their many discussions about e-business eventually led them to the joint conclusion: "Here's a better way to deliver bridal registry services."

By putting bridal gift lists online, they hoped that their new website would allow wedding guests to shop online from home and complete the gift-buying process in ten minutes instead of hours. Not only could the company make money by taking a commission on each bridal gift purchased through the service, but as Tim points out, brides and grooms are a tremendous consumer group because of the money they invest in their weddings and honeymoons and in setting up their new households. This allows the company also to benefit from advertising revenue.

The breadth of their vision (plus the higher costs of technology in 1996) caused Tim and Raj to raise venture capital money to support the development and launch of WeddingChannel.com. They used this money to build their website and start marketing the service to the department stores whose bridal registry services they were hoping to automate.

Their innovative use of the Internet to facilitate bridal gift purchases helped the young company attract two major partnerships that established WeddingChannel.com as the leading online gift resource for brides and grooms: Federated Department Stores and *Brides* magazine. By partnering with Federated, WeddingChannel.com became the official online registry for all Macy's and Bloomingdale's stores nationwide. The partnership with *Brides,* the most popular bridal magazine, brought the young company media reach and additional content for the website. Just as important, these partnerships brought the company credibility.

Today, WeddingChannel.com is the leader in online bridal registry services. The site serves more than 40 million page views per month and offers shoppers bridal gift registries from an unprecedented collection of top stores, including Bloomingdale's and Macy's, Tiffany & Co., Crate & Barrel, Neiman Marcus, Williams-Sonoma, Pottery Barn, REI, Restoration Hardware, and many more. Over 700,000 soon-to-be married couples manage their gift registries through the WeddingChannel.com website twenty-four hours a day, seven days a week, and guests can choose from more than 15 million products to purchase as wedding gifts online or in stores.

Tim Gray sees the Internet as a huge enabler for entrepreneurs because it breaks down so many barriers that traditionally limited the reach of startup companies. He recommends e-business by saying, "The Internet is a powerful tool for you because as an entrepreneur, you can quickly market to a worldwide audience without the huge costs that you would have incurred before the Internet arrived."

Tim is right. By lowering the costs of building and marketing a new business, the Internet has also dramatically reduced the risks of starting a new business.

INTERNET MILLIONAIRE SECRET

Tim 's experience shows that you are surrounded by business opportunities that you may not even see. The best of these are simple ideas based on making your customers' lives easier and more efficient.

Instead of being satisfied with the traditional process of buying wedding gifts, Tim and Raj saw that they could build a business by improving a difficult gift-buying process that the retail industry accepted as "good enough." Not even the major department stores that control the bridal registry business fully realized that the Internet was offering new and better ways to redistribute and monetize the information contained in their bridal registries. By focusing on the needs of its potential customers rather than accepting the traditional way of doing things, WeddingChannel.com became the dominant player in the bridal registry market before most others even saw the opportunity.

EFFICIENCY ENTREPRENEUR #2:
GENEVIEVE THIERS, SITTERCITY.COM

Because Genevieve Thiers grew up as the oldest of seven children, she spent much of her childhood babysitting. This experience came in handy during college because it helped her earn the money to put herself through school. She babysat for dozens of families in the Boston area while she was in college. From this experience, she saw that many mothers were desperate to find trustworthy sitters but didn't have ready access to the large pool of potential sitters on college campuses.

Once Genevieve graduated and realized that she hated working for a big company, she decided to pursue the business opportunity she saw in connecting parents and sitters using the Internet. Inspired by the success of online dating services, Genevieve realized that a similar matchmaking service putting parents and sitters together had great potential. The site has grown to become the number-one babysitting resource on the Web.

Genevieve kept her job just long enough to use the paychecks to launch Sittercity.com. She started by hiring some friends to build her initial website and paying them out of her company salary. Her father also helped her out with $120 to buy the Sittercity.com website address (which he still kids her about).

When I asked Genevieve if she raised any money to get started, she replied: "No, I spoke with some venture capital people and some angels, but they didn't get it. I only needed thousands, not millions, of dollars, which is too small for many investors to bother with. More important, they didn't understand the demand that moms have to find trustworthy caretakers for their children. It was seen as 'woman's issue,' not as a real business."

It took Genevieve about three months to get the site designed and launched. Then, she started building her business by inviting 650 babysitters to sign up, using names that she had collected by spreading flyers in dorms across college campuses in Boston.

Soon after that, the parents started showing up, too. She made her first sale about two weeks after launch, when the first mom signed up for the paying service.

The market inefficiency that Genevieve has so successfully targeted is the disconnect between individual babysitters (who are young and always looking for work) and older, more affluent parents who consistently have trouble locating desirable sitters in their local areas. Traditionally dependent just on word-of-mouth recommendations, many parents have judged it worthwhile to pay for a website service offering prescreened local babysitters.

Today, Sittercity.com makes money primarily by selling memberships to parents while babysitters can join the network for free. Sitters are able to post their information and references in a trusted environment. Parents can then search among them and contact those that best fit their needs. It's a great application of the Internet's ability to connect people, just like online dating sites do.

The future outlook for Sittercity.com is bright. Now based in Chicago, the company is highly profitable. It boasts more than 100,000 registered babysitters and nannies in 20 cities across the country and is expecting to grow that to 500,000 in the next year. It has also successfully launched a new corporate program where corporations can buy memberships in bulk for their employees as a fringe benefit.

Like most good ideas, Sittercity.com sounds obvious once you point it out. When I asked Genevieve why she thought nobody else had done this previously, she said: "Most people *talk* more than they *do*. As soon as I launched the original Sittercity.com website, I got lots of e-mails and calls from people saying, 'I was going to do that.' Of course, none of these people actually had done it, but I did. I think that if you have a good idea you have to pursue it."

She also echoed one of the themes I shared with you earlier in this book: "Your readers should realize that there are huge business opportunities everywhere. Just wait until you are inconvenienced. If you find something difficult to do, there's a company you can build to help solve that problem. That's all I did with Sittercity.com and tens of thousands of people agreed with me."

INTERNET MILLIONAIRE SECRET

By recognizing the inefficient distribution of information between babysitters and their customers (parents), Genevieve Thiers started a multimillion-dollar business in her spare time. Where other inefficiencies exist, so do opportunities—and it's getting easier and cheaper to turn those opportunities into e-businesses than ever before due to declining technology costs.

For example, instead of paying $120 for a URL website address, like Genevieve did in 2001, today you can pay less than $10. Similarly, instead of spending months developing a website, you can build one in a few hours nowadays using hosted services and design templates.

Perhaps even more important, Genevieve was able to start and grow her business with no outside investors or venture capital money. Even today, as Sittercity.com has grown into a national company, it has succeeded in financing its growth purely from its own cash flow and by taking advantage of the continuing decline in the costs of Internet software and services.

EFFICIENCY ENTREPRENEUR #3:
CONNIE METTLER, ARTFAIRCALENDAR.COM

A more recently launched example of an efficiency-based e-business is ArtFairCalendar.com. This is a website I know very well because I helped my own mother, Connie Mettler, start it last summer. While it hasn't made her a million dollars yet, it is growing rapidly because of its great appeal to a previously untapped audience: art fair customers.

Working with my brother and my mother to build a website that sells her husband's fine art photography online helped me realize that we could use the Internet to help attract more people to the art fairs where my mother and her artist friends exhibit their work. I proposed that we should build ArtFairCalendar.com as a site that would list all of the art show events taking place each weekend in several regional markets where art fairs are most popular. While this sounds obvious, no one in the art fair world had yet implemented this simple approach to providing better information to their customers. There are lots of websites promoting individual shows, but no one had put up a site that collected all that information in one place in a format most useful from the customers' point of view.

Connie thinks that this has not been done before because artists and the people who love art fairs are not very "techie." Many artists are still struggling to put up sites for their own art, and none of the individual art show promoters would create such a site because they are all competitors. It was only once my brother and I helped her build a website for selling her husband's photos (www.NormDarwish.com) that she realized just how many people use the Internet to search for information all the time.

She recognized the potential of building a business promoting all art fairs, not just the ones where she and her husband were exhibiting. The idea was also personally appealing to her because it would allow her to use her decades of expertise in the art festival world to make money from the whole art fair industry instead of only by selling her husband's photos at each individual show.

Today, ArtFairCalendar.com offers visitors a calendar listing of the top fine art fairs and craft shows in Michigan, Ohio, Illinois, and Florida, as selected by Connie, the editor-in-chief. Each state has its own page to serve the customers that live in those areas. Each state's page also offers a free e-mail newsletter that notifies subscribers about the shows in their area each month. Adding details like exhibition hours and parking instructions that the artists take for granted has been very popular with the audience of art fair attendees.

While I did most of the original work setting up the website for her, Connie has since learned to update the site herself, spending only a few hours each week on it. She says that the template system I used makes it very easy to post and update the site's listings. (Later in this book I'll share details on how to find affordable and easy-to-use website template systems that you can use, too.) Most of the work comes just once a year in the spring, when the new art fair schedules come out and need to be edited and posted online. Lately, updating the site has taken a bit more of her time, because she is now answering inquiries from people who want to advertise on the site or in the e-mail newsletters she sends out. Connie doesn't mind this time commitment because it leads directly to more income.

Connie was skeptical at first about the time we were both spending on building the service because she "just couldn't see why anyone would care about this information or how we would make money." Today, she realizes that the fundamental reason the site makes money is because it makes people's lives easier. (As you now recognize, this is the hallmark of Efficiency Millionaires!) The site is useful for customers who are looking for entertainment or shopping opportunities, and it even proactively e-mails them details on great art events. Art fair organizers love the site, too, because it offers a targeted, proven audience to which they can advertise.

The site helps Connie make money several ways now: It generates more attendance at the art fairs where Connie and her husband exhibit (which leads to more sales of his photographs); it has led to more online sales through her husband's website; and event promoters pay to advertise on the website and in its e-newsletters. She says, "We've created a one-stop shop for art fair and craft fair information that no one else had done before."

Connie recommends that you try e-business because she believes that it has much less risk compared to traditional business opportunities.

She says: "Never be afraid to try something new. The Internet seems complicated, but it is a powerful tool that can help you. You don't need to be intimidated by technology because there are new services that really make it very easy to use. I was really amazed at how easy it was."

I'm proud of the ArtFairCalendar.com business both because it's going to help my mother retire more comfortably than she expected, but also because of the Efficiency Millionaire theory it demonstrates for you.

INTERNET MILLIONAIRE SECRET

If there's an industry, hobby, or community that you know well, you should examine the inconveniences facing that community or its customers that hinder its growth. Each of those obstacles could be a business opportunity waiting to be solved.

Like my other examples of efficiency-based e-businesses, ArtFair Calendar.com demonstrates that redistributing information useful to an attractive target market is a simple approach that you should try to apply to your own interests to find a potential million-dollar e-business of your own.

As ArtFairCalendar.com, Sittercity.com, and WeddingChannel.com all show, information is not perfectly or conveniently distributed. It seems like it should be, but we all know that it is not. Many industries, topics, or communities have not yet fully recognized that a website (with an e-mail distribution list for publicity) can help them share information about their products and services more efficiently and cost-effectively than ever before.

If you are the one to bring that new efficiency to your target market, you will make money. You can earn income by charging advertisers to reach your audience, by charging audience members for access to the information, by selling things directly to that audience, by licensing the information you collect to other companies, or in other ways that the new interactive media marketplace is still creating.

YOUR "MILLIONAIRE IDEA JOURNAL"

To get the most out of this book, I encourage you to buy a notebook, small or large, open it up, and title the first page "My Internet Millionaire Secrets."

Internet Riches *includes many exercises that are designed to make you think. Since I'm confident that all that thinking is bound to stir up some valuable ideas, I want you to have a convenient and consistent place to write down your ideas and responses to these exercises.*

Every time I refer to your Millionaire Idea Journal, I want you to take advantage of your new notebook. If you follow along and make an honest attempt to participate in all the exercises, you'll soon see those pages filling up with great ideas that could change your life.

As you progress through the chapters, valuable ideas will start popping into your head as a result of the stimulation from the book's topics, interviews, and exercises. It may even happen in the middle of the night or while you're in the shower. Keep your Millionaire Idea Journal handy so can write them down before you lose any of these potentially valuable insights!

Identifying Efficiency Millionaire Opportunities for Yourself

The key to finding Efficiency Millionaire e-business opportunities is simply paying attention and keeping track of the needs of the people in your daily life.

Everyone has run into frustrating business situations. Once you put on your Efficiency Millionaire hat, you'll start to see that identifying and fixing problems like these can be the basis of very effective businesses. Think about the businesses with which you work or purchase products from regularly. Think back to times when you have asked yourself these questions:

▲ Why are these unnecessary middlemen involved when I try to buy that product or service?

▲ Why can't I just buy or receive the goods directly?

▲ Why is it so hard to find goods like X, Y, or Z?

▲ Why does it take so long to get a certain product delivered or a needed service completed?

▲ Couldn't these repetitive tasks that are unnecessarily difficult be automated?

▲ Why isn't somebody in my town offering product X or service Y? Don't other people need or want it like I do?

Please take a few minutes to review each of these questions carefully. Here is your first chance to use the blank pages of the Millionaire Idea Journal. To keep track of your ideas, write down each of the frustrating situations that you think of for future reference. Finding situations like these and coming up with solutions to these "million-dollar questions" can make you an Efficiency Millionaire.

Traditionally, improving business efficiency was a job only for high-priced management consultants. Today, things have changed in favor of the individual entrepreneur, especially when it comes to fixing business inefficiencies that result from poor distribution of information. This change is because of the Internet's arrival. Improving the flow of commerce by improving the sharing of information between businesses and their customers can help you create an Efficiency Millionaire business.

Later in this book, after I've helped you to identify some promising million-dollar business ideas, I'm also going to show you how to implement your ideas by building very cost-effective and efficient Internet websites to capitalize on them. These websites can service the needs of your customers while also making money 24/7. Don't worry; this technology is less complicated than you think, and I'll spend several chapters introducing it to you.

Efficiency Millionaire Exercise

Answer each of the following questions in your Millionaire Idea Journal. You can do most of this work in your head, but when you start to find original ideas popping up, be sure to write them down. You don't want to lose them!

▲ What are your five favorite websites?

▲ Do any of these online businesses help make your life more efficient, easier, or more fun? If so, how?

▲ What other Efficiency Millionaire people and companies can you identify in your life?

▲ What kinds of efficiency opportunities are being exploited by businesses like eBay, WeddingChannel.com, or ArtFair Calendar.com?

▲ Review again the questions I posed a couple of pages back. What businesses or situations did you write down?

▲ Can you imagine solutions to inefficiencies that are similar to those of your favorite websites or this chapter's Efficiency Millionaire example businesses?

▲ What processes in your day-to-day life are the most annoying?

▲ If you made it your goal, could you do anything to help reduce those frustrations that you and others must feel?

Be certain to write down in your Millionaire Idea Journal all of your responses to capture potential million-dollar ideas!

THE INTERNET'S SECOND MILLIONAIRE WAVE— PRODUCTS

MY SECOND type of e-business millionaire is the Product Millionaire. While many Efficiency Millionaire businesses could not have existed before the arrival of the Internet, most traditional fortunes were built on buying and selling physical products.

Almost every product and service is becoming available online. Even physical goods or services that have to be delivered in person are being marketed online. Entrepreneurs with interest or expertise in products have built many great companies online already, but many more e-business opportunities are still available.

Reseller Product Millionaires: Sourcing and Selling Other People's Goods

Product Millionaire businesses are closely related to Efficiency Millionaire strategies because reselling and brokering of goods implies that you are adding efficiency to the transaction. The difference is that

Product Millionaires generally carry and ship inventory themselves instead of just making introductions or confirming brokered transactions.

Product reseller businesses that offer physical goods for sale can be broken into two general categories: those that compete on price and those that compete on selection. The Internet has allowed an additional category of *information resellers* to emerge as well. These companies repackage information produced by others for their audiences.

PRICE-BASED PRODUCT RESELLERS

The Internet has allowed anyone to put up an online store to resell things produced by others. It can be as simple as someone selling random items from around the house (as many casual eBay users do) or a more focused business that builds a name for itself by focusing on sales of a specific product.

By picking a commonly needed product, you can start a store and be certain of demand for your goods. Good examples of these sorts of products are consumable items, such as socks, coffee, batteries, office supplies, or auto parts. Because these goods are regularly used by people worldwide, you can be sure of recurring consumer demand among the millions of people online. Unless the product reseller has an exclusive source of products, however, she must somehow ensure that her goods are more attractive to customers than those of competitors. This usually means that the goods must be cheaper.

SELECTION-BASED PRODUCT RESELLERS

Since competing on price alone makes for a tough road, I recommend alternative strategies for reseller entrepreneurs. These alternatives include variations on e-retailing that are based on the selection of goods you choose to offer—namely, specialty product reselling and product aggregation reselling—as well as information reselling. All of these strategies offer advantages that can make them much more profitable for you than reselling products based on competitive pricing alone.

Although prices are always important to customers, offering unique goods or a better selection than competitors is also a great way to differentiate your e-business. Other ways to differentiate might include offering better customer service, selling products that are rare or difficult for others to obtain, adding something to the goods or packaging that makes them more appealing, or nurturing a unique community of customers who buy your goods.

Amazon.com is a top example of a company that is so big that it can implement several of these strategies simultaneously, as well as compete on price. The Amazon model requires a lot of financial capital and technology expertise, however.

As a startup entrepreneur you're more likely to be successful implementing a smaller-scale approach to reselling that bases your new venture's competitive advantage on targeting a specific market niche or providing a unique selection of specialty goods. I call these two approaches to product reselling *specialty e-retailers* and *product aggregator e-retailers*.

SPECIALTY E-RETAILERS

While Amazon.com and Walmart.com have staked out the mass market for goods of all sorts, specialty retailers have had great success online, too. This is because they can cost-effectively provide a larger and more specialized product selection to online shoppers worldwide through the Web than a brick-and-mortar store can. They also often need only one central location from which to fulfill orders.

Like catalog retailers in the pre-Internet days, specialty e-retailers thrive because they can deliver specialty goods into markets that traditionally weren't large enough to support a store specializing in those goods. The best product specialist websites also provide product expertise, advice, and higher-quality customer service to their customers, often because the owners of these e-businesses are themselves avid consumers of the products.

SPECIALTY PRODUCT RESELLER:
SID KREIS, SEYBERTS.COM

Seyberts.com is a great example of these principles. Although it is based in a small farming community in the middle of Michigan, Seybert's Billiard Supply has established itself as a worldwide leader in sales of billiard equipment because of the expertise, product selection, and customer service it offers around its sale of high-end pool cues and accessories.

Sid Kreis built the Seyberts.com website simply as a favor to his pool league team buddy, Jim Tong, back in 1996. Jim was selling high-end pool cues out of his closet and Sid, a grocery store meat department manager, thought that he might be able to use the new PC he had gotten to build a little website to help out his friend.

Sid was inspired to try e-business when he went online to look for information about an obscure slot car that he had loved as a kid. He was staggered to receive thousands of results from his search engine query about the "Tyco Thunderjet AFX slot car." He immediately recognized that the Internet was aggregating huge audiences around previously obscure interests, and he seized the opportunity to build a business around his own hobby: shooting pool.

With no technical training and only a high school education, Sid used a free hosting service and some basic HTML he learned from a book to put up their first billiard supply website. Seyberts.com received its first order for a pool cue one week later; soon after they received an order all the way from France.

Within six months, Jim had offered Sid a partnership in the new business and gradually convinced him to leave his job as the meat department manager at a local grocery store to run the new website business full-time.

As a former meat department manager, Sid viewed the cluttered website stores he found online through the eyes of a grocer. This helped him identify his target market and business opportunity. As he puts it, "the aisles were too cluttered" on competitors' websites. Even though in some cases he would be offering the same products, he saw many things he could do differently to set Seyberts.com apart from competitors.

As a result, his focus in building Seyberts.com was to improve the product selection and customer experience available to online shoppers for high-quality billiards equipment. Similarly, he focused the business on a specific audience of high-end customers and has continued to limit inventory to top-of-the-line products only.

Sid sees little point in "wasting time on casual browsers who are just looking for pretty pictures." Proof of the success of this approach emerged when I asked him how many unique visitors or page views the website had (the traditional measures of success for website businesses). He didn't know! But he *did* know a much more important number— namely, the sales per day the website averaged and how much money they had made that month. That's the sign of a successful e-business!

Seyberts.com has grown to be recognized worldwide for its leadership in sales and service of the billiard supply industry, with revenues in the millions of dollars. It now has five full-time employees, plus several part-time ones as well. The company has launched a successful line of custom pool cues and even signed up top professional pool players as its representatives.

The company has also expanded into the "real world" by cleverly repurposing a former farm produce stand into a large showroom of billiard and game room equipment. This kind of new job creation and reuse of farming facilities is much needed in the Midwestern heartland and has been very welcome in Sid and Jim's local community.

The establishment of new businesses in previously isolated regions is one of the unexpected bonuses of the Internet's growth. Sid points out that it would have been impossible for a small town like Coldwater, Michigan, to support a specialty billiard supply store without the Internet's global reach to help customers find them. Being located in a small, rural town also helps the business keep its overhead low and recruit reliable employees. "Small town honesty and service with global distribution" is how Sid summarizes the benefits of combining their Midwestern base with the Internet's reach.

Thrilled with the success of his business, Sid enjoys going to work every day as part of his "dream job." He says, "I'm a meat cutter from the tiny town of Quincy, Michigan, who, because of my website, now gets to sign up and work with my heroes on a daily basis, including the number-one pool player in the world. When I go to conferences now, people from Japan come up to me, like I'm some kind of celebrity, all because of this website I built based on my favorite hobby—shooting pool!"

For entrepreneurs considering e-business, Sid describes the Internet as "a ladder that just keeps going up." He ascribes the success of Seyberts.com to its focus on a specific market and recommends that you do the same: "E-business is for the normal guy like me," he says. "It doesn't take a load of money. You can have a room full of lunch boxes to sell from your house without having to rent office space. If you sell what you know and what you've got in front of you, you can deliver quickly, too. Stay away from obvious general categories like jewelry and focus on the one percent of the population that shares your interests. On the Internet that one percent can equal millions of people."

With proper attention to the unique needs and interests of that small group of potential customers, you, too, have the chance to build a million-dollar e-business.

INTERNET MILLIONAIRE SECRET

Seyberts.com demonstrates that a commonplace product that you take for granted can be turned into a million-dollar e-business by clever application of the Internet's worldwide reach to create a specialty "boutique" online.

Even though pool cues were a long established and widely available product category, Sid Kreis and his partners built a successful business by providing more depth of selection than anyone in their chosen industry had previously realized that customers wanted. In fact, the highly specialized selection of high-end billiards equipment offered by Seyberts.com may not have even been sustainable by a traditional bricks-and-mortar store. It was Sid's recognition that the Internet enabled him to reach and aggregate previously widely dispersed customers that helped Sid and Jim identify the business model that has worked so well for them.

PRODUCT AGGREGATOR E-RETAILERS

Another successful strategy for reselling products produced by others is to collect a variety of them from different suppliers to aggregate a unique shopping experience based on selection. This "product aggregator" approach attracts a targeted market of consumers who share interest in the chosen mix of products.

PRODUCT AGGREGATOR RESELLER:
SHARON MULLEN, INVENTIVEPARENT.COM

InventiveParent.com is a website that retails unique children's products. Unlike most websites, it focuses on selling products designed by other parents instead of offering big brand names.

Examples of the products carried include Preggie Pops, intended to help pregnant mothers combat morning sickness; the Wee Block, which was invented by a father frustrated by his son squirting him when his diaper was changed; and the TP Saver, which was invented by and for parents tired of their kids unrolling all the toilet tissue in the bathroom.

Sharon Mullen started InventiveParent.com because she was a new mother frustrated when her baby's blanket kept falling off of his car seat. She decided to make herself a special fleece blanket with Velcro attachments to solve that problem. Like a good entrepreneur, she soon realized that it was a viable product and put up a website to sell it online as a "Car Seat Cozy."

Within a week, Sharon sold the first Car Seat Cozy online, but it was slow going for the traffic to build after that. Frustrated by the slow growth in her business, Sharon attended a trade show for juvenile products in Dallas. There she met other people who were in the same boat she was— trying to break into the retail business, each with a kids' product that they had created themselves. She recognized that the specific needs that these other baby products were designed to fulfill were complementary to her Car Seat Cozy, so she put some of these other parents' products on her website hoping that they might increase her traffic and her cash flow. She quickly found that presenting customers with a variety of new and innovative products designed specifically to serve the needs of a target market can be a big draw.

InventiveParent.com has had about 70 percent annual growth since it started in 1998. The business carries more than 250 different products now and is so busy that Sharon hasn't even had time to update her original product, the Car Seat Cozy, or send out as many e-mail newsletters as she would like.

Like most web-based businesses, InventiveParent.com has low personnel expenses. Sharon operates out of her home in Hampton, New Hampshire, with just two people and one part-timer to help her. The Internet allows her to outsource a lot of her administrative needs to other small businesspeople and keep overhead very low.

As with almost all the Internet millionaire entrepreneurs profiled in this book, Sharon did not raise any money to help establish her business. She kept her own costs low and, more important, believes that no traditional bank or venture capitalist would have invested in her business because it only sells unproven products from unproven inventors.

InventiveParent.com's success is even more impressive because it has spent zero on advertising. Its new customers come mostly from word-of-mouth or search engine listings. Because her product mix is so unusual,

Sharon has found that about 20 percent of her customers are referrals from other customers. Her appealing array of attractive products fills real needs in people's daily lives. This customer-focused product selection is the key to her success as a product aggregator reseller.

Sharon has put the strengths of the Internet to work in building her business at InventiveParent.com. She has identified unique products that appeal to a narrow audience but collected enough of those products to create a one-of-a-kind "virtual department store for kids" online. In some cases she doesn't even need to invest in the inventory she is selling because she has arranged to take and forward orders directly to the manufacturers of the items. What a great low-overhead business model!

INTERNET MILLIONAIRE SECRET

Diversify your product offerings. You rarely see stores that sell only one product. Why would you do that online, where it is even easier to stock additional products? Adding the products of potential competitors actually increased the sales and traffic of InventiveParent.com.

There are many reasons, both commercial and psychological, for diversification, but two of the most important are that (a) customers like to buy more than one item from online stores because it reduces their average shipping cost per item, and (b) consumers naturally trust businesses that seem larger and more established.

Stocking multiple products also gives you the opportunity to receive more than one sale from each customer. After all, the people most likely to purchase from you are those who have purchased before—why not give them additional products to purchase and continue your profitable relationship together?

Just as Sid Kreis started Seyberts.com as an offshoot of his hobby of shooting pool, and Sharon Mullen based her business on her personal experience as a mother, you can use expertise developed from your personal interests, hobbies, or needs to help develop a merchandising plan that reaches other people like you.

What interests or areas of expertise do you have in your life that could lend themselves to a product-based reseller approach?

INTERNET MILLIONAIRE SECRET:
Affiliate Advertising Programs

Did you know that you can start a business selling top-quality merchandise and services from name-brand companies with zero investment in inventory or customer service? Participating as a publisher in an online affiliate advertising program offers you exactly that opportunity.

An affiliate ad is an online advertisement for a product or service that entrepreneurs publish on their websites in order to collect a commission on every sale of that product or service that they deliver to the advertiser. If you post such ads on your site, you are referred to as an affiliate "publisher" in the lingo of affiliate programs.

For example, if you, as a consumer, see and click on a website ad for a credit card or a dating service, it's likely that the website owner ("publisher") who posted that ad will get a cash "bounty" for delivering your visit or sale to the affiliate advertiser. These bounties can be a percentage of each sale or a fixed dollar amount. The ads can be obtained for free from the advertiser or from affiliate program companies such as Commission Junction that act as brokers between advertisers and publishers. While some online advertisers only work through established affiliate program companies, many others run their own affiliate programs independently.

Thousands of top producers today offer affiliate advertising programs as an incentive to get entrepreneurs to publish their ads online. If you can convince enough people to visit your site to see the affiliate ads you post, some of your visitors will click through the ads to visit the advertisers' websites and/or purchase the items shown in your affiliate ads. Then, you'll eventually start receiving checks from the advertisers.

So, whenever you find a product or service you like, it's worth considering if you'd like to become an affiliate publisher for that company. If the affiliate advertiser approves your participation in its publisher program, this is as easy as simply sharing some of their affiliate ads with whatever online audience you might have access to!

The chief benefit of affiliate programs to entrepreneur publishers is that you can effectively sell other people's goods with zero capital required to invest in any product development or inventory. If you have

*an audience of online shoppers or you are interested in or good at pro-
moting things online, using affiliate ads to promote sales to your audiences can be very profitable because it requires so little overhead.*

AFFILIATE PRODUCT RESELLER ENTREPRENEUR:
MATT HENDERSON, TRAFFICMATT.COM

In 2002, Matt Henderson was a thirty-three-year-old father making his living by hanging wallpaper in Spartanburg, South Carolina. With just a high
school education and a family to feed, his career options were limited.

In search of better money and a more fulfilling career, he started a website after a friend explained the basics of affiliate advertising to him. Matt
saw the business potential of using affiliate ads for other people's products
to make himself money by marketing to the huge audience online.

Matt created TrafficMatt.com to discuss products that he liked and
thought would appeal to others looking for similar product information.
Today, he has more than a dozen niche-focused sites, each of which specializes in a specific product or service area.

Matt carries no inventory but simply focuses on providing helpful
information on complex products such as credit card accounts, auto vehi-
cle reports, online dating services, and digital-imaging software. These
products serve specific needs that people go online to research and are
also complicated enough that users appreciate his concise explanations
and recommendations of the features of each product. The value of the
information that Matt compiles and writes attracts users and keeps them
coming back, too.

More important, each product's advertiser also offers an affiliate program
to publishers like Matt (or you) who promote its products. These affiliate
ads offer a commission or bounty on each unit sold through the ads.

The beauty of affiliate ads is that they allow entrepreneurs like you
and Matt to sell products without ever having to invest in product development or buy inventory. Using affiliate ads to monetize your content
leaves you free instead to focus on developing the information you provide your website visitors and marketing it.

By creating simple websites that focus on popular but niche products that he thinks are interesting, Matt has built a publishing business
from his house that makes him more than $100,000 a year by simply

writing reviews of the products he chooses to focus on, offering online links to purchase them through affiliate ads from Commission Junction, and promoting his link-filled sites primarily through pay-per-click advertising.

Although Matt has focused on promoting affiliate offers to his audience, the key to his success is not just his use of affiliate ads. His success started with identifying products whose target audiences' needed better information before making their purchases. Although he's very successful, you can see that even with more than a dozen websites, Matt has barely begun to scratch the surface of the online audience's needs for more product and service information.

Matt says that his business is one anybody with enough interest and commitment can emulate. While he gives his first credit to God for having blessed him with success, he also admits to his amazement that "... I can sit here in my own house and sell things all over the world, day and night, while working less to make more money than I ever did hanging wallpaper."

Identifying the right niches to target is the critically important first step of this approach. Although it's hard to believe that one could make a living simply by offering more information about products as common as credit cards or website hosting, Matt (and many others) has proved the profit potential of such niches.

Even greater rewards await those entrepreneurs who manage to identify and exploit niche audiences seeking products that are even more profitable because of their high margins, complexity, or business demand.

These days Matt often works more hours than he did hanging wallpaper, but because he likes his new venture so much, it rarely feels like work at all. He says: "Anybody can do it if they want it enough. The potential of e-business to make money for you is really limitless."

INTERNET MILLIONAIRE SECRET

If you had top-quality products to sell but were completely free of the hassle (and capital requirements) traditionally required for buying, warehousing, shipping, and performing customer service, couldn't you come up with some good content and clever marketing strategies to push those products to audiences you know?

If you answered "yes," you should investigate publishing affiliate ads to your target market.

You'll still need to build an audience for your affiliate advertisements, like Matt Henderson has, but you won't need to develop your own products, employees, and fulfillment or customer service operations. Becoming an affiliate advertising publisher is a low-risk approach that could help you build a million-dollar e-business with very low overhead.

INFORMATION PRODUCT RESELLER E-BUSINESSES

As TrafficMatt.com's affiliate advertising e-business shows, information is the easiest and cheapest thing to distribute online, so it's not surprising that some very interesting and profitable businesses have been built by repackaging publicly available information online. Great examples include The Drudge Report, FARK.com, and Digital Media Wire.

PREMIER ONLINE NEWS PACKAGER:
THE DRUDGE REPORT

One of the first online news junkies to compete with the major media, one-man reporter extraordinaire Matt Drudge has created a news site that gets millions of visitors every day. Sometimes he even beats the TV networks to break big stories.

His business model is straightforward—he collects and posts links to the top news story of the day. The major reporting work is done by NBC, CNN, *The New York Times,* and the major newswire services, with Drudge consolidating links to the best stories on each topic for his audience's ease of use. He also includes links to the top columnists in a variety of fields including politics and business. The site generates millions of page views per day and is recognized as an important force in journalism.

This sort of success in a mainstream topic area like news may be challenging to replicate in today's more crowded online marketplace, but more focused approaches to repackaging information still offer excellent upside with limited capital investment required. Let's take a look at some other successful examples of repackaging information online but for more targeted audiences.

HUMOROUS INFORMATION RESELLER:
DREW CURTIS, FARK.COM

By focusing on a specific demographic (young males) and adding his own humorous perspective to coverage of the events of the day, Drew Curtis has made a business out of simply surfing the Web.

Visit FARK.com and you'll find a daily updated list of links to funny, entertaining, weird, or titillating stories from all over the Web (and the world). Primarily targeting bored office workers with Internet connections (a huge and growing audience), FARK's daily links collection attracts more than 50 million page views each month.

Drew identified an underserved audience and has given them what they want: entertainment. He has built this audience over several years but done it all from his home outside Lexington, Kentucky. In our first interview together, he even informed me that he had managed to change the diaper of his toddler while we were speaking!

Visit his website and you will quickly see that the key to success of Drew's business has been his unique sense of humor. The word "fark" is an example—he made it up so that he could curse on Internet message boards without getting into trouble.

FARK.com simply features links to publicly available content, from news stories to funny photos. Drew and his volunteers categorize each link and add a tag that describes the article they link to. News stories are categorized as Amusing, Spiffy, Obvious, Follow-Up, Dumbass, or Weird. Of course, for a site with a 95 percent male audience, it's not surprising that that FARK's most popular category of links is Boobies.

Attracting this targeted audience of young male office workers has allowed Drew to develop a profitable advertising business. His business has grown even faster since the resurgence of online advertising started in 2004. In addition to FARK's ad business, he also charges $5 a month as a subscription fee for people who want to get access to the latest FARK links before they are even posted on the site.

FARK.com started simply because Drew surfed the Web a lot. Each morning he would collect links to things he thought were funny to send to his friends. Demand from friends and friends of friends grew this daily e-mail into a larger habit of five or six e-mails a day. Naturally, building a website to post the material was his next step.

Like many entrepreneurs, Drew's success was at least partially due to some luck: His first choice for a website was to focus on curry recipes! The popularity of FARK's humor links has far exceeded his expectations (and the probable upside of any curry website). I was especially inspired by his answers to two questions I asked him:

Q: How much time did you put in to get started, and how much do you spend now each day?

Curtis: To tell the truth, I have never even stopped to ask that question. I have been having so much fun doing FARK every day that I don't even count my hours and never have.

Q: Did you try to raise money to get started?

Curtis: No. No venture capital person would ever invest in a business based on free content and staffed by volunteers that targets people who are bored at work.

Busy people, like investors, don't get my business because they are busy. They aren't even aware of my website, even if their assistants or employees are surfing the site every day.

FARK.com has zero employees, most of the website publishing is automated, and Drew's only regular help consists of unpaid volunteers who enjoy being involved in the site so much that they contribute time and content for free.

In fact, it turns out that most of FARK's content comes from user submissions. Readers actually compete to send in the best material. This clever leveraging of the audience's free time and enthusiasm gives Drew inexpensive content that he has made a business out of repackaging for other audience members.

Another aspect of FARK.com that impressed me is that the business didn't originate in any of the "cool" major cities, like New York or San Francisco, thought to be meccas for hip, young professionals. The Internet allows FARK.com to reach the whole world from Drew's home in Kentucky.

Drew's advice to aspiring entrepreneurs considering an Internet-based business is simple: "Don't give up under any circumstances. Do whatever it takes. There will come a point just right before you succeed when you want to just bail completely, but you need to stick with it. That supposedly good job with the stable salary just isn't worth it compared to the flexibility and satisfaction you can have being your own boss."

Spoken like a true entrepreneur!

INTERNET MILLIONAIRE SECRET:
K.I.S.S.

"Keep it simple, stupid." FARK.com's business model is very simple, yet Drew Curtis has a keen sense of what his target audience is interested in seeing each day. He profits from their spare time by simply repackaging publicly available information into a fun and easy-to-use format.

Your e-business doesn't have to reinvent the wheel or deliver an earth-shattering new product to be very profitable. Focus on the interests and needs of your target market instead, and then apply "Occam's Razor" (see sidebar below) to find the easiest and most cost-effective solution to profitably meet their needs.

Drew's success with FARK.com is inspiring. He has built a great business by simply doing something he enjoys. Plus, he has very low overhead because he works from home in low-cost, rural Kentucky and has no employees. FARK.com is a great example of a business that could only have been created by taking advantage of the Internet.

OCCAM'S RAZOR

An English philosopher, William of Ockham, popularized a fundamental theory of logic used to test the relative merit of differing propositions. Today, these principles are summed up in the statement: "The simplest solution is usually the correct one."

You should put the principle of Occam's Razor to work in building your e-business, too. When deciding on what to sell, don't overcomplicate your life or your business by choosing products or services that are too complex to produce or for customers to understand. Occam's razor suggests that most problems can be correctly solved by drawing on as few complicating assumptions as possible.

> You can offer more complex products later—getting started today
> with the simplest approach will help you demonstrate the profitabil-
> ity of your new e-business (and put money in your pocket) sooner.

B2B INFORMATION RESELLER:
NED SHERMAN, DIGITAL MEDIA WIRE

Ned Sherman has built a million-dollar e-business by taking advantage of
another Internet Millionaire Secret: the business-to-business target market. His daily "Digital Media Wire" e-mail is a free newsletter that reaches
a desirable business audience of tens of thousands of media professionals
worldwide. Ned has parlayed this audience into a sizable business supported by advertisers that pay him to reach his readers with their ads.

As an attorney, Ned realized that there was a shortage of information
available to his clients who were interested in the latest legal and business
information about deals in the new entertainment-technology-media
industry. While some trade magazines covered the emerging digital con-
vergence industry, they were published only weekly or monthly and did
not feed the audience's demand for daily updates in the fast-moving
new field. He recognized that e-mail was the ideal way to cheaply
deliver business-to-business (B2B) information about the latest deals in
digital-music licensing, video games, interactive TV, intellectual prop-
erty issues, and strategic relationships between the companies active in
those markets.

In late 2000, Ned quit his law firm job and started publishing daily e-
mails. The newsletter focused on the financial transactions, legal details,
and new strategies that his target market wanted to know more about. By
simply summarizing publicly available information on the latest deals,
announcements, and events in the digital media industry, he was able to
create an in-demand product with little overhead.

Ned used a simple text-only format to start, both to save money and
to ensure that everybody who received the e-mails could read them easily. He simply forwarded his first efforts to a few hundred friends, family
members, and former clients. Then, Digital Media Wire took off. With no
advertising, Ned had 3,000+ subscribers after the first month. Advertisers
soon started calling him because of the desirable audience of media executives his new publication had collected.

Since then, Digital Media Wire has grown almost exclusively through word-of-mouth. Ned has done no advertising of his own, other than handing out promotional postcards at media company offices and appropriate industry conferences, plus a few small barter deals with magazines. Additionally, he is proud to point out that Digital Media Wire's mailing list is 100 percent opt-in. He's never needed to rent a list of e-mail addresses to grow the business because the newsletter's content is so important to its audience that new subscribers seek him out every day.

Today, Digital Media Wire has 30,000+ subscribers to its daily, ad-supported e-mail newsletter. This targeted, self-selected audience attracts top advertisers interested in reaching its executive audience. Law firms, technology companies, and media firms, including RealNetworks, PricewaterhouseCoopers, Apple Computer, the British Consulate, and Hewlett-Packard, have taken advantage of the newsletter's display-type advertising or its classifieds-style section that is often used for job postings.

With only four full-time employees (including Ned), Digital Media Wire has grown into a very successful company with more than $1 million in sales annually. Ned has also been able to create a "brand" for digital media industry information that he is using to organize Digital Media Wire conferences and to publish industry directories, too. Global media powerhouse VNU recently bought out Digital Media Wire's part ownership of a conference they organized together, and it's clear that more deals are on the way to increase the profitability and reach of the startup soon.

Ned says that he's been amazed at how great an impact a small business like his can have on such major industries as media and technology. "I sometimes have to pinch myself when I realize that I did this out of my apartment with almost no money where big companies with teams of top journalists and engineers have failed," he says.

He is convinced that there remain similar opportunities for new entrepreneurs to start similar B2B-focused information reseller businesses. "We have just hit the tip of the iceberg," he says. "There are tremendous opportunities for entrepreneurs to use the Internet and e-mail, plus the newer distribution channels like SMS [simple messaging services], podcasting, mobile, and RSS [the "really simple syndication" format for distributing news content], to build profitable new publishing businesses by targeting business audiences."

Last, I asked Ned why he would recommend e-business to other entrepreneurs: "Owning your own business gives you the ability to control your own destiny," he says. "There's nothing more satisfying than controlling both your business and life. If you have the passion, a good idea, and are willing to work hard and be careful with your costs, anyone can succeed with the tools available today online."

INTERNET MILLIONAIRE SECRET

Like the Drudge Report or FARK.com, one of the best things about Ned Sherman's approach to building his million-dollar e-business is that he obtains his content virtually for free.

Although Ned employs an editor to review and rewrite the hundreds of submissions they receive, most of the information carried in each day's Digital Media Wire newsletter is obtained at no cost. In fact, it is usually sent directly to him by publicists and businesses worldwide that want publicity in his newsletters for their latest achievements.

Ned also keeps his costs very low because his newsletters focus simply on reporting the latest industry news instead of offering opinion, commentary, or investigative reporting (which would require more expensive reporters as employees). By simply repackaging and sharing information that is difficult to obtain concisely elsewhere, Ned's small team has created a profitable e-business by providing a news "filtering" service for a busy audience.

The success of Digital Media Wire shows that there's no need for you to limit your new e-business's approach to providing consumer-oriented products or services. In fact, people are often more willing to spend money on business needs than personal ones. That's because they expect that a business product will help them make more money in their own business, and also because such business expenses are usually tax-deductible.

As you develop your own million-dollar e-business idea through the exercises in this book, be sure to give some extra thought to how a B2B approach might be right for you, too.

WHAT CAN YOU CREATE?

The fascinating thing about The Drudge Report, FARK.com, Digital Media Wire, and many other, similar sites is that their owners don't actually create much, if any, original content. They've created very profitable e-businesses primarily by filtering and repackaging professional-grade content created by others.

Your unique perspective on the world can help you create an information reselling business, too. If there's a topic or an industry that you find interesting, you can quickly build a website that simply collects links to news stories in that field. You are adding value by playing the role of editor for your readers, directing them to the most relevant news or entertainment in that field. Consistent publication and promotion of your link collections, using techniques such as those detailed in Part 4 of this book, could transform your website into the next FARK.com, Digital Media Wire, or even a Drudge-sized money machine!

Original Product Millionaires: Inventing or Improving a Product

Another way to create a million-dollar business is to invent or improve a product. This Product Millionaire route tends to require more mechanical or manufacturing expertise than the others, but it is a proven way to wealth.

The easiest way for an individual entrepreneur to be successful with this approach is to come up with a simple idea that can be mass-produced. The infamous "Pet Rock" craze of the 1970s is a perfect example of this phenomenon.

Once you have an attractive product, you can make money by selling it yourself (retail), selling it to distributors (wholesale), or licensing the product to a larger corporation that may do the production and sales for you. Many entrepreneurs manage to do all three.

Because the Internet is so good at reaching and aggregating formerly dispersed audiences (as I'll discuss further in Chapter 5, on Niche Millionaires), there are now more markets for more specialized products than ever before. Successful identification of a million-dollar product idea will quickly lead you into additional questions involving the "Three Ps" of product development: prototyping, production, and patents.

1. *Prototyping.* For inventors with a good idea for a physical product, the first step is to develop prototypes, or examples, of the concept. A prototype can be made in your basement or garage out of plastic, bananas, felt, or whatever materials are relevant, but it must demonstrate the functionality and features that make your new item attractive. The best part about this stage of becoming a Product Millionaire is that you can do most of the work yourself (and test the results on your friends!).

2. *Production.* If your friends and family find the new gadget useful, your successful prototyping can soon lead to production. Depending on the type of materials and the complexity of assembly, production of your new million-dollar gadgets will most likely start out in your garage, family room, or kitchen. Many successful food, decorative, collectible, and gift e-businesses have started this way and thrived on the Internet.

3. *Patents.* While developing your prototypes and moving toward production, if your product is a functional article, you'll also want to investigate patents for your original product. Article I, Section 8 of the United States Constitution is the foundation of U.S. patent law. These laws provide protection for the inventors of useful objects. In practical terms, to patent your gizmo means that you are the only one who can make money from selling it for a defined period of time (traditionally seventeen years in the United States, but now more often twenty years due to international treaties).

Patenting your invention is a process you should start as soon as you believe that you have a viable product, otherwise publication or widespread public knowledge of your product's concepts could destroy your ability to patent it later. Consult an attorney to pursue these matters further.

Because patent law is a highly technical specialty, my recommendation would be to go beyond your usual circle of acquaintances and only consult a lawyer with a specialty in patent law. (Your average business lawyer or divorce attorney is likely to know only enough about patents to hurt your case.)

The best part about patents is that they grant you the exclusive rights to make money from your new invention. If you succeed in obtaining such a patent, you may then be able to simply license your invention to a larger company in exchange for royalties from sales. This approach can keep you from needing to get involved with production at all!

INTERNET MILLIONAIRE SECRET:
You Can Make Money Selling to "Nobody"

You may have an interesting product or service but doubt its marketability. More often, you are excited about its marketability, but friends or family, the people you trust, doubt its potential! These naysayers will spend a lot of energy trying to convince you that "nobody will buy that." But is that really true?

The fact is that nobody can predict retail consumer behavior. Pet rocks and hula hoops are examples of crazes that no one could have predicted, while sophisticated consumer research supposedly guaranteed the success of Sony's Betamax videotape format and Ford's Edsel cars.

Part of being a successful entrepreneur is learning to "trust your gut." This often means acting despite conventional wisdom and taking risks that would scare others.

Luckily, the Internet offers entrepreneurs a chance to reach more people than ever before, and that's a reason to have confidence in your new product's potential: If you find your product interesting, the chances are that others out there in cyberspace may, too.

When your naysayers claim that "nobody" would buy your product or service, do they really mean absolutely zero customers would be interested? "Nobody" probably really means "nobody I know" or "nobody in our town" because, in the past, that's as far as most entrepreneurs could afford to market their goods. Most people's vision of customer markets is limited by geography because industrial-age businesses could not afford to reach a wide audience without a huge marketing budget.

Enter the Internet: Perhaps your naysayers think that only one person in 1,000, or even one person in 10,000, would be interested. If that's the case, what they are really saying is, "Somebody might be interested, but you'll spend all your money on marketing before you can ever reach him." That's a valid business critique in a traditional economy, but not on the Internet!

Because the Internet destroys the limitations of geography, it can help you reach millions of people inexpensively. If you can find interest from even one in 10,000 potential customers, you have an exciting e-business possibility on your hands because the cost-effective reach of the Internet is so broad.

Remember the Law of Large Numbers from Chapter 1? Little niches add up to a lot of "nobodies." The Internet represents the first time in human history that communities can be built purely on common interest instead of around accidents of geography. Niche interests and demand for niche products thrive online because the Internet's cheap communications allow communities to aggregate around relatively rare interests and hobbies. Whether your interests and products involve rare Japanese goldfish, Lawrence of Arabia, collecting antique typewriters, the latest medical research, or extreme skiing, you're sure to find collections of people online pursuing those same interests. This means that you can sell niche items to those groups even if each of the participants is a rare individual in his own town. Online, people can cheaply and easily find each other (and your targeted product). You can reach them with a website and e-mail list much more cheaply than you ever could build and stock and advertise a real store.

The moral of this story: Don't be afraid to pursue your entrepreneurial dreams. The Internet is here to help you reach hundreds of millions of people online, even one percent of one percent of one percent of those people is a lot more than nobody—and all those "nobodies" can make you rich!

It takes courage and perseverance to build a business focusing on an original product. But when an innovative new product captures the audience's interest, it can be very profitable. So profitable, in fact, that success stories in this category do not stay independent for long. An independent retailer with a successful original product usually enters into wider distribution relationships and then receives buyout offers from larger retailers.

To find a good example of an original product entrepreneur who has found success online but has not yet been bought out, I merely interviewed my own wife.

ORIGINAL PRODUCT ENTREPRENEUR:
KATHERINE LEE, SWEATERBABE.COM

Knitting has always been a passion for my wife, Katherine. She has turned her expert knitting and crochet skills into a business online by selling original knitting and crochet patterns through her website. Her experience is a good example of how you can take advantage of your own interests to make money once you produce a website that can reach millions inexpensively.

In 2001, Katherine was fed up with the politics in her corporate job and decided to quit. After a couple of unfulfilling jobs in the fashion business, she decided to strike out on her own by founding SweaterBabe.com. The decision to pursue self-employment was reinforced when she became pregnant with our first child.

Unlike many product entrepreneurs, Katherine identified her target market (knitting and crochet enthusiasts) before she decided on her products. Careful analysis of competition online and from local yarn stores nationwide convinced her that there was a business opportunity for a new website that offered hip, young knitting and crochet patterns for sale instead of the dowdy grandmotherish styles most often published by knitting and crochet magazines.

Her patterns are sexy and fresh designs for garments like scarves, sweaters, hats, and ponchos, as well as accessories like purses and baby blankets. These design differences may be subtle to many consumers, but such styling details are a big deal in the fashion world.

She also saw that by selling her patterns online she could reach a lot more customers than by just selling them in a traditional yarn store. Because a website could cost-effectively reach far more people, it had a better chance of connecting with the less common and younger, hipper knitting/crochet audience that she wanted to target. (These target customers are also more likely to be online, just like the bored office workers who visit FARK.com.)

To set up her first website, my brother helped Katherine learn Macromedia Dreamweaver (a common website production and editing software program) and install the shopping cart software. It took her about two months of part-time work to set up her first site. This demonstrates how even just a couple of years ago, it took relationships (and fees) with several different vendors to get various e-commerce features working together on a website. Today, she is certain that setting up a similar site would be much faster because now many hosting companies provide design templates that also include integrated e-commerce shopping carts.

Her startup costs were about $500. Most of that was fees for the credit card processing account and signing a long-term hosting contract. (Today, however, competition in the hosting and credit card markets has largely eliminated those costs.)

The most interesting part of Katherine's business is in how she delivers her products. Although when she started she would print out and mail each pattern purchased, last fall she discovered a digital-downloading service that allows her to upload each of her pattern documents one time and then it handles all the transaction-processing for her customers' purchases.

Now customers visit SweaterBabe.com, select and purchase their patterns, and download them all without any work on Katherine's part. She simply checks the sales reports and bank balances whenever she wants to take a break from designing new patterns.

SweaterBabe.com is a great part-time business because, as a mother, Katherine only has a few hours per week to keep it going and growing. For very little effort her website is out there generating business for her, and more people are finding it and buying her patterns every day. Plus, she is confident that if she had more time to put into SweaterBabe.com, it would pay off further.

Lately, Katherine has not found more time to invest in SweaterBabe.com because she is so busy with media deals generated by its success. For example:

▲ Because of the website's popularity, she has been approached and had her designs published by several major knitting and crochet magazines.

▲ She has also been asked to contribute patterns to several books.

▲ Her own book of crochet patterns, *SweaterBabe.com's Fabulous & Flirty Crochet Patterns,* has just been published by a publisher who found her through her website.

▲ She was even called by two sets of TV producers to audition for new television shows about knitting and crochet!

Like many of our other featured entrepreneurs, Katherine's advice is straightforward and encouraging: "Go ahead and build your own e-business. I'm still amazed that something as simple as selling patterns can work online, but I've found a great market. If you can come up with something to offer that people haven't seen before, it can work for you, too. It's easier to do than ever before, and with less risk, because it's entirely up to you how much you put into it. Find a simple concept and just do it. You can create an income stream that you might never have imagined."

Katherine says that the Internet has been critical to her success story because, quite simply, SweaterBabe.com couldn't exist without it. Like the local yarn stores that are in every town, she could never afford to reach as many people in the real world as she does online. E-business also allows her the freedom to set her own hours and build up the business on the side whenever her other responsibilities allow.

Katherine's favorite things about being an e-business entrepreneur are, not surprisingly, this flexibility and the money. She's making very nice money and, perhaps more important, she's successfully pursuing a life-long dream that also allows her time to care for our children. She also enjoys the compliments she gets by e-mail from all over the world from people who love her designs. Even better is when she visits yarn stores or knitting events these days and people call her "the Sweater Babe"!

Katherine's success with SweaterBabe.com shows how turning a hobby into a business can bring a variety of benefits into an entrepreneur's life, including money, flexibility, and even a little fame. You should be on the lookout in your own life for opportunities to create and sell unique items that you enjoy producing, too.

INTERNET MILLIONAIRE SECRET

SweaterBabe.com shows that there is room on the Internet for original products, especially those that are uniquely creative or useful. Although your hobbies may not become sustainable businesses if you can only afford to market to customers in your hometown, on the Internet you can reach millions of people very cost-effectively with your creations.

SweaterBabe.com also highlights the great potential of digital downloading. If your original product can be contained in a digital file (using words, graphics, or music as opposed to physical objects), you too could run an almost entirely software-based business. That frees the entrepreneur to focus on developing new products, marketing, and growing the business while the sales are automatically fulfilled online.

How Can You Become a Product Millionaire?

The first step is to draw on your own experiences for answers to these two questions:

- ▲ Are there products that you've created or adapted to serve needs or interests in your own life?

- ▲ Are there activities or processes in your life that are overly difficult because of lack of specialized tools or gadgets?

I know this sounds too easy to be true, but even the simplest Product Millionaire ideas can be very lucrative: A young father was frequently "splashed" by his baby boy when changing his diapers. He invented a "Wee Block," which does exactly what the name says. It's now sold worldwide, including at InventiveParent.com (profiled earlier in this chapter).

PRODUCT CRITERIA

As you can see, creating Product Millionaire businesses is easiest if your product (1) meets a need that already exists in the marketplace, and (2) is easily explained. These two factors will help it become popular through word-of-mouth much more quickly than gadgets that are complex or are designed to meet uncommon needs.

Additionally, it's best if the product fits easily on store shelves and in shipping boxes, so it's easy for retailers to stock the product and ship it to buyers. (Even better is if you can make your products deliverable simply by downloading them from the Internet.)

The bottom line is that Product Millionaires make money by helping improve people's lives much like Efficiency Millionaires do. They just use innovative products to do it instead of new processes or distribution methods. Even the simplest ideas can be turned into million-dollar businesses if they meet the audience's needs. If you do it right, those simple product ideas can quickly grow—and your business might just get acquired by a major corporation as well.

Product Millionaire Exercise

Take some time to consider your answers to the following questions:

▲ What needs can you identify in your own life that could be fulfilled with better or more specialized products, packaging, materials, or parts?

▲ Are there products that you've customized to serve needs in your own life?

▲ Are there any off-the-shelf products that you regularly modify or rearrange or recombine to improve their efficiency?

▲ Could you market the technique you use to customize the product, or market the modified products themselves?

▲ What are the everyday items in your life that need a redesign or an upgrade?

▲ Can you turn any of these ideas into products?

Write down in your Millionaire Idea Journal the ideas that these questions should stimulate. They will be valuable ammunition for the continuing business development exercises later in this book.

5
THE INTERNET'S THIRD
MILLIONAIRE WAVE—NICHES

THE THIRD WAVE of Internet millionaires have profited by recognizing that communities are formed based not only on common social interests, but also on shared purchasing interests. Because of the Internet's ability to aggregate previously dispersed audiences, now any community is a market for specialized products that in the past might not have been profitable when their reach was limited to local markets.

By identifying these communities, large or small, you can target their members as potential customers for appropriately targeted goods and services that address the needs of their specific hobbies, lifestyles, products, industries, or services. I call this the Niche Millionaire strategy.

To implement this strategy, set yourself up as an expert in whatever niche you are qualified for, and that has business potential.

By targeting a niche that you know and like, you can use your credibility to create a business for yourself that you can enjoy and could also make you rich. Because you can keep your costs low as an e-business entrepreneur, you will also be able to target smaller markets that big companies neglect. This means less competition for you and probably higher profit margins, too.

Niche Millionaires

Historically, businesses could only reach customers within their local or regional markets. Only truly large companies could invest in advertisements or branch offices or stores to reach customers nationally or worldwide.

A major difference between such Industrial Age companies and today's Information Age e-businesses is that Internet companies are not limited by geography. This means that you can reach customers worldwide more cheaply than ever before possible. As a result, even small ideas that offer only a small profit per purchase that are purchased by only a small fraction of the reachable audience can still yield *really big* profits for small e-business entrepreneurs like you. So even small businesses with limited appeal and no staff can make a lot of money these days because of the worldwide 24/7 reach of the Internet (remember the Law of Large Numbers from Chapter 1). Two concepts in particular enable e-businesses: Internet distribution and virtual communities.

INTERNET DISTRIBUTION

Both product and information industries were historically based on control of distribution. After a popular item like a vinyl record was manufactured or an important decision about a big financial deal was made, those who controlled how that product or information was distributed almost always made money by positioning themselves as middlemen. It was similar with service businesses—services traditionally were delivered in person and their distribution was consequently restricted to local markets.

The Internet explodes these traditions because now information can travel worldwide instantly and essentially for free; products can ship directly from their warehouses to consumers without middlemen distributors; and many services, especially information-based ones, can be distributed virtually for free online. For potential Niche Millionaires like yourself, this means that you have the chance to market your niche expertise worldwide unlike any generation in history.

VIRTUAL COMMUNITIES

The Internet brings people together around their shared interests and needs, creating virtual communities of like-minded people who interact using e-mail and websites. This results in a fundamental change in the way both society and business can be organized because these people may develop deep relationships and even do business together but never meet face-to-face in the real world.

WHAT DOES THIS HAVE TO DO WITH YOU?

The definition of a community is simply a group of people who share a common interest. For a business person like you, if you have expertise or products relating to the common interest of such a community, you instantly have a potential million-dollar business opportunity!

Virtual communities are a major trend that you should get behind because each online community can be viewed as a new market. If you can understand the needs or interests of such groups of people, you can sell them goods or services that meet those needs. This can be even more rewarding for you if you happen to have a passion or hobby for such a niche yourself. Just as doctors or airline pilots or Porsche mechanics make money by delivering specialized services, you may also be able to leverage your own specialized knowledge to create a million-dollar business serving a niche community.

Your Hobbies Can Make You Rich!

The most exciting part about the Niche Millionaire business model strategy is that you can draw upon your own hobbies and interests to create your own profitable e-business niche. The wide reach of the Internet means that almost any niche interest is sure to be shared by others online. By addressing a smaller target audience with products or services specifically matched to that audience's interests, you may uncover unprecedented opportunities to make money while pursuing your own interests.

In fact, by using today's software and e-marketing tools, you can inexpensively run a business yourself from home, keeping overhead low and profitability high while pursuing your own interests and developing social and business relationships with others who share them.

EVERY NICHE AUDIENCE IS A POTENTIAL CUSTOMER GROUP

E-business entrepreneurs like you should realize that the hundreds of millions (and soon to be billions) of people online worldwide have all brought their real-world interests and needs with them to the Internet. There are millions of virtual niche communities emerging online. Each one is full of people from all over the world pursuing their shared interests and needs 24/7 around all kinds of subjects. There are thousands of websites, chat rooms, e-mail lists, buddy groups, and online stores servicing big, popular social interests—from pop music to sports, movie stars, clothes, electronics, and dating. More prosaic interests like shoe shopping, health insurance, termite removal, cleaning supplies, and recipe swapping are also huge hits and offer business opportunities as well.

There are also business-oriented online communities built around work-related topics. These virtual communities exist in every industry, from architecture to zoology, and include many subspecialties such as industry-specific research, equipment and supplies directories, and conferences.

In addition, every online store or e-mail newsletter has its own community, even if the owners of that website have not yet realized it. Each collection of customers or subscribers shares the common interest that inspired them to visit the site and purchase goods or subscribe to the e-business's newsletters. Even though they can't see each other, the pooling of these common interests among this collection of people creates niche communities that can be turned into profitable markets.

Smart businesses are nurturing these audiences to increase their customer loyalty. The easiest way is to offer the online community the ability to offer feedback. This is why you see more and more message boards, e-mail newsletters, live chat support, and online polls on the websites you visit. These businesses recognize the power of interactivity to create community. The community effect in turn reinforces the audience's loyalty to that brand and customers' purchasing activity.

NICHE GROWTH

There are considerable business opportunities for entrepreneurs who recognize that any online audience of customers or readers or viewers or poll participants can be seen as a target market. Businesses have hardly begun to tap all of the micromarkets that the World Wide Web has enabled. In addition to the more mainstream virtual communities, there are still an almost unlimited number of million-dollar e-business opportunities in narrower niche communities online. While some opportunities are large and others small, the Internet is still very young. Experts have compared the growth of the Net to a baseball game by suggesting that it is still only in the second or third inning!

Moreover, as time goes on and more people come online across the world, the number of these niche markets will increase. Simultaneously, the amount of time spent online by people who are already "wired" is continuing to increase, as is the reach of digital media and commerce through new platforms such as mobile phones and podcasting. Virtually every niche community on the Web is going to continue to grow and represent increasingly large business opportunities. (In other words, if you have a niche you love but are afraid is too small or, conversely, is already filled by competitors, don't worry. There will eventually be more than enough customers to go around!)

A good example is iVillage.com. Founded during the go-go 1990s, this website has been the most successful online venture targeting women; it even went public during the dot-com boom. Although iVillage is still very successful, it's obvious that the hundreds of millions of women online today are creating demand for many more niche businesses targeting specialized aspects of the female experience. Online communities about women's fashions, pregnancy, education, religion, hobbies, careers, and sports are all flourishing separately from the iVillage portal.

For example, before the Internet, there may have been only one person in every town who was interested in an obscure subject. Because of the Internet, however, all of these people with an obscure but shared interest—whether it's Egyptian pyramid building or raising pet cockroaches or collecting vintage spoons or playing volleyball blindfolded—can now find each other! Although just one person per town was not even enough to have a conversation, when each small town's representative of that interest group or hobby gets online, you suddenly have a community of thousands of them!

And that's just in the United States. If you look abroad to include foreign fans of whatever specialty topic interests you, there may be hundreds of thousands or even millions of people whom you will never meet but who share the same seemingly obscure interests. *Identifying and developing products or services to serve such communities is the goal of a Niche Millionaire.*

YOUR TARGET NICHES

So what million-dollar niche should you target? Do you have hobbies, business expertise, personal relationships, unique experiences, or access to goods/services that others do not?

Such niches don't need to be as broad or as deep as you might think. Because of the Net's ability to aggregate an audience around almost any topic, even very narrow niche specialties can represent viable million-dollar targets for your new e-business.

What about your life, industry, hobbies, or region might be fascinating to others? Just because it's common where you live or work doesn't mean it wouldn't be fascinating to people elsewhere.

Every aspect of your life and occupation deserves examination as a potential million-dollar e-business opportunity that you could exploit online by serving others with similar niche interests or needs.

Niche Millionaire Strategies

If you can find an audience niche that you think has potential, you'll next want to think about how to make money from that niche audience. Niche Millionaire businesses are most often based on selling either products or content (i.e., information) to targeted audience groups. (Yes, my Millionaire Types often overlap, and this first niche strategy, the product-based Niche Millionaire business, demonstrates that perfectly.)

Niche Product Businesses

Selling products is the traditional way of making money from an audience. For example, you would find (or manufacture yourself) products relating to that specialty for resale to the niche audience.

For example, All Handmade Baskets is an online business that specializes in selling the handwoven baskets traditionally made in the Northeast United States. Although handmade baskets may not be an interest you share, imagine how widely dispersed the enthusiasts and collectors of such baskets were before the Internet arrived. To the niche audience that collects American baskets, this website is a big deal because it aggregates handwoven basket information and products that were traditionally difficult to find.

Amazon.com provides a larger example of the niche product strategy as it continues to add additional stores focused on specific interests that go far beyond its original focus on books. For example, Amazon has started selling local and regional gourmet foods on its websites, recognizing that local niche food specialties can have wide appeal when put online where customers from other areas of the world can purchase them.

If you can identify local products that merit wider audiences, you could similarly start your own Niche Millionaire business by putting them online for sale. (I'll be introducing you to the easy-to-use software tools needed to do so later in the book.)

The simplest examples of niche products, however, are those that are handmade. Because they are produced one at a time by hand, they are by definition limited to a niche audience. This care and attention to manufacturing often means that they are high quality, uniquely creative, or personalized, too. A great example of this kind of online niche products business is Bathboats.com.

NICHE PRODUCT ENTREPRENEUR #1:
DANA MCDILL, BATHBOATS.COM

Dana McDill and his wife, Mary, are working artists. For decades, they have made their living by traveling around the country to art shows and craft fairs to sell their handcrafted toy boats. In 1999, Dana put up a website to help promote their boats. He has been surprised and pleased at its profitability ever since.

The boats that the McDills sell at Bathboats.com are bathtub toys that they craft themselves from local wood in Princeton, Minnesota. There are three different basic designs that they sell, but they also take custom orders. Bathboats.com customers are all interested in unique gift items. Many are grandmothers and grandfathers who want to order a custom present for their grandchildren.

The McDills have been pleasantly and consistently surprised about their success with e-business. Most of their peers in the artist community just use the web to show their work. Dana points out that there's a bigger opportunity in e-commerce for anyone with an existing business selling a niche product because they can sell it online now too.

The costs of running their e-business are so low that the McDills make a profit by selling just three of their boats each month. They have been so pleased with their sales that they haven't even started publishing an e-mail newsletter or advertising their work online, and they have not raised their prices in years.

Site maintenance is also minimal and consists of changing the pictures on the website quarterly and updating the McDills' calendar of art fair appearances. For technical issues, Dana just calls his friend Lee for help.

For the McDills, the best thing about their website business is that the revenue it generates means that they can do a lot less traveling. Just checking the e-mail each day, they find new bath boat orders—often from states and countries that they have never visited!

The Bathboats.com website business was profitable from its very first month in 1999 and has been ever since. While the McDills still make the majority of their income from exhibiting at art fairs around the country, revenues from their website greatly enhance their lifestyle by providing an extra $20,000 a year in income without much work. As Dana puts it:

> That money is great. It keeps me from having to apply for that job at Wal-Mart as a greeter! Plus, the profit per boat from online sales is much higher than from sales we make at shows because we have no costs for travel or lodging. It also keeps sales coming in for us all year round. That's important because there aren't too many art fairs in Minnesota between October and April.

Dana believes that there are still great chances to build successful new e-businesses today. He measures this opportunity by the fact that he used to get many phone orders, especially from grandparents who had never shopped online. Today, he doesn't get those calls anymore, so he concludes that shopping on the Internet must be more popular than ever. Here is his advice for you if you are considering starting an e-business today: "Just try it! Nothing ventured, nothing gained. With the Internet, you can have a presence for your products in every town in the world right away."

Bathboats.com is a great example of a niche product e-business because the product is so unique that it would probably never be able to support the overhead costs of a traditional store-based business. Just the lease on a physical store dedicated to selling handmade bath boat toys would probably cost more than its monthly profits. But in cyberspace, the McDills can reach the whole world with their wonderful boats, and enjoy the profits all year round!

I was thrilled talking with Dana because his e-business shows how working online can really improve your life even without making a million dollars. He had no technical training to start his site; he spends almost no time maintaining it; he does almost zero marketing—and it still brings him tens of thousands of dollars per year! He and his wife find their lifestyle easier (because they don't have to travel so much) and more profitable since establishing their e-business. Plus, they have the satisfaction of working from home in rural Minnesota doing what they love.

When we spoke, I advised McDill that there is also a significant opportunity for him to expand his business by simply starting an e-mail newsletter. A simple monthly newsletter sent to customers who've ordered from him online before, reminding them of the company's great bath toys, would be sure to increase his sales further with very little effort. If he then also collected e-mail addresses at his art shows, he could quickly build a larger clientele than he and Mary could probably serve with their handmade manufacturing process.

The principles demonstrated by Bathboats.com can be applied to any existing "real world" business: by putting up a website that can take additional orders for you, incremental revenue is likely to follow.

INTERNET MILLIONAIRE SECRET:
A True "Mom and Pop" Business

Bathboats.com proves that with the low cost of doing business online today you can base a business on almost anything. Before reading this story, would you have believed that there was a successful business based solely on selling handmade wooden toy boats?

The success of Bathboats.com shows that you don't have to make a million dollars for e-business to positively change your life. Thanks to help from the Internet, Dana and Mary McDill live on their own terms, take and fulfill orders from their home studio at their own speed, and enjoy the flexibility of an e-business-enabled lifestyle that was unknown just a few years ago. As artists living in rural Minnesota, the McDills have modest income expectations anyway, so an extra $20,000 each year is a huge bonus. Their e-business has helped them live more like millionaires without killing themselves in the rat race.

INTERNET MILLIONAIRE SECRET:
Free Niche Merchandise E-Business
from Café Press

If you are considering starting a merchandise-related e-business or have a niche you'd like to target but are still looking for the right products to offer, you need to know about a specialty e-commerce provider called Café Press. This exciting young company provides free online storefronts so that entrepreneurs like you can take advantage of completely out-sourced manufacturing, fulfillment, and customer service of logo-branded apparel and promotional items. Café Press offers print-on-demand pub-lishing services also.

This means that you can set up an e-store selling your own T-shirts, coffee mugs, or other personalized goods very quickly and with no startup capital required. The Café Press service includes all website hosting, design, and shopping cart services. It even includes an e-mail collection utility and newsletter mailing capability.

HOW DOES CAFÉ PRESS WORK?

Café Press bases its business on the just-in-time manufacturing and delivery of customized apparel and related items. You can upload a photo or logo design to the company's website and use it to create personally branded hats, shirts, coffee mugs, calendars, notebooks, or any of fifty or more other popular items.

Unlike traditional printers or merchandise producers, you can order small quantities (or even just one) of each item you create at an afford-able price because Café Press doesn't manufacture them until you place your order. Café Press makes its money by providing you with the merchandise and website services at a comfortable margin that covers all of its costs. For example, T-shirts cost $14.99 and coffee mugs cost $10.99 each. These prices include your design or photo custom-printed on the item, even if you buy just one. You can then sell your goods at whatever price you choose above those levels and keep the difference as your profit.

The really interesting part is that Café Press encourages you to use its system to open an online store to sell your own customized goods. You can add whatever markup you would like to the base prices and promote your goods in a personalized online store on CafePress.com, while the company handles all order taking, manufacturing, delivery, and customer service. A basic store (limited to a few items) is free, and an upgraded one that can offer more products and allows increased HTML customization of the store's look costs only $6.95 per month more.

This is an easy, fun, and very inexpensive way to get started in e-commerce. It's an excellent opportunity for entrepreneurs new to e-business because it requires no startup capital and leaves you free to concentrate on creating and promoting cool products to your targeted niche audience instead of wrestling with technology or administrative duties.

EASY AND PROFITABLE NICHE PRODUCT STRATEGIES USING CAFÉ PRESS

I recommend four ways to take advantage of this great service. In fact, just to show you how easy it can be, I've included examples of ways that I have used Café Press stores myself:

1. **Launch your own line of clothing or other merchandise.** Visit CafePress.com and search on the keyword "milkaholics" to find a store I built to showcase some cute baby clothes as a test.

2. **Use Café Press as a test environment for your product line or e-business.** Before investing in a traditional merchandise manufacturing and fulfillment operation, use this online service to test new products and customer demand for them, as I did when building an e-business for Larry King of CNN.

3. **Use the service to start a side business that can add additional revenue to your existing website business or current job.** Visit SweaterBabe.com (or visit Café Press and search on keyword "sweaterbabe") to find a store that my wife put up to sell logo-branded goods related to her knitting and crochet business.

4. *Launch a promotional clothing or merchandise line to promote an existing real-world business, too! Visit InternetMillionaire Secrets.com (or visit Café Press and search on keywords "internet millionaire secrets") to find a link to a Café Press store selling Millionaire Idea Journals, T-shirts, and coffee mugs for fans of my books.*

Since selling apparel through Café Press costs you nothing, your piece of every sale is 100 percent profit directly into your wallet. Talk about an Internet Millionaire Secret!

NICHE PRODUCT ENTREPRENEUR #2:
EILEEN DESCALLAR, THETSHIRTNEXUS.COM

Anybody can open up an online store selling custom-printed T-shirts and apparel by capitalizing on the "free" merchandise inventory offered by Café Press. Eileen Descallar has had great success by applying this approach to her favorite hobbies. Maybe you could, too?

An avid video gamer, fencer, rock climber, and chess fan, Eileen has built not just one but several Café Press stores to sell apparel relating to her hobbies. She started by creating T-shirt slogans and logos based on catch-phrases and geek slang from the video games she loves to play. Her motivation to start selling T-shirts using Café Press services was simply to try to cover the monthly expenses she was spending on online video games.

Drawing on her background as a graphic designer, it was easier for her than most people to come up with attractive logos to put on her goods. Her design skills are not the key to her success, however. Rather, it is Eileen's focus on developing products that target her own specific hobbies.

The insight that has driven her business (as well as that of many other entrepreneurs) is that traditional clothing companies don't produce "fun" clothing for niche audiences. Most of retailing is based on mass production of mass designs for mass consumer audiences.

The print-on-demand technology behind Café Press changes that and allows anyone to offer customized items one unit at a time instead. Eileen's business profits from this by offering clothing personalized to the interests of her niche audiences—clothes that her customers can't get anywhere else. Examples of Eileen's goods include T-shirts emblazoned with the word "Geek" and baseball caps that say "Gamer," fencing-themed apparel for fans of the classic sword-fighting sport, rock-climbing designs for female climbers, and other items for subcultures not served by mass market apparel retailers.

After putting up her first Café Press store, Eileen made her first sale in three days. Her business has since grown largely through word-of-mouth in the several hobbyist communities where she is active and sells merchandise.

She has spent some money on targeted pay-per-click advertising of her goods but more on visiting trade shows and conferences relating to each of her targeted interests. Because she is a longtime member of the various sporting communities, her mere presence at these events often inspires people to discuss and purchase her merchandise. She also often hands out flyers promoting the goods she makes available. (Since she likes to go to gaming conferences, fencing matches, and rock-climbing events anyway, she doesn't even really count these costs as business expenses since they are part of her normal activities!)

Eileen has grown her online apparel sales into a full-time business from her home near Santa Barbara, California. Recently laid off from her job as a graphic designer, she was pleased to find that the extra attention she's now been able to devote to her online business has more than made up for the salary she lost. Her e-business has brought her the added bonus of flexibility in her schedule, greater incentives to pursue her own hobbies, and significant financial upside as the business continues to grow, too.

Today, Eileen's mini-empire of niche-targeted online stores includes her original Café Press store, OfflineTshirts.com (for computer geeks and video gamers), plus FencingWear.com (selling goods targeted at collegiate fencing athletes), Rockgrrl.com (for women who like to rock climb), ChessMatch.net (for chess players), and FlipsideTshirts.com (targeting Filipino-Americans like Eileen herself). The online shops are also featured together in one place under the brand name TheTshirtNexus.com.

Eileen recommends e-business for many reasons, especially the fact that the ratio of income potential to time investment is very high. She says, "Stick with it. You might put out a lot of effort in the beginning designing the logos for your shirts or whatever your product is, but then you can be making money from that one-time investment for months or years to come as you sell online."

She also has valuable tips for aspiring entrepreneurs looking to identify their own niche target markets. "You have to be truly interested in what you are starting up," she says. "Niche markets are easy to identify and market to, but you need to love it—both because you are going to spend so much time at it and also because the fans of that activity who you're trying to sell to will quickly realize if you are not genuine."

Eileen definitely recommends Café Press to aspiring entrepreneurs, adding, "To start a business, even an e-business, you usually have to have some capital up-front, plus a website, shopping cart, credit card processing, etc. But with Café Press you can just try it!"

INTERNET MILLIONAIRE SECRET

Opening a Café Press store can help you pursue e-business in a targeted subject area you love with all of the capital investment, technology needs, and customer service outsourced to the service provider. Eileen Descallar's use of this strategy has helped her create a profitable, full-time job pursuing her own interests for a living. If you were to follow Eileen's lead and let Café Press do most of the hard work of manufacturing, shipping, and customer service, you too could find yourself free to focus your efforts on the fun parts of the business that any entrepreneur would enjoy: creating cool new designs and marketing them to niche communities by simply enjoying your own hobbies.

Niche Content Businesses

Niche information businesses rely on creating or publishing information (called "content" in the Internet world) appealing to a niche audience's interests. Traditionally information-based businesses were dominated by mass-media publishers and broadcasting companies that created and published content with broad appeal to entertain and inform mass audiences. Today, however, the Internet allows anyone to make money by publishing to a large audience, even if their shared interest is a narrower one than could have supported a magazine or TV show in the past.

The key to a niche publishing business model is finding or creating the specialized information or entertainment content attractive to your audience. If you have the content, then you can make money by selling advertisements to companies that want to reach your niche audience. You may also be able to charge membership or subscription fees for access to the information or to communities built around the content.

Both personal interests (e.g., gardening, gossip, garage bands, etc.) and professional interests (e.g., pharmaceutical sales, farm equipment, dental floss distributors) are good targets for this approach.

In fact, some entrepreneurs are making such good money at niche content ventures that they did not want to be interviewed for this book. While this may surprise you, it is because they want to keep the lucrative niche content markets that they have identified to themselves!

Niche content can be exploited in many ways online to meet the information needs of a target market, including:

▲ Publishing an information-rich e-mail newsletter such as Digital Media Wire (discussed in Chapter 4)

▲ Building a compelling website such as Bookslut.com

▲ Publishing a "blog" like MobileTracker.net

▲ Combining elements of all these approaches with your own creativity to create new business models for niche content

Read on for examples of successful niche content businesses started by people like you.

NICHE CONTENT ENTREPRENEUR #1:
JESSA CRISPIN, BOOKSLUT.COM

Even though she dropped out of college, Jessa Crispin loves books. She loves books so much that when she had a job she didn't like, she spent her free time peppering her sister and friends with e-mails filled with commentary on the latest books she read.

Jessa decided she should post her commentary online so that her e-mails didn't overwhelm the in-boxes of her friends and family. Although she had no particular technical training, in 2002 she taught herself how to use some basic website software and launched the Bookslut.com website from her apartment in Austin, Texas.

Although her site's book reviews and comments were originally intended just for her friends and family, the worldwide reach of the Web surprised her: Just a month after she launched her site, Jessa received an e-mail from a reader in Hungary commenting on a book review that she had posted!

As the traffic and attention to Bookslut.com grew, Jessa started to realize that her articles and commentary on new books and literary issues were filling a void. Although there are many book-related websites, most of those e-businesses focus simply on selling books. The niche audience of readers of literature and contemporary works was hungry for high-quality, original commentary and criticism about books.

After relocating to Chicago for a new job, Jessa realized that she liked reading and writing about books far more than she liked her new job. She quit her job to focus on Bookslut.com full-time. You might think that Jessa now spends lots of time on marketing the site or recruiting advertisers, but in fact she still focuses on reading and writing about books. She has never advertised and is not entirely sure how people find her website.

Lucky for her, the Internet has rewarded the original niche content written by Jessa and her contributors: Bookslut.com's articles about new books are often the only reviews online for many authors ignored by the mainstream literary press. Search engines such as Google and Yahoo often display Bookslut.com's reviews as top results when surfers search online for those authors. This brings thousands of unique visitors to Bookslut.com every day.

Today, Bookslut.com has evolved into a webzine (a magazine-style website) that publishes new "issues" each month that are full of new articles and commentary. Jessa has also recruited volunteer columnists who cover topics such as mystery novels, libraries, feminist literature, and book-to-film adaptations. The most popular feature on the site is a blog that she (along with her coconspirator Michael Schaub) update daily with witty commentary on the latest literature and related topics.

Jessa attributes part of her success to the much lower capital outlay and expenses required for a "virtual" Internet business compared to a traditional, real-world business. Having lower startup costs and overhead allowed her to focus instead on having a creative vision for her business that created a new niche for literary journalism online.

Part of this vision has been to publicize and give credibility to the literary scene outside of the East Coast media center cities. By writing from the Midwest, and also sponsoring well-attended "Bookslut.com Reading Nights" at bars around Chicago, Jessa and her collaborators have brought visibility to a literary scene usually ignored by the largely New York–based publishing industry.

Jessa says that she absolutely loves her "job" now. She feels blessed to be able to sit at home and read the free books that are delivered to her door daily by the big publishing companies—all of whom now crave Bookslut.com's endorsement.

She also recommends niche content e-businesses to you. "Most people on the Web are too busy selling things," she says, "but I believe that people respond even better to original content. Anybody who is willing to work to create truly original content can successfully find an audience online. I'd really like to encourage people to put more interesting content on the Web so I could have more to read!"

INTERNET MILLIONAIRE SECRET

Given the low cost of publishing online, developing your own niche content business is a low-risk way to start a business. By targeting a demographic you know with content that you are excited about and qualified to write up (or can gather from qualified sources), you can quickly start building an audience.

Starting a website in your spare time focused on one of your hobbies may even enable you to emulate Jessa Crispin's career switch. Building an audience this way will open opportunities to profit from advertisers who want to reach your target audience, too.

You will have an especially good chance of making money using this approach if you provide information that helps buyers and sellers of high-priced items such as homes, cruises, or cars transact more efficiently. The Internet makes that easier than ever before.

The Blogging Phenomenon and Its Impact on Entrepreneurs

As you have probably heard by now, a revolution is under way in the publishing and media worlds. The media establishment is under assault by a new form of journalism called "blogging." A blog is shorthand for "weblog" and simply refers to regularly updated Web pages that contain the thoughts and writings of unofficial commentators on subjects of all sorts. Blogs can focus on the mundane and trivial or serious politics, professional issues, or anything in between. (Visit www.bloglines.com/topblogs for one list of top blogs, and check my website at InternetMillionaireSecrets.com for more.)

Blogs are viewed as a revolution because they allow anyone to communicate with a mass audience without the traditional intermediary of a newspaper, radio/TV station, or publisher. As a result, virtual nobodies are able to establish themselves as authorities (or at least commentators) on every niche content subject that you can imagine.

What do blogs offer entrepreneurs? The inexpensive and wide reach of Internet-based publishing once again means that entrepreneurs have a significant business opportunity in the blog space.

If you have something to say that is interesting enough to attract a regular audience, a blog can quickly become an addictive hobby and possibly even a lucrative business based on advertising sales. Many bloggers have also used their newfound fame and influence to capture book contracts, broadcasting jobs, and jobs in traditional journalism, too.

TECHNOLOGY EXPERTISE NOT REQUIRED

I know that many of these strategies sound promising but out of reach because of their technological complexity. Don't worry. I promise that in Part 3 I will detail for you the specific steps you can take and the vendors you can use to create your own professional-looking websites, online stores, and e-mail newsletters. All of these services are available today through the Internet on an outsourced basis.

Once you've determined what target market you want to tackle, I'll show you exactly how to get started—and you don't have to be a computer wizard to succeed!

**NICHE CONTENT ENTREPRENEUR #2:
BLOGGER JON GALES, MOBILETRACKER.NET**

MobileTracker.net is the brainchild of Jon Gales, a twenty-year-old blogger based in Florida. Although he still lives with his parents, Jon has built a profitable e-business by establishing himself as an authority on the latest and greatest in mobile phones through daily publishing on his blog.

Audience demand for his content is so high that he's making more than $70,000 per year from advertising on the site without even working full-time.

Like many of the other successful entrepreneurs profiled throughout this book, Jon identified a target market that matched his own niche interests to build his business. A cell phone "geek," he started his blog in 2003 simply to share his own opinions and industry news with other mobile enthusiasts. He particularly wanted to share his reviews of the latest handsets being released for sale in the U.S. market. He also hoped that he might be able to convince the phone manufacturers to share some advance models with him before release.

The launch of MobileTracker.net was well timed because Jon's posting of information on the latest-model mobile phones paralleled the increase in complexity of their features such as color screens, built-in digital cameras, and e-mail capabilities—all of which are appealing yet confusing to the consumer audience interested in buying phones.

MobileTracker.net has capitalized on the need for new details on the latest handsets by sharing in-depth information and wireless industry news with an audience that happens to include mostly affluent, educated consumers who are attractive to advertisers and difficult for them to reach through other media.

Voila! An advertising business was born, and it is so healthy that Jon has "taken time off" from college to pursue his lucrative blogging career. (He also gets all the free phones he could ever want!) In addition to his love of mobile phones, Jon is a big fan of the business of blogging. Because blogging software is available for free and website hosting costs almost nothing these days, his overhead is extremely low. His only product is daily written commentary on an industry whose products he loves.

There's no reason that you, too, can't build a profitable blogging business similar to Jon's. *By targeting a market of desirable consumers with timely and concise information that is hard to find elsewhere, it's possible to build a blog publishing business with no employees and minimal overhead, using cost-effective marketing and administrative software services and the Internet to freely distribute your commentary.* You just might be able to turn your hobby into a flexible, fun new career as a blogger!

As Jon says, "There's a big potential readership waiting in nearly any industry that interests you. You just need to start with one reader, then make it your goal to reach two. The Internet is a fantastic delivery mechanism for information—why not try it?"

INTERNET MILLIONAIRE SECRET

Blogging is a hot topic these days because it's a low-overhead way to share your commentary with the world, but it's not that big a deal technically. You can get free, easy-to-use software to start your own blog on the Web by visiting sites like www.blogger.com.

What makes a blog popular and potentially lucrative has little to do with the fact that it's a "blog" at all. Instead, you should recognize that blogs are just easy-to-use tools to put your writing on the web each day. The key to building a successful blogging business is identifying and nurturing an audience community interested in the topics you cover and finding advertisers interested in reaching them, too.

In other words, blogs are great, but they are just a means to an end in your establishment of a successful e-publishing business. If you have a message you want to get out or a topic that you want to cover regularly, becoming a blogger may be your road to e-business success. Look past the buzzword to focus instead on how your content can best appeal to your target market first. If starting a blog is the best way to reach them, go for it!

As Bookslut.com and MobileTracker.net both demonstrate, the most likely revenue stream for publishing e-businesses is online advertising. Many of the entrepreneurs I interviewed agree that there are still lots of opportunities to launch new, niche-targeted advertising-based businesses online. In fact, this approach gets easier every year. With the value of advertising online now well established as a way to reach consumers, you can focus on finding and providing value to your advertisers and making money for yourself.

Niche Community Businesses

Interactive communities are another area of possible focus for today's e-business entrepreneur. By creating a website that offers targeted information and interaction between members of a niche community, an entrepreneur can make money by advertising, by selling goods or services targeted to that community, or by charging them for membership. Often a mix of these strategies is applied.

The increasing numbers of people online looking for entertainment, information, or distraction represents an opportunity for you to tap their attention to build an interactive community. Role models for your endeavors should include pioneering online brands such as *The Wall Street Journal* (almost 1,000,000 paying online subscribers) or ConsumerReports.org (2 million paying online subscribers),[1] both of which have used their well-regarded print publications to extend their brands online and offer their readers additional opportunities to interact with one another.

The rapid growth of advertising online can be used instead of, or in conjunction with, subscription-based revenue models to build your niche interactive community, too. Advertisers are increasingly recognizing the value in advertising to the targeted audiences that online communities offer. According to Nielsen//NetRatings and its AdRelevance service, revenues for general community websites jumped 214 percent in 2005.[2] The report stated that "general community sites tend to have a higher level of engagement or interactivity with their users, making the sites very attractive to advertisers." This trend is only going to accelerate as more people come online and continue to integrate online interaction into their daily routines.

An example of a successful niche community business is one of the success stories on my own resume: BillOReilly.com.

NICHE COMMUNITY E-BUSINESS #1:
BILLOREILLY.COM

Although Bill O'Reilly of Fox News' nightly television program *The O'Reilly Factor* is a major national star in many media, including TV, radio, books, and newspapers, he had not used the domain name he owned until he commissioned the construction of BillOReilly.com to tap the enthusiasm of his fans.

In 2002, because of our prior work together, I received a call from O'Reilly's agents asking for my help in creating an online business for Bill. We developed a plan to extend the popularity of his No. 1-rated cable TV news program and nationally syndicated radio show onto the Internet. Our work together created a multimillion-dollar business based on nurturing the fan community around Bill O'Reilly and his TV program, radio show, newspaper column, and books.

By recognizing that his fans shared common interests in politics, current events, books, and his opinions, we created a menu of content and services attractive to his audience. While much of the content is free, we also developed a Premium Membership program that charges fans $4.95

a month for access to exclusive "behind the scenes" content and interactions with Bill, e-mail newsletters, weekly previews of his newspaper column before it is published, petitions that members can sign on current issues, and streaming audio of his daily radio show.

In addition to these content offerings, we introduced message boards that allow O'Reilly's fans to talk to each other, as well as BillOReilly.com-branded merchandise that allows fans to publicly display their enthusiasm for his programming. These features have become extremely successful and demonstrate a blueprint for any entrepreneur interested in building a profitable online community.

The resulting creation of BillOReilly.com is a great example of how a community established offline can be nurtured and built into a profitable business online. This experience yields the following suggested strategies.

How to Profit from an Online Community

1. Identify a target group with shared offline interests.

2. Provide them a place to meet and interact online.

3. Offer logo-branded merchandise that they can purchase and wear to show their affiliation.

4. Develop enough exclusive content that you can charge a monthly subscription fee for access to the community.

NICHE COMMUNITY E-BUSINESS #2: COOKSILLUSTRATED.COM

CooksIllustrated.com is a good example of a more narrowly targeted online community. Although there are many websites that offer free recipes, CooksIllustrated.com succeeds in charging $3.95 a month, or a discounted $24.95 a year, for access to its premium recipe content.

The approach at CooksIllustrated.com is similar to that of BillOReilly.com: The business provides enough free information to attract visitors to the site and then upsells the most enthusiastic fans into paying for access to additional, exclusive content.

CooksIllustrated.com reportedly has had tremendous success with this approach and now reports more than 80,000 paid website subscribers (in addition to the 800,000 circulation of its print magazine). The high quality and exclusive nature of the content supports this revenue model: CooksIllustrated.com positions itself as the "Consumer Reports" of food. As an independent company, it accepts no advertising but focuses solely on developing and publishing top-quality recipes based on exhaustively tested ingredients, techniques, and equipment. The business is based on sharing this exclusive information with its readers (both online and offline).

Management of the company has obviously gotten the message that subscription-based membership sites are well worth the investment if an enthusiastic target market is available. Given CooksIllustrated.com's lack of advertising, the subscription business it has built is a clever (and probably very profitable) solution to extending its brand and content.

It's not too hard to believe that a broadcasting star like Bill O'Reilly or a magazine publisher like CooksIllustrated.com can drive traffic to a website to make money, but how about other communities without broadcast or magazine reach to promote themselves? What about the opportunities that individual startup entrepreneurs, like you, are more likely to face today? Here is an example of a small e-business based around a very targeted hobby that may be similar to one you enjoy.

NICHE COMMUNITY ENTREPRENEUR:
KEVIN DONOFRIO, SCOOBYMODS.COM

The limited production runs of Subaru cars mean that consumers who buy them tend to be devoted fans of the brand. Many Subaru owners are so enthusiastic about their cars that they enjoy customizing their vehicles and making modifications (or "mods") to improve their appearance or performance.

While this sounds like a very narrow niche, once again the Internet shows that it can aggregate an international audience that allows a previously obscure topic to support a business.

Kevin Donofrio lives in Phoenix, Arizona. He loves nothing more than working on his Subaru and has done many "mods" to the five Subaru vehicles he has owned over the years. In 2000, he started the ScoobyMods.com website along with two friends, Aaron and Pete, who share his enthusiasm for Subarus.

Kevin was frustrated when he realized that he and his fellow Subaru enthusiasts were spending almost as much time trying to track down and trade information about various modifications as they were working on or enjoying their cars. He decided to use his skills as a computer technician to create a centralized location on the Web where he and his friends and others in the Subaru mods community could congregate.

Although he had started the website as a charitable gesture to help support and promote the Subaru mods community, the site's high traffic started to incur expenses. When he lost his job at the end of 2003, Kevin found that supporting the site was costing him money every month that he could no longer afford. So Kevin and his partners launched efforts to support ScoobyMods.com through a mix of advertising, voluntary membership donations, and occasional T-shirt sales. These initiatives bring in approximately $400 a month and cover expenses.

ScoobyMods.com today allows users worldwide to discuss and trade information about the latest and greatest Subaru modifications, parts, techniques, and events. It has grown to more than 21,000 members who keep its message boards busy day and night. By paying $12 a year in premium dues, you get access to the latest plans, pictures, and instructions to modify your Subaru into a hot rod.

With its enthusiastic user base, it's clear that there would be room for revenue growth if Kevin and his friends wanted to commercialize ScoobyMods.com further. For example, signing up for Google AdWords would be an easy way to attract advertising dollars, as would raising the site's sponsorship rates or requiring everyone who uses the site to pay a subscription fee. Using Café Press to install a store that would offer a consistent, easily administrated, and profitable supply of ScoobyMods.com T-shirts and gear would be easy, too.

Those steps would probably greatly increase the revenues available from the community, but they would also be counter to Kevin's original intention of simply helping support the community, so it's nice to see ScoobyMods.com thriving purely on the enthusiasm of its members.

If you can identify a similar community in your own life, the example of ScoobyMods.com, along with BillOReilly.com, Cooks Illustrated.com, and many others, provides proof that the Internet offers new ways to turn community interaction and enthusiasm into businesses. If you are serious about developing your own million-dollar e-business, creating an interactive niche community is an excellent place to start.

INTERNET MILLIONAIRE SECRET

I recommend online communities as one of the top e-business trends for new entrepreneurs. The Internet is continuing to attract more and more users worldwide and usage of digital services by users already online is increasing, too. This growth is only going to be compounded by the arrival of wireless phones that increasingly become interactive enter-tainment devices as bandwidth and technology advance.

Once people are online, they naturally seek to extend their real-world interests onto the Web. By creating friendly virtual environments where people can meet and interact with others who share similar interests, you can recreate profitable business models that have existed offline for as long as there have been coffeehouses and bars in the real world.

Whether you build your interactive community around a website, a newsletter, a blog, or some other strategy, you should recognize that niche communities can go hand-in-hand with niche products and niche content to reinforce your message and profit potential.

As in all of my other e-business examples, the software needed to monetize such communities through membership charges, advertising, or merchandise sales is increasingly affordable and easy to use.

Selecting a Niche

I have two simple criteria to evaluate Niche Millionaire business ideas. You should use them, too. They are very handy for helping to decide which of your Niche Millionaire business ideas have the best potential to make you rich.

1. *Are you a believable expert in the field?* If you're trying to sell goods or services to people who are big fans of your selected niche interest, will they believe that you know what you are talk-ing about? Their belief in your credibility is critical if they are going to buy from you. (This factor is less important if you are selling name-brand products. Then, credibility is important to assure potential customers that the products are real, that your delivery is reliable, and that any warranties will be honored.)

2. *Can you offer a product or service that members of that niche will pay for?* Everyone appreciates free content or products, but

creating enough value that people are willing to *pay for* is critical for business success.

Being able to answer "yes" to both of these questions is the key to the success of any Niche Millionaire idea.

Your Niche Millionaire Idea List

To start your own list of Niche Millionaire ideas, I'm first going to help you to find and exploit your own interests and hobbies to create products or services that interest you personally.

Most business strategy advice is the opposite: It suggests that the best way to start a new business is to look for what the market is demanding. While that approach is valid, especially for existing companies looking to expand, I instead recommend that you start by examining your own interests. Starting with topics that are personally interesting to you is more likely to yield business possibilities that excite you over the long term.

You'll need to answer a series of questions in order to develop a list of potential million-dollar niches where you have something to offer. Don't worry if the some of the ideas you create don't yet seem significant enough to build a business upon. I'm going to help you evaluate all of them. The odds are good that some of your thoughts actually are quite valuable, especially given the tools and techniques this book is going to share with you.

Please take the following questions seriously. Spend time on answering them thoughtfully and maybe even get together with someone who knows you and your skills well enough to discuss these ideas with you. Creating your own e-business and attaining your "millionaire" lifestyle depends on it!

FIRST-LEVEL QUESTIONS

Write down as many answers as you can think of to the following questions in your Millionaire Idea Journal.

▲ Have you developed any professional expertise from your work?

▲ Are you particularly good at anything in particular?

▲ What are your hobbies?

▲ Do any of your hobbies involve skills that may be of interest to others?

▲ What hobbies did you used to enjoy that you have dropped over the years?

▲ Are there any topics or subjects that you are deeply enthusiastic about?

▲ What's unique about your town, your friends, or the way you live?

▲ Is there anything unique about your upbringing or family history that may be marketable?

▲ Are there regional or local specialties from your neighborhood that are ripe for sharing with the world?

▲ Do you have special access to any unique goods, services, celebrities, or information?

Please focus on these first-level questions for as long as it takes to come up with several solid responses to each question. Write down your thoughts in the Millionaire Idea Journal. Don't be skeptical—include everything you can think of. The more ideas you have to work with the better.

SECOND-LEVEL QUESTIONS

Take the various niches you've identified from the previous question set and now ask yourself these additional questions about those niches, to help narrow the list down.

▲ Are other people interested in the topics you identified in the first-level questions?

▲ Is there anything unique about the audience you want to address that makes them an attractive potential market for you?

▲ Would this audience be local/regional/national/foreign, wealthy/poor, online/unwired, educated/less educated, religious/irreligious, urban/rural, professional/blue collar, old/young, etc.?

▲ Are you aware of any online businesses that are already addressing this opportunity?

▲ Could you add something to present the goods/services/information in an entertaining way that differentiates you from competitors?

▲ If you were going to pursue a business based on these niches, what would your initial product or service be?

THIRD-LEVEL QUESTIONS

Review the answers to the first- and second-level questions. From among the ideas you've listed, choose the *five* niche interest areas that you think may have the best business potential for you. Preferably pick five areas where you know the most or have the best idea of how your business would be different from potential competitors.

Brainstorming five target niches may sound like a lot, but try to force yourself to find five—it's usually the hard work of thinking of the last few that will stimulate your brain's creativity to produce the best million-dollar ideas.

Add your latest thoughts on these topics to your Millionaire Idea Journal. We will revisit your responses to these questions in Chapter 8, using them as the basis for further development of your potential e-business.

Notes

1. Subscriber data for *The Wall Street Journal* online is from editorial page Publisher's Letter: "A Report to Our Readers," by L. Gordon Crovitz, Publisher, August 1, 2007, p. A14; subscriber data for *Consumer Reports* is from a company press release, September 26, 2005.

2. Nielsen//NetRatings study quoted in Center for Media Research "Research Brief," August 26, 2005.

PART TWO
DEVELOPING YOUR OWN
E-BUSINESS MODEL

APPLYING MILLIONAIRE TYPES THEORY
A CASE STUDY

HERE IS A CASE study that demonstrates the Millionaire Types theory. It goes through the steps that an entrepreneur like you can take to evaluate your own interests to find a potential million-dollar business idea.

Webster Loves Cars

Drawing on the Millionaire Types theories from this book, an entrepreneur who loved cars might consider starting an automobile-related business. The traditional route for car enthusiasts to make money might be to get a job working for someone else as a car salesman or mechanic. Although those are respectable jobs, neither immediately allows you the freedom to be your own boss or the potential to make a million dollars.

After reading *Internet Riches,* an entrepreneurial individual may look at the automobile market much differently than most other people. He would recognize that there are a variety of ways to target his chosen field of cars that also allow him to work from home and take advantage of the low overhead costs of starting his own e-business online.

Let's call this model entrepreneur "Webster."

Choosing Webster's Target Market

Webster's goal is to spend his working time involved in the world of cars, so he chooses car buyers, sellers, and owners as his target market. Knowing that there are existing big companies already targeting the general car market online through the Internet (e.g., CarsDirect.com, Edmunds.com, Autobytel.com, CarandDriver.com), he narrows his focus to select a niche.

Instead of trying to cover all kinds of cars like the big players already in the online marketplace, Webster decides to focus on Classic Cadillacs, a type of car that he admires and grew up with.

By drilling down from the general to the more specialized niche audience for Classic Cadillac cars, our model entrepreneur will have much less competition as well as more enthusiastic audience members. He also has credibility and knowledge about the niche because he grew up working on Cadillacs in his spare time.

Car-Related Business Models

Drawing on our three Millionaire Types, Webster could come up with several possible business models for his business about Classic Cadillacs.

EFFICIENCY MILLIONAIRE APPROACH

Webster knows that buyers and sellers of collectible Cadillac cars have difficulty locating each other. This inefficiency suggests that he could create a website service to help match them together and take a fee from each introduction or simply charge the sellers for advertising to the buyers.

Another efficiency-related approach would be for Webster to put together a list of repair problems common to classic Cadillacs. He could expand the list by also including the parts, repair processes, and the costs associated with fixing them. Creating a directory of mechanics who specialize in repairs of classic Cadillacs may also be a worthwhile investment of Webster's time.

Each of these approaches would allow Webster to create or rewrite and/or repurpose publicly available information to serve the needs of his target market. Each is also likely to lend itself to the creation of an advertising-supported business model. If he is clever and has the technology resources to do it, Webster may also profit by finding a way to broker the transactions between the car owners and mechanics or buyers to whom his online services provides introductions.

Each of these examples would help members of his target market (i.e., car buyers and owners) by making it more efficient for them to buy, sell, and repair their cars. And in no case would Webster have to invest in any inventory or deal with shipping.

PRODUCT MILLIONAIRE APPROACH

If he wants to pursue a *product reseller* business model, Webster could identify the top suppliers for the rare parts needed to fix old Cadillacs. He could then buy and resell the parts from them to his niche audience of Cadillac fans through his website, or through an auction website like eBay or LiveDeal, or through a classified advertisements site like Craig's List.

He could also resell such parts virtually (i.e., without taking an inventory himself) by helping to promote existing Cadillac parts businesses online. In this case, Webster could either work through direct relationships with those parts vendors or through an affiliate program relationship, such as those provided by Commission Junction. (Each of these online services mentioned is explained more in Part 3.)

Webster could also take an *original product* approach. He knows how he has long been frustrated by the difficulty of storing compact disks when cruising in his favorite cars. He comes up with an inexpensive nylon and Velcro pouch that attaches to the dashboard to store these small but valuable items. He can outsource the manufacturing of his new product to the many contract manufacturing and promotional goods companies he finds available online.

An even easier product-based approach would be to identify car-related products manufactured by others that would appeal to his niche audience of Cadillac fans. He could build a boutique store around these products on his website. Webster could increase the appeal of these products and make them more unique by having the logo of his Classic Cadillac website printed on the products, too. He could even use Café Press (see Chapter 5) to set up his own online store for free using merchandise that this company provides.

NICHE MILLIONAIRE APPROACH

Webster could also tap the enthusiasm of Cadillac fans worldwide by publishing a free or subscription-based e-mail newsletter or blog, repackaging the types of information mentioned in the previous examples. He could also include interviews with top Cadillac collectors, mechanics, and fans, plus photos of members' cars, discounts on parts, and merchandise.

He could also offer Classic Cadillac–related message boards and photo postings by fellow enthusiasts to create a virtual community where they could interact with each other, and he could use his newsletter or blog to promote it.

Multiple Opportunities, Multiple Revenue Streams

By focusing on the Classic Cadillac niche, Webster has positioned himself as an expert in a field he enjoys with multiple potential streams of income. Regardless of which approach (or combination of approaches) he chooses, creation or repackaging of all this Cadillac-related content would help Webster develop a critical mass of specialized information that has great appeal to his target market.

Once he has built that audience, attracting advertising business from auto-parts retailers and manufacturers won't be too far behind. That advertising business may be the sole revenue stream in his business model, or it may be in addition to retail sales, leads brokering, affiliate program commissions, or community subscription revenues, too.

(If Webster's fictional "Classic Cadillacs" e-business sounds too good to be true to you, I encourage you to look elsewhere in this book for similarly narrow-focused e-businesses that have had great success. These include BirdsJustWannaHaveFun.com, which only sells "foraging and enrichment toys" for parrots, or Seyberts.com, which only sells high-end billiards equipment, or Sittercity.com, which has built a national business just by helping parents find babysitters.)

As you can see, the Millionaire Types can help you evaluate your own million-dollar ideas to see how they might work in each category to create a successful business model for you.

THE ICICLE BUSINESS MODEL METHOD

AS DISCUSSED in Chapter 2, a "business model" is simply a fancy MBA phrase for having the right product or service for the right target audience at the right price. Your business model is the key to creating a successful business.

Once you learn to recognize the strategies that your can use to create a business model's revenues, you can conduct a business model analysis for yourself similar to the one we did together for our fictional entrepreneur, Webster, in Chapter 6.

I'm going to help you go beyond simple discussion, however, to begin identifying a successful business model for yourself using a process that I call "ICICLE." It is an equation that states:

$$I + C + I + C + L = E$$

As an acronym, it sums up my approach to helping would-be entrepreneurs find the right million-dollar e-business. It breaks down as follows:

I	+	C	+	I	+	C	+	L	=	E
Your Interests & Ideas		Customers in Target Market		In-Demand Products, Services, or Information		Competitive Advantage		Leverage		Your E-Business Model

Unlike most business authors, I believe that there is more to success than simply creating a profitable business. To help ensure that you create a successful life in addition to a successful business, I believe that it's critical for you to find a business model that fits your skills and interests, as well as market demand, to generate profit from work that you enjoy doing and managing on a daily basis. That's why the first letter in my ICICLE formula stands for "Your *Interests* and *Ideas*."

The next few chapters are going to help you analyze your interests and compare those interests to the available target customer markets to find the best products, services, or information for *you* to sell online. The exercises will also help you to choose between the many opportunities available by helping you discover your personal competitive advantages.

Once you've uncovered a good business model by understanding the I (interests and ideas), C (customers), I (in-demand products/services), and C (competitive advantage) aspects of this process—which we'll explore together soon—I will walk you through the the best ways to build your website and market its products to "leverage" (the L in *my* formula) the wide, cost-effective reach of the Internet.

The resulting revenue-generating sales approach is the "e-business model" for your new e-business, also known as the E in the ICICLE equation.

Webster's ICICLE Equation Application

If we apply the ICICLE business model equation to Webster's search for the right car-related business for him to start, it looks like this:

Webster's Interests & Ideas:	Cars
+	
Customer Target Market ID:	Classic Cadillacs
+	

In-Demand Products/Services:	Repair and parts information
+	
Competitive Advantage:	His personal passion for and knowledge of cars
+	
Leverage of the Internet:	Online research that can quickly find information useful to his target market
	A templated website to display that information
	Easy publishing of a customer e-newsletter or a blog to promote the site
	Advertising and sales revenues from his new website
	A worldwide audience of hundreds of millions of potential readers reached inexpensively through the Internet
=	
Webster's New E-Business Model:	Publishing of Classic Cadillac–related parts and repair information to a worldwide audience, paid for by advertising and referral links to vendors

In Chapter 8 we'll apply the ICICLE formula to your life, so you can identify the lifestyle, activities, and content you want to spend your time on and get a clearer idea of the kind of e-business you want to start.

WHAT E-BUSINESS SHOULD YOU PURSUE?

OKAY, YOU'VE read this far. You've learned a new way of looking at business opportunities and gained a new appreciation for the reach and business effectiveness of the Internet.

The remaining question that you are asking is, "**What business should I start?**"

My answer may surprise you. Unlike most business strategy books, I want to spend this time talking about you.

It's time to start applying the ICICLE formula to your life. The goal of this chapter (and the other chapters in Part 2 of this book) is to help you identify the lifestyle, activities, and content you want to spend your time on and then use that knowledge to identify the best e-business for you. Together with you, I'll try to help you find a successful business model, one that will allow you to offer the right products to the right audience at the right price.

As the ICICLE formula suggests, this process starts with you and your interests and the ideas that you have about exploiting them.

I	+	C	+	I	+	C	+	L	=	E
Your Interests & Ideas		Customers in Target Market		In-Demand Products, Services, or Information		Competitive Advantage		Leverage		Your E-Business Model

You Are the Expert

Don't worry, we're not going to get too touchy-feely. I'm still going to share with you my Internet Millionaire Secrets for the business models, techniques, and tools that can help you build a millionaire e-business. But both my experience and my research attest to the fact that having a good business model is not enough to truly succeed unless that business is also one that excites you and fits your personality.

My theory is simply this: When you start a new business, there is no one more important to understand than yourself.

I believe that "you are the expert." *You* are the expert on you, on what you like to do and how you prefer to spend your time. The best person I know of to explore million-dollar business opportunities for you is *you*.

Most people have worked for years but never stopped to ask themselves why they chose what they do for a living. They don't ask themselves, "What else could I do instead?" Even more important questions to ask are, "What would I prefer to do today and why?"

INTERNET MILLIONAIRE SECRET:
You Already Have the Answers

I believe that you already have several million-dollar business ideas inside you. The fact is that you are special. You're not special because you have the best education or resume, but because you are the world's top expert on you! No one knows you, your capabilities, and your situation better.

Most million-dollar business ideas are simple and grow out of their inventor's personal experience. I am going to show you how your decades of life experience in dealing with people and life's issues can fuel your million-dollar business fire. If you can learn to listen and have faith in yourself, you already have the materials and knowledge necessary to answer your own life's big questions and develop an e-business that both makes you money and makes you happy.

Where's the Business Stuff?

Aren't we wasting valuable time with this discussion about you and your feelings? Shouldn't a book about the pursuit of internet riches focus instead on profit and loss, marketing strategy, inventory management, or other business topics?

Yes, we'll get to that soon. But even more important is to help you build a business that reflects who *you* are and who you want to become. My definition of success is making good money by doing something you love. You have to focus first on what you like to do so that you'll have the passion to charge out of bed every morning excited to build your website into a million-dollar success.

Identifying a Business Opportunity That Fits You

Starting a new business is an exciting time. The possibilities are endless, and so is your potential upside. (Hopefully, the interviews in this book have started you thinking constructively about a business that would work for you.)

The key to finding the right new business for you, however, is to combine your skills, interests, and hobbies to target the right group of customers with in-demand products/services that help those customers solve their problems in a cost-effective manner. Ideally, the approach you develop will be one where you have a competitive advantage and the business can operate over the Internet to gain the leverage of its low costs and wide reach. Figure 8–1 outlines the phases and steps for using the ICICLE equation to identify an e-business model that suits you.

Figure 8–1.

STEPS FOR IDENTIFYING THE RIGHT E-BUSINESS OPPORTUNITY FOR YOU

Phase	Steps
Interests & Idea Generation	▲ Identify interests, ideas, skills, and relevant personal attributes.
Customer (Target Market) Research	▲ Identify customer groups with whom your personal background suggests you would enjoy working and to whom you have something to offer.

	▲ Evaluate the purchasing behavior of those groups. ▲ Compare those customer groups with the business models and competitors you identify as most relevant.
In-Demand Product Identification	▲ Research which products are most in demand. ▲ Research product suppliers and competitors online and get pricing
Competitive Advantage	▲ Analyze situation and personal resources to determine differentiating factors that could make your approach unique and profitable.
Leverage	▲ Apply results of analysis to the unique capabilities and reach of the Internet.
E-Business Model for Your New Business	▲ Compile the results of the previous steps to define the business model for your new e-business.

If you've been putting to use the blank pages of your Millionaire Idea Journal as I suggested earlier, you should have lots of interesting business opportunities to review. Now let's use that material to work through each step of the ICICLE equation to further develop strategies for your new business.

Interests and Idea Generation: Your Personal Review

Who are you? This is the most important question in the whole book.

Are you a member of (or aware of) any demographic group that has potential as a target market? Groups that are underserved with products, information, or publicity are primary candidates. Consider all aspects of yourself, large and small, including:

Gender	Expertise
Hobbies	Ethnic background
Religion	Relatives
Education	Career
Affiliations	Location

Now consider whether these interests and personal attributes combine to give you a unique appeal to a desirable target market by asking these questions:

- ▲ Do any of these communities that you are affiliated with represent a potential customer market that you would be interested in targeting?

- ▲ Who are the types of people you most like to deal with?

- ▲ What target market would you be most comfortable with?

- ▲ What would make you excited to get out of bed each morning?

- ▲ What do you care about more than your current job?

- ▲ Is there a way to commercialize that interest online?

Build on the ideas that these questions stimulate by also consulting your Millionaire Idea Journal. Review all of your notes from the topics we've covered in chapters 3 through 7 to try to identify interests of yours that are as broad as possible and also involve people spending lots of money, either in a large lump sum or on a recurring basis.

Customer (Target Market) Identification Techniques

Three techniques—cash flow analysis, business models, and "evergreen" business ideas—will help you evaluate and decide upon the first "C" in ICICLE, your target market.

CASH FLOW ANALYSIS

Review the customer bases you've identified to discover when and where they spend the most money. Are there any ideas that jump out at you? Here are just a few examples to jump-start your thinking.

Large consumer purchases that can yield profitable e-businesses include:

- ▲ Real estate

- ▲ Weddings

- ▲ Medical-related products/services

▲ Financial planning

▲ Cars

▲ Home improvements

▲ Vacations

Smaller but recurring consumer cash flows that you may be able to build a business around include:

▲ Coffee

▲ Cell phones

▲ Association or gym memberships

▲ Magazines or newspapers

▲ Taxes

▲ Pet food

▲ Prescription medicines or medical supplies

Targeting businesses, rather than consumers, as your customers can often provide more stable cash flows, although the sales cycle is often longer, too. Business needs that are constantly in demand include:

▲ Office supplies

▲ Insurance

▲ Industry gossip

▲ Good salespeople

▲ New promotional ideas

▲ Commercial real estate

Can you identify groups of potential consumer or business customers who have problems or unnecessary difficulties in any of their significant purchasing decisions that your e-business could help remedy? Positioning yourself in the middle of a transaction as the answer to customer problems is a great way to make money. Ideally, those money problems are large or recurring (or both).

BUSINESS MODELS

Given the list of potential target markets you have created, can you apply one or more of the business models we've identified to any of them to create an e-business for yourself? Try reviewing this list of potential e-business models and comparing each to the customer target markets you've generated.

The intent of the business is to:

- ▲ Improve the efficiency of a process through services or software.

- ▲ Create or improve a product and sell it.

- ▲ Resell someone else's product to your target market.

- ▲ Create and sell products with relevant logos.

- ▲ Sell accessories appropriate to your chosen market area.

- ▲ Create a directory of vendors or suppliers.

- ▲ Write reviews of products or services in your target market.

- ▲ Build a community of fans of that topic.

- ▲ Place affiliate program or other advertising on your or other people's websites.

- ▲ Publish an e-mail newsletter or blog that offers your views on some aspect of the target market.

- ▲ Start a blog or compile an e-newsletter that contains the latest news and gossip for your target market.

- ▲ Use the Internet to introduce your topic or product to foreign markets.

- ▲ Consult with other online entrepreneurs to improve their advertising or traffic.

- ▲ Offer your expertise as a customer service expert in that target market.

What kind of e-business opportunity makes the most sense to you after you've taken into account your personality type, your interests, the kind of work role you want to play, and the resulting best business models? Be sure to write down your concepts in your Millionaire Idea Journal.

TOP "EVERGREEN" BUSINESS IDEAS

What should you do if you've diligently completed all of my exercises but still haven't identified a million-dollar business idea of your own?

I encourage you to keep trying to find your own million-dollar ideas by reviewing the earlier lessons in this book and brainstorming with family and friends. Most millionaire opportunities grow out of personal experience and take a lot of personal enthusiasm to nurture and harvest.

If you still don't have a particular passion, here are some "evergreen" target markets that you may want to consider. Each of them has strong, recurring demand from customers at both the retail and wholesale levels. Many are probably also fields where you have personal experience that you can draw upon to make one of them your own:

Weddings	Personal computers
Real estate	Industry gossip
Coffee	Funeral arrangements
Health care	Coupons
Vacations	Cars
Baby-boomer services	Medical supplies
Information brokering	Pets
School information	Religion
Insurance	Spanish-speaking, Chinese, or Indian markets
Sports	New technology (e.g., cell phones, WiFi, TiVo, iPod)

Most of these evergreen target markets have both consumer and business customers. If you have reviewed the list with consumers in mind, try going through it again while envisioning serving business customers in that market instead.

If you are still stuck after considering each of these target markets, try applying the various business models from the list on page 114 to each of the various industry targets listed here in the evergreen business ideas section.

If you've read chapters 1 through 7, you can probably evaluate the potential of each of these million-dollar business ideas faster than before. One of them is bound to help you come up with a new angle for your e-business idea. Record your thoughts in your Millionaire Idea Journal so you don't lose any valuable data.

In-Demand Product Identification Techniques

Once you have some good ideas about the customer markets that you would like to target, it's time to decide what product or service you can sell to them. Here are a couple of techniques to help you evaluate and decide on the second appropriate "I" in ICICLE for your new e-business.

PERSONAL REVIEW

Once again review your Millionaire Idea Journal notes. Having learned about Efficiency Millionaire, Product Millionaire, and Niche Millionaire strategies, as well as the secrets behind the success of many e-businesses, you should have decided on some ideas of your own.

As a reminder, here are some of the key questions from Chapter 3 to get you thinking about product ideas:

- ▲ Are there inefficiencies in the daily life of your target customers that you could help solve?

- ▲ Are there products that you have customized for your own use that you could sell to your target market?

- ▲ Do you have the capacity to create products of your own for sale?

- ▲ Are there types of information that are unreasonably difficult to get that you could find and provide to others?

Spend some time on this exercise. It may be difficult to find the product most in demand by customers, but the solution is usually a simple one once you identify it.

INTERNET MILLIONAIRE SECRET:
Rethinking Startups

Our educational and media institutions tend to focus on large corporations rather than small business. They promote the goals of climbing the corporate ladder, increasing employee headcount, and going public as the highest callings for business people.

I disagree. This presumption bothers me, and it's one of the principal reasons that I wrote this book. After years of working in some of the biggest and most prestigious corporations in the world, I recognized that these career goals are fine for many (maybe even most) people, but they don't fit everyone. This includes me, a refugee from corporate America, and probably you, too, if you're reading this book. The creativity, excitement, constant learning, and huge potential upside of owning a business of your own combine to make entrepreneurship the most stimulating and potentially lucrative career path available.

I'm going to promote another idea, too: that the e-business you build should stay small. In the Industrial Age, small meant limited reach and limited profits. But in the Information Age, even small businesses can reach the whole planet inexpensively; and they can be easier to manage but still highly profitable. This approach keeps you in control, doing a job you love, and it can make you rich without all the corporate B.S. of working for someone else.

By aiming for profitability rather than corporate advancement or growth for growth's sake, your e-business can be another example of the new breed of companies: Internet-enabled, profit-driven, and even lifestyle-enhancing.

FINDING THE MOST IN-DEMAND PRODUCTS

If you're still unsure of what product or service would be best for you to sell online, you can put the power of the Internet to work for you once again. You can use the search engines and publicly available software tools to discover what products/services your potential target market is most interested in.

Once again, be sure to record the results of your work in your Millionaire Idea Journal for future review and inspiration.

▲ *Surf the Web.* Visit a number of websites that cater to your target market. Examine the ads that those websites carry. What products seem to be selling to that community?

▲ *Search by keyword.* Visit your favorite search engine and type in a few keywords about your potential target market customers. Examine what results pop up in the "sponsored links" or "sponsor results" that run down the right hand side of the page. Try varying the keywords to get different ads. What products do these ads suggest are in demand by your target market? Can you provide similar products or improvements upon existing products?

▲ *Pursue the buzz.* Both Google and Yahoo offer free information about the most popular current searches on their sites. Yahoo calls this service "Yahoo! Buzz" and Google calls it "Zeitgeist." Through these sections you can find out the hottest topics of the day. Armed with this information, you can create new websites, e-newsletters, blogs, T-shirts, e-books, bumper stickers, or whatever else you can dream up based on that consumer interest. It's a surefire way to attract attention to your new business.

▲ *Do "AdWords" testing.* Google's AdWords service is responsible for many of the sponsored search results and sponsored links that you see all over the Web these days. If you sign up for this service, you can create hypothetical, text-based ad campaigns that Google will run across its network of websites. (It's free to sign up and use the tools I'm discussing, but it will cost you money if you want them to start actually running the ads. That's not necessary for our current purposes, though.)

Once inside the AdWords system, you will be asked to choose keywords relating to the products or services you are considering offering to your target market. The AdWords system will then display to you how many clicks each one is likely to receive each day!

This is highly valuable product research for free. If you play around a bit and try different keywords and different products, you'll be able to prequalify the interest of your potential audience in your potential products before you spend a dime.

Some of these services are brand new, so be sure to visit the InternetMillionaireSecrets.com website for updates. There are sure to be even easier-to-use product identification services available online soon.

Competitive Advantage

Once you have identified your personal *interests and ideas,* potential *customer* target markets, and their most *in-demand* products (the ICI part of the ICICLE formula), it is time to narrow your choices to those that offer the best profit and happiness potential.

Although only you can decide which activities make you happy, I can help you with some additional analysis that should help your profitability potential. This analysis applies the concept of competitive advantage (the second "C" in your personal ICICLE equation) in order to determine the best e-business model for you.

The key to most successful businesses is that they do their chosen activity better than their competition. A "competitive advantage" is a unique connection, resource, idea, timing, or other factor that means you can produce or deliver your product or service faster or cheaper or better or more profitably than the other guy. As a new entrepreneur, a competitive advantage can be a good reason to pick one business idea over another. A sustainable competitive advantage can make the difference between success and failure whether you currently have many competitors or they only show up later to copy your success.

As a potential Internet millionaire, you need to assess your own skills and experience and look for something or someone in your background that will help push your new business over the top into million-dollar territory. If you have an area of expertise, connections, or even just enthusiasm, it may yield a competitive advantage for you.

Let's do an exercise: Write down your best answers to the following questions in your Millionaire Idea Journal. Do any of them apply to your list of potential million-dollar business ideas? You can also consult the many notes you should have written in your journal by now to see what other opportunities come to mind.

Are you really good at anything that you can turn into a product or marketable service?

Are people always telling you: "You are so..."? Could that skill or personal attribute be marketable online?

Do you have:

▲ Unique knowledge of an industry, product, service, or target market?

▲ A "first-mover advantage" (meaning that you're the first person to act upon this business idea)?

▲ Strong partners to help you?

▲ Personal connections to an important supplier, customer, or celebrity?

▲ Product ideas that can be protected by patents?

▲ Products or services that no one else can source or deliver?

▲ Strong, unique opinions that other people enjoy hearing or find useful?

▲ Lower operating costs?

▲ Free or low-cost help from family members or friends?

▲ Free or low-cost advertising?

▲ Ownership of or exclusive rights to a product, service, celebrity, or brand name?

▲ Special skills that would be hard for a competitor to recreate?

If you're thinking about Efficiency Millionaire ideas, do you have an advantage such as a new product design, better software, a more complete database of potential clients, or inside connections that can make the targeted product easier to use or the targeted process easier for customers?

If a Product Millionaire approach is in your future, what can you add to existing products that will make your goods unique and valuable to the customers? What can you do to keep competitors from simply copying your idea?

If you're focusing more on being an expert in a Niche Millionaire business, what or whom do you know that will set your business apart from competitors?

Ideally, using the combination of these several techniques has helped you to come up with an approach that is innovative, potentially profitable, and has some sort of a competitive advantage.

Leverage

You have completed the idea-generation stage of building your million-dollar e-business. Congratulations! You've determined your personal interests, your target customers, the most in-demand products/services desired by those customers, and your competitive advantage in meeting their needs.

Now it's time to explore the "L" in our ICICLE business model equation—leverage. You want to exploit the vast distribution leverage of the Internet to launch your business. If you can successfully integrate all of the elements discussed so far, and leverage them using the Internet, you'll be on the path to creating a million-dollar business model that you also enjoy building. Parts 3 through 6 are going to discuss the many specific recommendations I have for leveraging the Internet to help you build, run, and market a profitable e-business.

PART THREE
BUILDING YOUR INTERNET MILLIONAIRE E-BUSINESS

TECHNOLOGY SECRETS AND STRATEGIES OVERVIEW

Until only a few years ago, the possibility of a person becoming successful in the "B" quadrant (Business Owner) was only available to those who were brave or rich. . . . Today, primarily due to changes in technology, the risk in becoming a successful business owner has been greatly reduced. And the opportunity to own your own business system has been made available to virtually everyone.

Robert Kiyosaki, *Rich Dad's Cash Flow Quadrant,* Time Warner Audio Books ©2000 by Robert T. Kiyosaki and Sharon Lechter.

NOW IT'S TIME for you to get going—here are practical and specific steps you can take to start your new e-business.

Remember, although the technology may seem intimidating at first, I'll explain everything in detail so that you can see how easy to use it has become in recent years. More important than any technology is you. It is your creative new business idea that contributes the crucial value to transform lifeless software into a vibrant new million-dollar e-business.

The Outsourcing Revolution

Technology makes today's entrepreneurs more powerful than any generation of entrepreneurs in history. Today, from your home you can log on to the Internet and build e-commerce storefronts, stock them with goods, market to millions of people, and build profitable business relationships worldwide. Furthermore, using the software and services offered by others to build your business lowers your overhead costs and allows you take advantage of millions of dollars worth of software and technology expertise.

This process is called outsourcing, and the easy-to-use software services you use to do it are available from application service providers (ASPs).

ASPS: WHY BUY WHEN YOU CAN RENT?

Over the last decade, competition among technology companies has made online business services increasingly easier and cheaper for entrepreneurs like you to use. As long as you have a PC with an Internet connection you can, without leaving your house, find every type of technology or service you need to successfully operate an online business. Instead of investing in all kinds of hardware and skilled staff—buying and configuring your own computers to host a website, building your website from scratch, writing the software code that operates e-mail and e-commerce programs—you can simply rent these functions online at low monthly rates by working with ASPs.

ASPs are the answer to the prayers of the modern entrepreneur. Today you can simply pay a few dollars and an ASP will offer you hosting services, secure e-commerce, e-mail management, and any of the other "heavy lifting" parts of the website business.

While in traditional business you might want to invest in building assets yourself, software and online services are so inexpensive today (and depreciate so fast) that you will find it much more affordable to outsource these activities to a third-party party ASP that specializes in technology services and maintenance.

By outsourcing the technology components of your business, you can inexpensively replace many of the most expensive parts of operating a traditional store. You can rent software monthly from an ASP, instead of purchasing it, and the support staff needed to keep it humming will be included in the monthly fee. This keeps your overhead costs down because you don't need to hire administrative or technical teams in-house. Outsourcing to third parties also means that you can worry less about technology details and focus instead on doing what only you can do best—developing your killer business!

Outsourced services that are available now through the Internet include:

▲ Website hosting

▲ Website building

▲ Credit card sales-transaction processing

▲ E-mail list management

▲ Advertising sales and management

Every type of technology or service you need to successfully operate an online business is available today through your PC without leaving your house.

PRICES DROPPING

The competition among these technology service providers is such that prices are dropping dramatically all the time. Just as PCs themselves are getting cheaper all the time, other services you need are dropping rapidly in price also. For example, two years ago it was easy to pay $40 a year to register a domain name. Today, $8.95 a year is a common price for annual domain name registration, and many vendors offer them for less or even for free when included with other services.

Similarly, major companies like Microsoft have begun offering small business versions of their corporate-level e-mail management software for as little as $19.95 a month instead of the tens or hundreds of thousands of dollars it would cost a Fortune 500 corporation to license them.

TECHIES HATE ME FOR THIS!

If you discuss this strategy with technology-oriented people, they are likely to disagree with my recommended strategy of using out-sourced ASP services to build your business. That's because they already understand technology and may make their living by providing technology know-how, so they are threatened by my suggestion that you don't need their help, at least for the first phase of your business's growth. (Because they are technologically sophisticated themselves, it is also a good bet that they have never tried the easy-to-use services I recommend!)

You can tell your techie friends that I recognize that eventually you will probably want a complete software "platform" that integrates the different services provided by these ASPs into one easy-to-use, enterprise-grade system.

However, while you are still in the early stages of your business, you should be focused on getting your product out to the public, to make certain that there is a profitable market available to you. It is not the time to invest in customizing systems that may not be right for your needs a year from now and certainly will be expensive.

The bottom line is that you can save a huge amount of money and time while establishing your business by using ASPs. That's why I recommend avoiding the expense and delay of building customized systems until you are confident of the need.

Although stitching together the services of several different ASPs may require you to remember several different passwords, and potentially confuse a few sharp-eyed customers slightly by passing them back and forth between different third-party services, the savings is more than worth it. With good branding and website navigation, you can weave ASP services into a compelling user experience that will make your new business look like a million bucks. (Your customers never have to know that your new dot-com business is a part-time operation that you run using a PC set up on a card table in your spare room!)

The Critical Components for Starting Your E-Business

Here is my list of the most important technology components needed to create a successful million-dollar web-based business.

FIRST-STAGE TOOLS (ASP SERVICES)

Before you can sell anything you'll need to have at least four services in place to be able to serve customers:

1. *Professional-Looking Website.* It's critical that visitors to your site get the impression that they are dealing with reliable, professional people or else they won't buy anything.

2. *E-Commerce Shopping Cart Software.* If you are selling products or services, you have to be able to collect the money from your customers via credit card. The world moves too fast these days to wait for a check in the mail!

3. *E-Mail Address Collection and Management.* Collecting contact information on your visitors and customers is crucial so that you can continue to communicate with and sell to them. You can start collecting e-mail addresses even before your website is complete or products are ready for sale.

4. *E-Mail Newsletter Publishing.* Continuing contact with all of the people on your mailing list is the best way to sell, upsell, and reinforce your product/service message. Regular publishing of e-mail-delivered newsletters (e-newsletters) is the most cost-effective way to do this.

Again, don't worry! Finding and implementing these technologies is easier than you think. All of the companies that provide them have spent years trying to make their services as easy as possible for new users like you to take advantage of. Additionally, my research has focused specifically on finding the ASPs that are the easiest to use (and have the best technical support in case you ever get stuck).

Additional or different tools may also be applicable if your business specializes in certain niches. For example, if your new business includes webcasting of music or videos, you'll also need to contract with a webcasting ASP that provides streaming media services that can, like the other services listed, be "rented" on a monthly basis to support your business.

TOOLS YOU CAN'T RENT

Years of experience and research have taught me and my many clients that keeping your overhead low is a key to the success of a new business like yours. *That's why I advocate an approach that minimizes and delays the amount of money you invest in tools and services until it is really necessary. You should only spend money when you have a specific reason and a strategy for how that investment is going to make you money in return.* Using ASP services is one of my proven techniques for keeping your expenses down. This book is full of more suggestions.

That said, what's left are three categories of resources that you can't rent but must provide yourself:

1. *Products or Services.* Obviously, you must have something to sell on your new website. Our work together in parts 1 and 2 should have helped you decide what product or service is best for you to sell.

2. *Content.* You or your team will create the words, pictures, and environment that showcase your products and encourage customer purchasing. Informational material of all sorts is collectively called "content." Whether you need a little or a lot of content depends on your business model. We'll deal with this topic more in Chapter 12.

3. *A "Hollywood Pitch."* Summarizing how you describe your business can be very helpful when dealing with search engines, customers, and potential partners. This is a critical part of both your business model and your content approach that will also be discussed in more detail in Part 4.

BEWARE OF "SALESPEOPLE"

Many "experts," especially if they have technology backgrounds, will encourage you to add other tools or services to your action plan. These might include expensive "bells and whistles," such as fancy graphics, custom database programming, Macromedia Flash animations, advertising campaigns or tracking tools, audio/video streaming, search engine optimization, dedicated servers, or much more.

Although their job titles may not say so, these folks are basically salespeople. Of course they recommend more expensive features than you actually "need"—it's their job.

Because it's difficult for a nontechie to evaluate the worth of these services, Internet services providers and "consultants" love to push overpriced and often unnecessary services to newbie entrepreneurs like you. In the early stages of your new business, you need to conserve both your time and money as much as possible.

Stick with the basic e-business startup tools and action plan that I outline in this book and I promise that you will save a lot of money. You can always upgrade later!

PRACTICAL FIRST STEPS

Almost every day new service providers (or new services by old providers) appear online in a continuing effort to make things easier and cheaper for small-business owners. I encourage you to use the Internet to research and compare these many ASP services available to new business owners like yourself. A convenient first stop on your search should be the website that's freely available to readers of this book: www.Internet MillionaireSecrets.com. Here, my team and I regularly update our vendor recommendations to help readers like you.

Regardless of whether you choose to use the companies I recommend or you choose companies that you have researched on your own, the next steps are essentially the same—you must choose a domain name and build your first website.

Starting Your E-Business: A Project Outline

Assuming that you already have your own ideas, or that you have used chapters 1 through 8 to determine the products/services you want to sell, here are the seven specific initial steps that successful entrepreneurs take when launching a new e-business.

1. Domain name selection

2. Choosing a website hosting company

3. Website design and construction

4. Copywriting

5. Optimizing

6. Marketing

7. Operations

In chapters 10 through 25, I'm going to walk you through each of these steps. Then I'll offer my advice on how to evaluate the vendors of those services. My latest recommendations for the best ASP suppliers are available online at InternetMillionaireSecrets.com.

10 CHOOSING YOUR DOMAIN NAME

A DOMAIN NAME is the part of your website address between the "www" and the ".com" or ".net" ending. For example, "internetmillion-airesecrets" is the domain in the address for the website for this book (www.internetmillionairesecrets.com). Domains are also often referred to as URLs (pronounced either as "you, are, ell" or simply as "earl"). It stands for "universal resource locator," which is the technical name for the full address of a website.

Your domain name should match your business's brand name as closely as possible. Whether you choose to include the ".com" extension in your advertising graphics or not, the basic branding of your business should tie your products and business name and domain name (URL) tightly together. This will help consumers recognize and remember your company better and also reduce customer service confusion later.

Most short and obvious domain names have been taken due to the explosive growth of the World Wide Web in the past ten years. Don't be discouraged, however! There are still many good URLs left if you are a bit creative.

Size Does Matter

The best domain names are easy to remember. Ideally, you will create a name that is short, easy to spell, and says something positive about your business. Finding a domain name that fits your business and also meets these criteria can be a challenge these days, but it is more than worth the effort.

Because most all-one-word or short two-word domain names have been taken by other businesses or by speculators, you are most likely to find a better domain name if you cleverly combine two or even three words. The days of simple one-word businesses like Amazon.com are generally gone. Longer and more descriptive URLs for new businesses, like BillsFineBooks.com or TopQualityPaperbacks.net, are more likely to be available today.

The "URL Brainstorm" Domain Name Selection Technique

The method that I recommend to find a suitable domain name involves brainstorming lists of keywords associated with your products or services. Try the following six steps to generate your own URLs:

1. Mentally review the business you are proposing to build.

2. Start a list with three columns in your Millionaire Idea Journal (or create a document in Microsoft Word).

3. Fill the first column with *nouns* associated with your business's products or services. You should think of as many nouns as you can, using your imagination to come up with different ways of expressing the primary service that your business offers.

4. The second column should be a list of *adjectives* that can be used to describe the nouns in your first column.

5. The third column should be additional *descriptors* that can modify the phrase you create from the keywords in the first two

columns. Most useful are possessives or nouns that suggest that your website is a retail space.

6. Try combining the nouns and adjectives from the different columns to create different URLs.

By putting the nouns and adjectives together, you can create a list of possible domain names that have a much higher probability of being available than a simple one-word URL. For example, if you were launching an online shoe store, your URL brainstorm lists might look like this:

COLUMN 1	COLUMN 2	COLUMN 3
Shoe	Quality	My
Shoes	Best	Your
Footwear	New	The
Heels	Discount	Central
Pumps	Sale	HQ
Sneakers	Italian	Outlet
Sandals	Fashion	Plaza
Kicks	Athletic	Shop
Loafers	Clearance	Store
Boots	Cheap	Place
Slippers		

The results of this word combination exercise can be a wide variety of potentially useful URLs for your new business. For example, Quality Shoes.com, MyItalianLoafers.com, YourFashionFootwear.com, and Discount SandalStore.com all have much higher probability of being available to you than Shoes.com. They are also more memorable for your customers. If necessary, use a thesaurus to help find synonyms for words you like.

- -

INTERNET MILLIONAIRE SECRET

The name and Internet address of your business are so important that you should be ready to spend days or even weeks to come up with just the right combination of words that are also available as URLs.

As Sid Kreis, the founder of Seyberts.com, the billiard supply website profiled in Chapter 4 on Product Millionaires, says: "Try to pick a brand

*name and URL that is clear, concise, and easy for people to pronounce
and spell. One of our biggest mistakes was using the name of our business's previous owner, Mr. Seybert, for our website and our brand name
when we could have picked something better."*

Buying a URL from a Speculator

Another alternative is to buy a domain name from speculators. If there is
a domain name already registered that would be absolutely perfect for
your new business, but no one seems to be operating a business using
that URL, chances are good that the domain is owned by someone who is
hoping to sell it for a profit.

In many cases, simply typing in the URL to your browser will call up
the domain with a page listing the owner's contact information and sometimes even the desired sales price. You can also usually find out the registered owners of any domain in which you are interested by referencing
the WHOIS database (www.whois.com); contact information is usually
available even if the owners have not made public their intention to sell
the URL.

Of course, trying to buy something that another business has bought
for the specific purpose of selling at a profit means that you probably
won't get a very good deal. As soon as you express your business interest
in the domain name, the owner is likely to raise the price. A notable case
occurred back in 1999, when a speculator succeeded in selling the URL
"business.com" to a startup company called eCompanies for $7.5 million!

If there is a URL that you just have to have, try approaching the owner
as an individual and try to downplay the fact that you are hoping to profit
from the URL that he owns.

URL Availability

Once you have made a list of possible URLs for your new business, the
next step is to check on their availability. The easiest method I have found
is to keep your list of potential URLs in Microsoft Word document, then
you can copy and paste your choices into a domain name registrar's
search page. As you find domains that are available or taken, you can note
that in your master list of URLs for easy future reference.

URL RESEARCH SECRET

If you visit the GoDaddy.com home page (or other domain registrars such as Register.com or NetworkSolutions.com), you will see that you can type in domains one at a time to see if they are available. However, if you used

Figure 10–1. Bulk URL Reaseach Tool.

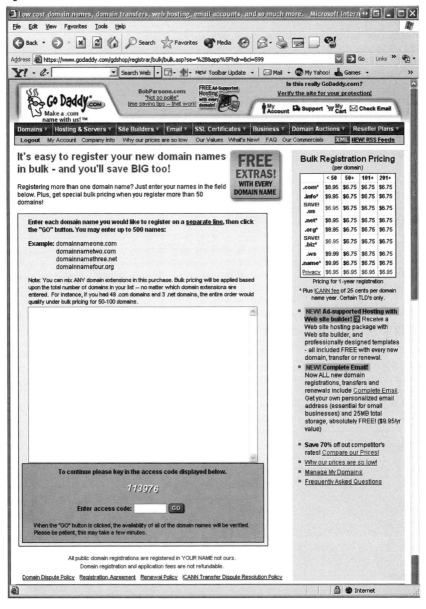

my URL brainstorm technique, you should have a bunch of domains that you want to test at the same time.

Instead of laboriously typing them in one at a time to check their availability, you can use the link shown on the GoDaddy.com homepage, "bulk registration," to test multiple URLs simultaneously. Click on the bulk registration link on the home page and you will see that you can copy up to 500 variations from your list of favorite potential URLs into the box that appears. Figure 10–1 demonstrates this helpful tool. Type in the access code displayed at the bottom and hit continue to get instant results about all the URLs in which you are interested in one shot!

This tip can save you lots of valuable time.

URL VARIATIONS

Once you have located a URL that you like, you should also consider purchasing variations on the name you have chosen. This is a good idea to protect yourself from competitors launching similar websites and also to make sure that any advertising you do draws users to your site, not to one with a similar but different URL.

Don't forget to try variations like .net, .us, .org, or whatever else may be appropriate for your business. Be careful, however, that you don't register a .net domain name to build a business where the .com version of your domain is already hosting a competitor! Not only is that bad for your business, but it can lead to a trademark infringement lawsuit from the competitor if you are in similar businesses.

So, for example, if you are launching FineClassicCadillacs.com, you should probably also try to register FineClassicCadillacs.net and .org, just to make sure no one else does! Similarly, you should also register common misspellings of your URL like FineClassicCaddilacs.com or other variations.

It's not necessary to register all these URL variations right away, but once you have finalized your URL choice and begun to spend money on promoting it, it is wise to protect your URL investment with purchases like these. Using a low-cost domain registrar like GoDaddy.com makes this defensive strategy much more affordable than it was just a few years ago. GoDaddy.com will allow you to forward any visitors to those URL variations to your main site automatically and for free.

URL COSTS

You cannot "buy" a URL. Instead, URLs are licensed on a year-to-year basis under the authority of the International Corporation for Assigned Names and Numbers (ICANN). Registrars license the rights to administer domains to the public from ICANN and pass the URL "products" along to the public.

Today, the annual cost of URLs can be as little as $5.99, especially if you sign up for multiple years. However, some domain name registrars still charge $20, $30, or more per year, so be careful which company you use!

How many years should you buy? Like all my recommendations, I recommend that you sign up for the minimum to start. I know that you might save money by buying multiyear packages, but experience shows that entrepreneurs often change direction early in the business establishment process. If you decide that you need to change your URL, you don't want to have "saved money" by paying up-front for three or five years for a name that you no longer need!

DOMAIN REGISTRAR RECOMMENDATION

As you might have guessed, GoDaddy.com is my recommended domain-name registrar. I have used this company's services and recommended them to my clients for years with consistently strong results. This well-recognized and professional company has grown to be the world's largest domain registrar and has been ranked number one among all registrars in total new domain registrations for several years.

As you can see in Figure 10–2, GoDaddy offers easy-to-use administration of your domain names. Free services include domain forwarding, e-mail accounts, and locking, which prevents your domain names from being transferred without your permission. The technical support team is also first-rate and responds quickly to inquiries. If you visit InternetMillionaireSecrets.com, you'll find a link to my own GoDaddy-powered domain registrar service, InternetMillionaireDomains.com, as well, which donates its profits to charity and entrepreneurial education efforts. At less than $10 per domain name, these registrars are both much cheaper than bigger-name providers like NetworkSolutions.com, which still charges 1990's style prices of $34.99 per year.

Be careful to choose a responsible company for these services because there is a lot of deceptive advertising in the domain registration business.

Figure 10–2. The GoDaddy.com Account Manager

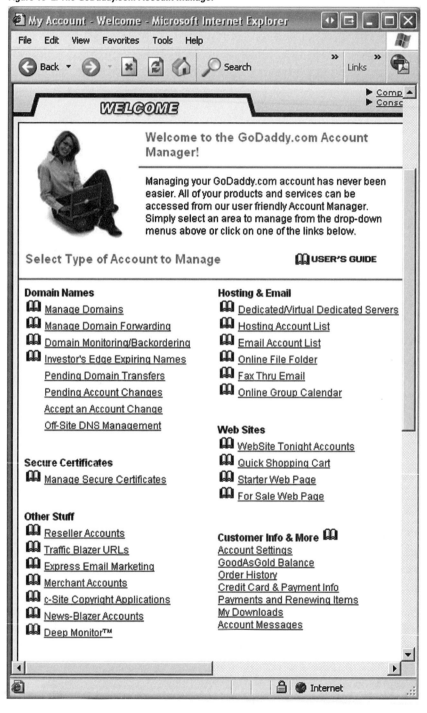

For example, registrars that advertise prices of less than $5 usually require multiyear purchases up front or limit you to only one domain at that price. They also rarely provide much in the way of additional features or good technical support in case you get stuck.

DOMAIN REGISTRATION EXPERT:
BOB PARSONS, GODADDY.COM

Bob Parsons is the president and founder of GoDaddy.com, a provider of domain name registrations as well as many related services that enable the use of domain names (including my own domain-name registrar service, InternetMillionaireDomains.com).

Bob is also a very successful, serial entrepreneur. In researching this book, I spoke with him about the amazing growth of his business from a startup to the number-one domain registrar in the world, with almost $200 million in annual sales. While he started with more technology experience and capital than most entrepreneurs in founding GoDaddy.com (the result of the successful sale of his first company, Parsons Technology, to Intuit in 1994), he still has an entrepreneurial spirit and lots of good advice for new e-business owners, gleaned from his years of building technology companies.

Bob attributes much of the success of GoDaddy.com to being straightforward about products, pricing, and customer service. His companies deliver top-rate products and customer service for very competitive prices. This approach generates so much positive word of mouth from users that more than 90 percent of GoDaddy.com's new business is generated by personal recommendations from existing customers!

You should consider this straightforward "no tricks" approach for your own e-business, especially because today's Internet marketplace is so crowded and often deceptive. As Bob puts it, "There are many opportunities to build successful new e-businesses today, but your focus should be on providing value to consumers in a way that takes the hassle away for them. By offering a good deal on an in-demand product with good service, you'll create repeat and referral customers." This is common-sounding wisdom for traditional businesses, but the Internet is so full of get-rich-quick schemes and misleading promotions that it's valuable to see it so successfully demonstrated by an online business.

From his vantage point as the founder of such a successful e-business, Bob also has a strategic vision that should be very encouraging to aspiring entrepreneurs like you:

> We are still just at the frontier of what the Internet is going to become. The sooner you get involved and learn about the Internet, the sooner you could find success in e-business. You don't have to learn it all at once; just a little every day can help you find the appropriate opportunity for you. You don't need to spend a lot of money these days to start an e-business, either. From anywhere, including your kitchen at home, you can use the tools of companies like mine to learn and put them to work inexpensively building your own e-business, too.

Like me, Bob suggests pursuing business opportunities that excite you personally. His commonsense rationale is, "If you love something it will tell you all its secrets. People who love their jobs can deliver so much more to their customers. If you love what you are doing, you'll be willing to work harder than if it was just a job."

As discussed at length in Chapter 5 on Niche Millionaires, this enthusiasm for your topic should translate into better products or services for your customers, as well as motivation for yourself and the team you hope to build.

INTERNET MILLIONAIRE SECRET

The biggest lesson to be drawn from Bob Parsons and his business success is the importance of following and nurturing your own entrepreneurial vision. He says that when he started his domain registration business, "We were told all the negative stuff like, 'If that would work, how come someone else isn't doing it already?'" He has proved the naysayers wrong with several hundred million dollars worth of sales.

Today he says, "I've found that sometimes a good sign that you're on the right track is that what you're doing causes others to question your good sense." In other words, in pursuit of your own million-dollar e-business, it's not always bad if others think you are crazy!

Critical Questions for a Domain Name Registrar

By the time you read this, other domain name registrars may have introduced newer or better services than GoDaddy.com (or my own InternetMillionaireDomains.com). No matter which company you are thinking about using, however, there are important questions you must ask of any domain-name services provider. Be sure to ask about the:

▲ Cost of URLs

▲ Ease of access to technical settings

▲ Services included in the price, such as:

Free domain forwarding

Free domain locking

Free e-mail accounts

Other features available

▲ Ease of transfer of the domain to other registrars (in case you ever need to move your e-business to another provider)

▲ Technical support

CHOOSING A WEBSITE HOSTING COMPANY

"HOSTING" A website means storing the digital files of your website's design and information on a computer that allows Internet users to view it. Although any Internet-connected PC can theoretically do the job, hosting companies use computers called "servers" that are specially designed to host websites and "serve" their files quickly and consistently to web surfers visiting the site.

In the 1990s, web hosting was a big deal. It was a new field for which the Internet explosion had suddenly created huge demand. Multibillion-dollar corporations such as Cisco Systems grew by providing expensive, specialized computers and equipment to build out vast hosting facilities worldwide to help serve and manage the surging demand for Internet content.

Today, however, the importance of hosting has declined. Like all other computers, server prices have dropped drastically. Concurrently, hundreds of companies compete for customers to fill ever-cheaper hosting capacity.

As you may recognize, this trend is your friend. Basic website hosting services can now be had for $3.95 a month or less. In many cases, hosting is now even "bundled" in with other related e-business services in package deals that make it even cheaper or essentially free.

Nonetheless, engaging a reliable hosting company for your website is critical to the success of your e-business. Since it is the hosting company that actually delivers your website to customers interested in your products, you need to be sure that the company will reliably store (i.e., host) and deliver (i.e., serve) your website twenty-four hours a day, seven days a week, 365 days every year, with minimal downtime.

Web Hosting Recommendation

Because website hosting is so inexpensive these days, I don't have a specific vendor recommendation in this space any longer. The capacity of most hosting companies that survived the dot-com crash is so large that the server needs of a startup e-business are unlikely to stress their resources at all.

In most cases today you will be well served (pun intended!) by simply purchasing your hosting along with your domain name or website design templates in package deals from one reputable provider.

Critical Questions for a Hosting Provider

Here are the decision factors to consider when choosing among the many potential hosting vendors available today:

- ▲ Fees: up-front vs. monthly vs. usage-based.

- ▲ Contract length: the best deals are usually available only with one-year (or longer) contracts. You'll want to balance this up-front cost against the savings it offers before purchasing. I recommend simple month-to-month contracts for hosting unless you can get a particularly good deal from a reliable company.

- ▲ Traffic limits: How much traffic and data storage are you allowed? What do overages cost you?

- ▲ Scalability: Will the hosting company's systems accommodate or crash if you get an unexpected surge of visitors to your site?

▲ Uptime guarantees: What percentage of time does the provider guarantee your site will be live for visitors to see? What penalties are assessed if the provider does not meet these guarantees?

▲ Data transferability: If you decide to take your business elsewhere, how difficult will it be to retrieve your files from the company?

▲ Security: What defenses are in place to protect your site and customer data from hackers?

▲ Included services: What other services are included in their fees? These might include traffic reporting, website building tools, discounts from other providers, and the like.

HOW TO BUILD A WEBSITE IN ONE HOUR

THE FASTEST WAY to build a professional-looking website is to use a "website template." A template is a prebuilt package of graphics that allows you to simply type in your text information through your Web browser to create a customized site for your e-business without knowing any computer code at all. If you have prepared your new site's text, layout, and graphics beforehand, by using such templates, you can copy and paste your information into the template to build a site very quickly.

Website Templates Defined

Many companies today offer these professionally designed website graphics packages premade for your website use—and often include them in package deals with website hosting. Although the designs offered in templates are not completely original, they are a fast and easy way to create a site that looks better than if you tried to design one yourself.

As with most of my advice, a template is one of the strategies that I recommend simply to get your business started. Once your business has revenue of its own, you can easily customize and upgrade later. You might even consider hiring a professional graphics designer in the future, though they cost a lot more money, of course. For now, my goal continues to be getting your million-dollar business online ASAP with the least expense to you.

By using a template, you can have a professional-looking website without having to pay a designer or a technical team to build one for you. In fact, you don't have to know anything more about computer programming than the username and password you set up when you purchase the service!

My Favorite Website Templates

You can tell that the online industry is still mostly run by technology people because few domain name registrar companies offer really good-looking templates. My theory is that because they understand already how to build websites themselves, they don't see the large demand for easier-to-use products from nontechnical entrepreneurs like you. Unfortunately, GoDaddy.com, Register.com, and other registrars that I have worked with over the years offer poor or no templates at all. Although Network Solutions offers a nice selection of design templates, it has not updated the collection in years.

My current recommendation for website templates is iPowerWeb. Because its templates are bundled with their hosting service, you would also have your website hosted by this company. It charges just $7.95 a month for 3,000 megabytes of hosting storage and a design template for a website. This is more than enough to get your new e-business started. The company even includes free domain name registration with a one-year contract and a money-back guarantee.

Also, iPowerWeb offers dozens of website templates in many business categories to help you make your business look legitimate very quickly. You'll have your choice of different color schemes and even some stock photos to use to personalize your layout. Additionally, their website editing system is very easy to use. You can just point, click, and type to add material to your website, including images and photos of your own if you want to get fancy.

Although you can easily pay less for hosting alone, lower-priced providers usually only offer hosting without the professional-looking templates that make iPowerWeb's slightly higher cost worth it for a beginning e-business entrepreneur.

WYSIWYG Website Building

WYSIWYG (pronounced "wizzy wig") is an acronym for "what you see is what you get." This sort of website editing system allows you to enter data, make changes in real time, and even preview your work online to see exactly what it will look like once published to the Web.

As an example of an easy-to-use WYSIWYG service, I have included here details and a series of screenshots that show how the iPowerWeb Web Builder online application works. There are many providers of similar WYSIWYG services, so this outline should be roughly applicable in many cases.

The point is to show you how easy it is to build a website using hosted templates. Advancements in these services make them easier to use every year. Today, by following the steps outlined here, you'll find that you can build a professional-looking site in just one hour with no technical training necessary!

The skills needed to build and publish a website are simply extensions of the skills you learned in Microsoft Word or other WYSIWYG word-processing programs. This means that you can sign in to one of these services and simply start typing away to create new Web pages that you can post on the Internet with just a few clicks of your mouse.

INTERNET MILLIONAIRE SECRET

If you can use a PC to type a letter or an e-mail message, you can build a website today. Widely available website templates help automate the process so even users with minimal technology expertise can now quickly and cost effectively build websites.

Step-by-Step Instructions for Building a Website

Once you have used the guidelines shared in other parts of this book to find, compare, and choose the best providers for your new e-business, it will come time to build your website. To get started, you need to visit the hosting company's website and purchase the service plan most suited to your needs.

As part of the purchasing process, you are likely to be asked for the domain name you'd like to use, as well as to choose a password that will secure the account you are opening. Entering that domain name, along with your personal information and credit card number, should soon have you on your way to successful setup.

You will then receive e-mails from your new hosting company partner. One of these e-mails should be a receipt for your credit card purchase. The other e-mail (or perhaps more than one) will contain information about where to go on the Internet to log in and start using your partner's services.

There is often a delay of as much as forty-eight hours before these services become available to you online. That's because the hosting company's computers need to reconfigure themselves to recognize your new account and the hosting services that they now need to provide to that domain name. So, if you are planning on setting aside a weekend afternoon or an after-work weeknight to build your new site, be sure to go online and purchase your hosting package a couple of days beforehand. That way it should be ready to go when you are ready to build.

Figure 12–1. The control panel screen of an iPowerWeb hosting account.

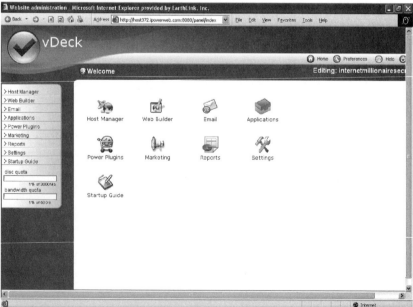

Once you have taken care of these administrative steps, it is time to log in to your new hosting account and start building. Here is a preview of seven things you are likely to see on your computer screen, since most WYSIWYG editing systems offer similar data entry, saving, and publishing methods.

1. *Log in and choose the website building tool.* The "control panel" of this Web hosting account (see Figure 12–1) offers many useful options that you can benefit from as your e-business grows more sophisticated. These include a variety of different settings, e-mail accounts, marketing tools, databases, applications like e-commerce shopping carts, and reports.

For now, we're just talking about building your website, so in this case you would just click on "Web Builder" to access the website building tools.

2. *Choose your design and colors.* The first part of building your site is to choose a design and layout that reflects your business. A new screen for creating such a design is the first choice on the menu you are offered after clicking on "Web Builder" for the first time.

Figure 12–2. Main Web Builder screen.

As you can see in Figure 12–2, this page is also the main menu for you to work with when modifying your site later. It offers links to online tools with which you can edit the individual pages you create, create a custom logo, preview the site you have built, and publish it to the live Internet. By clicking on "Create Design" or "Change Design," you will be offered the design templates about which you have been hearing so much from me in this book.

You can see in Figure 12–3 that Web Builder offers many choices of templates. You can browse by categories dedicated to different kinds of businesses, and also vary the colors and graphics included in each template, to create thousands of combinations. You don't have to know anything about graphic design or image-editing programs like Adobe Photoshop to choose from among these professionally designed website templates. Simply clicking will allow you to browse through them to find shapes and colors and photos that best fit the image your new e-business wants to present to its customers.

Figure12–3. Website template menu.

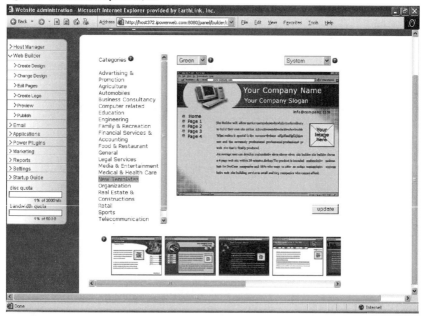

3. *Create a logo and tagline.* Once you have settled on a look and color scheme that you like in the "Design" section of the Web Builder tools, you'll want to save your work and return to the previous menu. There you can play with the "Create a Logo" tool. As you can see in Figure 12–4, this tool allows you to customize the main titles of your website, as well as add a "tagline" or slogan that helps identify your e-business to website visitors. You can also easily vary the font styles and sizes using pull-down menus.

Figure 12–4. The "Create a Logo" screen.

4. *Create and name your pages.* Once you've nailed down these basics of site design, colors, titles, and slogans, next up is to start building the individual content pages. These pages are the meat of your website and contain the information, products, or services that you want your e-business to share with the world. Figure 12–5 shows details. Simply clicking on the button that says "add new page" will do exactly that to get you started. You can create as many pages as you'd like.

Of course, each of your new pages needs a name. You can name them simply by clicking on the small page icon with a "T" in it. A small box will pop up and you can type in names appropriate for each of your pages.

Also shown in Figure 12–5 is that you can easily add more pages by clicking on the "add new page" button, or rearrange the order of your pages by changing the numbers in the boxes in the right hand column.

Figure 12-5. Point-and-click buttons for adding new pages or updating page order.

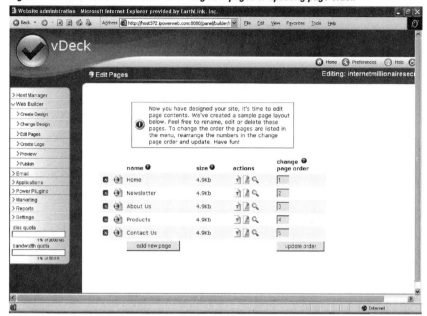

5. *Enter your page content.* Clicking on the pencil icon next to each new page's title will bring up a screen like the one shown in Figure 12–6. This is the WYSIWYG page editor. You can start right away by simply typing into the central box to replace the text that is there. Go crazy! Type away and share with the world the brilliant million-dollar e-business idea that inspired you to begin this process.

Even better is if you have already composed what you want your website to say. That way you can open the editing program in your browser and simply copy and paste from a Word document into the editing system. With this kind of clever preparation, you can build a great-looking website in less than an hour.

From the screenshot shown in Figure 12–6 you can also see that there are many small boxes and icons along the top of the screen. These are Web Builder editing tools that allow you to customize the look, spacing, fonts, sizes, colors, and links of your page. Many of these control buttons are similar to those used in Microsoft Word. "Bold," "Italics," "Left Justify," "Insert Bullets," and "Font Size" are all common word-processing commands with which you are probably already familiar. You can also cut, copy, and paste text and images just as if you were working in Word. You can even "drag and drop" text and images to rearrange them on the page. In fact, of the thirty buttons in the top two rows of the WYSIWIG page editor, only four or five are different from what you would find in Word.

You can also now start learning a few new tricks by clicking on the additional formatting buttons displayed. The most important of these are on the second line toward the right: "Insert Image" and "Insert Web Link." As their names imply, even these functions are easy to understand because all they do is help you insert an image (such as a photo, logo, or banner ad) into your Web page and add links to other pages on the Internet. A little practice and you'll master both of them, too.

The third line of buttons looks intimidating but it is not. All it is is a collection of specific commands for editing table layouts. Use of tables is what will allow you to insert a photo or other image next to text, as you can see in the screenshot in Figure 12–7.

The other Web-specific editing button you should be aware of is the second from right on the second line. It looks like this: <>. This is a powerful tool because clicking on it will switch you out of WYSIWYG mode

Figure 12–6. Screen for editing your website pages.

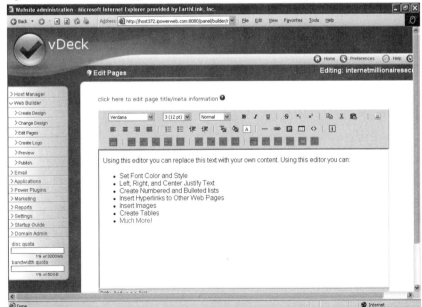

Figure 12–7. WYSIWYG page editor.

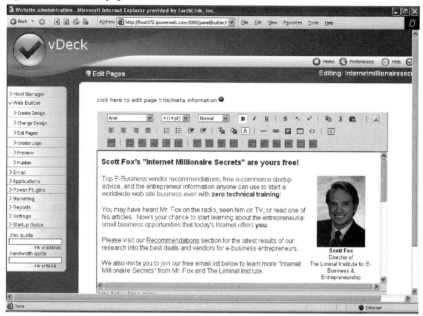

into HTML mode, so you can see the computer code behind the pages you just created. Although the point of using predesigned templates is so that you don't have to learn HTML, switching over to view the HTML code doesn't hurt the work you've done. This button is valuable because, although the WYSIWYG editor is very user-friendly, it doesn't allow you as much flexibility as writing and manipulating the underlying code does.

Writing HTML code yourself is beyond the scope of this book, but you will probably find yourself learning some as your e-business grows. Knowing that this "<>" button is available will allow you to put that knowledge to good use if you ever want to add additional customization to your pages that is beyond the Microsoft Word–type simple editing capabilities of the WYSIWYG editor.

Clicking on "Save Changes" at the bottom of the main editing screen will save your work to create your first Web pages. Be sure not to click away to other parts of the Web until you have saved your work, or it will be lost.

Once you've started typing and played with the buttons a bit, you'll soon be able to create a page like the one shown in Figure 12–8.

INTERNET MILLIONAIRE LAYOUT SECRET:
Web Page Tables

You'll find that making a Web page display nicely can sometimes be a bit of a challenge, especially if you combine text, images, and different fonts and spacing. The difficulties in making a page appear the way you envision it can often be solved by clever use of tables. Tables define the relationship of different bits of text and graphics to one another and force them to sit where you want them to be displayed.

Once you've gotten your basic text and images into a page, use of the table-editing buttons available in Web Builder (and most WYSIWYG editors) is the easiest way to build and modify tables that will squeeze the content into the shapes you desire.

----

6. *Preview your work for quality assurance.* Once you save your work on an individual page, the Web Builder system will take you back to the previous page listing all of the pages on your site.

Now is the time to take advantage of the little icon that looks like a magnifying glass. Click on it to preview your work. Take advantage of

Figure 12–8. Preview of completed website page built using the WYSIWYG editor.

this preview to examine the typing you've done for any spelling mistakes. Also, be sure to click on any website links that you've inserted. If you go to the trouble of building a website you want to be sure that it works!

This process of review and correction is generally called "quality assurance" or simply QA. Don't skip this step or you might be embarrassed by mistakes on your site that you could have easily corrected.

7. *Publish your website.* The last, and even easier, step to take your website "live" is to publish it on the Internet, as shown in Figure 12–8. Once you have done a thorough QA preview of your site to make sure it's ready for prime time, simply click on the "Publish" link. This link will take you to a page that reminds you of what you are doing to make sure that you are ready.

If you are ready, then click "Publish now." Then, within seconds, your new website will appear live on the Internet for anyone in the world to see!

As you can see, it is possible for you to build a website in just an hour without any technical training and with minimal technical effort on your part. Provided you have first created a detailed outline of the site's content, you can take advantage of tools like these to build a business online more quickly than has ever been possible before.

What are you waiting for?

Choosing a Website Template Provider

At these early stages of your new e-business, whichever provider you use for hosting should offer website design templates with point-and-click editing capabilities, plus the ability to go back and forth between text and HTML easily (so you can preview your work easily and for when you get better at HTML and want to enter code directly into the system).

Critical decision factors include whether the provider offers:

▲ Multiple design templates to choose from with current, stylish looks appropriate to your business

▲ WYSIWYG editing capabilities

▲ The ability to add your own images, including photos and logos, to the site

- ▲ Online storage for your images, preferably in a separate and easily accessed folder

- ▲ Easy publishing of website changes to the Internet

- ▲ E-mail accounts included with the hosting service

Templated Website Example

The beauty of website templates is that they are easy to create and maintain without knowing much about technology. In addition, they are inexpensive because they are usually provided as part of hosting/serving package deals that start at less than $10 a month. My website, Internet MillionaireSecrets.com, is a good demonstration of an effective use of templates to create a site that's functional and professional in appearance and quickly offers visitors the information they seek.

Figure 12–9. Template-based home page for InternetMillionaireSecrets.com.

Although I could have spent a lot more time, energy, and money on designing a fancy and impressive site full of bells and whistles to impress you, my intention with InternetMillionaireSecrets.com (as it should be with any entrepreneur's website) is to offer the user quick access to valuable information and hasten her conversion into a customer. Templates serve this need admirably, without requiring the website owner to reinvent the wheel by developing customized graphics.

When visiting InternetMillionaireSecrets.com (see Figure 12–9), the first thing you'll see is the top header where the site's title displays, as well as the dominant graphic of the PC in the upper left-hand corner. Along the left-hand side is a menu that offers each page of the site to you for easy clicking. In the center of the page is the text copy I wrote to explain the site and its services.

While the design of this site isn't likely to amaze any of your friends who may be graphic artists or Web designers, it should impress you as an entrepreneur because it was built quickly and cost effectively and still looks professional. Admittedly, templated websites won't serve all needs, but for startup ventures looking to get online quickly to start attracting an audience, they are the best solution available.

FINDING A WEB DESIGNER

YOU MAY WANT to consider hiring a professional Web designer or design firm if your website needs a unique, more customized look. This might be worth the expense, for example, if:

▲ You have custom needs such as unique products that require a lot of original photos to display properly.

▲ You are offering services where the look of your website is critical (such as fashion, advertising, or something particularly cool or trendy).

▲ Your business has outgrown the limitations of a templated system.

Professional Web design is more costly and takes much longer than using templates, but it can also yield fancier and more professional-looking results.

How to Choose a Web Designer

Finding a designer appropriate for your website is more complicated than choosing a domain-name registrar or hosting company. The decision is tricky because it must include subjective factors such as the "vibe" of your products, your desired image, and your own personal tastes, as well as more objective criteria like your timeline and budget.

If you want to hire a designer or design firm, here are four ways you can find appropriate vendors:

1. Surf the Web or get recommendations from friends to find sites that you like. Find out who their designers were by consulting the "credits" section of the home page (if available) or contact the site directly to ask.

2. Put a posting on CraigsList.org to ask for submissions.

3. Post a description of your needs to BuyerZone.com to get bids from a variety of vendors.

4. Search for "Web designer" on Google or your favorite search engine. You'll get thousands of results, both in the plain results and in the sponsored search results that run down the right side of the screen.

Critical Questions for a Web Designer

Here are some critical questions to ask anyone that you consider hiring to help design your website:

▲ What kinds of websites have you built previously?

▲ Do any of them offer goods/services similar to mine? If so, what unique aspects of your design helped their businesses grow?

▲ Do you have experience designing for e-commerce sites, or just in making pretty pictures?

▲ How long will it take you to deliver your proposed design for me?

▲ What other services can you offer (e.g., hosting, updating, tech support, etc.)?

▲ Who will own the copyrights in the designs that you provide to me? (You should insist on a written contract that clearly transfers all ownership of the work to you.)

▲ What amount of updating is included in your pricing?

▲ How much usability testing is included in your pricing?

Remember that if you are having custom work done, you need to commission it early in your website-building process because it can take longer than you think.

INTERNET MILLIONAIRE SECRET:
STOCK GRAPHICS

Top-quality marketing requires good-looking graphics. I recommend using templates. Templates often contain high-quality stock photos and designs that can help you create a professional-looking website.

If you are going to do any advertising or marketing beyond your website, however, you will soon need to invest some time in creating, or some money in commissioning, a good-looking logo and advertisements that will make your site look more professional.

You can commission these elements from designers or simply shop around online for preproduced "stock" photos or graphics. There are many online sources for stock photographs and illustrations that you can use to put together your own website and advertising graphics, and they are much less expensive than having custom work done. These websites allow you to purchase both color and black-and-white photographs, as well as illustrations, shapes, graphics, and a wide variety of useful designs.

Because there is a lot of competition in this space, many different pricing and service and rights options are available. For example, you can license or purchase images individually or on a subscription basis. And depending on the images you select, the rights available to you may be royalty-free or may include a provision that gives you exclusive use.

Logo Development

If you have a designer's eye and computer graphics (e.g., Adobe Photoshop) skills of your own, you may be good enough to create a logo for your company. If not, you may want to consider hiring a graphics designer to develop your company image.

Traditional graphics designers can be quite expensive, so I recommend either finding a friend who is handy with graphics software or using an online vendor.

DON'T BE A "TWEAK FREAK"

I'll have more to say on this topic later, but I want to warn you now not to be a perfectionist who wastes weeks or months tweaking your new website to make it perfect. Your goal at this early stage of your new business is not perfection but to get the website operational ASAP so that you can start generating revenue. Keep your eye on the ball!

Graphics can be easily developed and delivered via the Internet, so there are many, many designers you can find online. A simple Google search on "logo" will return a list of many companies offering designers to do your work. Generally speaking, they will inexpensively (for under $250) create several logos for you to choose from so that you can develop a corporate image that best represents your new business. However, since many of these professionals are not native English speakers and/or based in the United States, it can often be challenging to communicate the subtleties needed for design work via e-mail.

14 E-COMMERCE SHOPPING CARTS

TO UNDERSTAND e-commerce, let's start with a few definitions of the key concepts of shopping carts, payment processors, and merchant accounts.

Shopping Carts. A website "shopping cart" is a piece of software that mimics the use of a shopping cart in the real world. In other words, it is software that allows the online shopper to choose and hold items for purchase until she is ready to check out and complete the purchase process by making payment. The best e-commerce shopping carts:

- ▲ Are easy for the shopper to use
- ▲ Are easy for you to install on your website
- ▲ Offer easy visibility of the cart's contents
- ▲ Make it easy for the customer to add/subtract goods
- ▲ Display the current total cost of the items in the cart (ideally including sales tax and shipping costs, if any)

Payment Processors. An online payment processing company (some-times also called a payment "gateway") is the link between the customer's purchase and your credit card merchant account.

For example, in Figure 14–1, the payment processor receives a request from your shopping cart when a customer wants to check out and pur-chase goods from your website. The payment processor then electroni-cally checks with the customer's credit card company to authorize the expenditure and communicates back to your shopping cart that the pur-chase is legitimate and can be completed.

Merchant Accounts. A merchant account is the account that your busi-ness has with a credit card processing company. Again, as shown in Figure 14–1, it receives the authorization instructions from the payment processor and then collects the money from the customer's credit card account for deposit into your bank account.

In practice, the payment processor and the merchant account are often indistinguishable from one another. They can even be owned by the same company.

Online Merchant Accounts. Traditionally, any business accepting credit cards needed to have its own merchant account in order to process trans-actions. Like everything else we're discussing, however, the Internet has disrupted the traditional credit card merchant-account industry to again make things easier and cheaper for new entrepreneurs like you.

Not only has the Internet forced the industry to do away with the requirement that merchant account holders operate traditional stores, but competition in the merchant account business has driven down applica-tion fees from hundreds of dollars to zero. It has also caused major drops in per-transaction fees and discount rates (the percentage-of-sale-price fees charged by the credit card companies). Approval processing time for new accounts has also been cut from weeks to just hours in many cases.

A new online business like yours can quickly be approved online for a merchant account, often with no application fees and monthly charges of less than $20. Increasing standardization of online payment processing also means that you can integrate most major payment processing and merchant account providers into your website's shopping cart software with simple online forms and clicks of your mouse.

Figure 14–1. Overview of credit card payment processing.

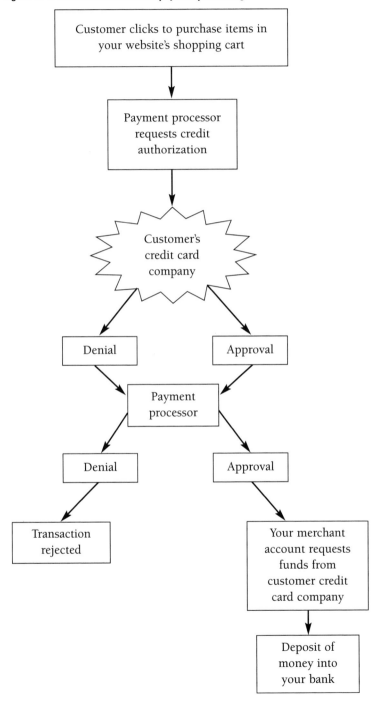

The Best Website Shopping Carts

The best kind of shopping cart for your new e-business will be a reflection of the kind of business you are starting. If you have a wide variety of products, each with its own unique attributes, you will need a shopping cart that can accommodate and display a wide variety of product details and images. On the other hand, if you are selling familiar products for a narrow range of items, you can probably use a much simpler shopping cart.

Because the technology and pricing of e-commerce shopping carts changes so rapidly, it is difficult to provide specific recommendations that will stand the test of time. Instead, I am going to provide you with several examples as well as a list of questions that you can use to help evaluate the best shopping cart fit for your needs at the time you read this book.

INTERNET MILLIONAIRE SECRET:
Payment Processing from PayPal

Recent progress in online payments technology has created a new breed of payment processors that are very helpful to e-business entrepreneurs. The leading example is PayPal, which grew from a startup in 1998 to become a major public company by early 2002.

PayPal's innovation was to develop technology to allow customers to send and receive money to one another directly from their bank accounts, eliminating the need for credit card transaction-processing capabilities. Although the service has since grown to include credit card processing also, this innovation is still having major repercussions on the previously closed world of credit card payment processing. (PayPal was acquired by eBay in late 2002.)

Today, the service offers e-business entrepreneurs the unprecedented ability to accept credit card transactions without a traditional merchant account. Your new e-business can accept online payments by directly debiting the consumer's PayPal account, checking account, or credit card. The service is free to set up, has no monthly costs, and charges a smaller percentage of sales than traditional merchant accounts. Compared with the cost and hassle of applying for and maintaining a traditional credit card merchant account, PayPal is a great deal for entrepreneurs.

My Current Recommendations

Here are four website shopping cart solutions that I currently like and why.

1. *PayPal.* As mentioned previously, PayPal offers a simple shopping cart that works very well with its own payment system. It can easily be installed by copying some HTML code (which PayPal provides) and pasting it into your website template.

If you are selling just a few simple items or are concerned about the costs of a merchant account, the PayPal shopping cart works nicely. A sample screenshot of the PayPal shopping-cart checkout screen is shown in Figure 14–2. You can see that it offers a nice clean design that is straightforward for the customer to use when checking out. You can also see, however, that it does not offer any graphic customization, so it is obvious to a customer that you have not invested in custom e-commerce design.

Figure 14–2. PayPal shopping-cart checkout screen.

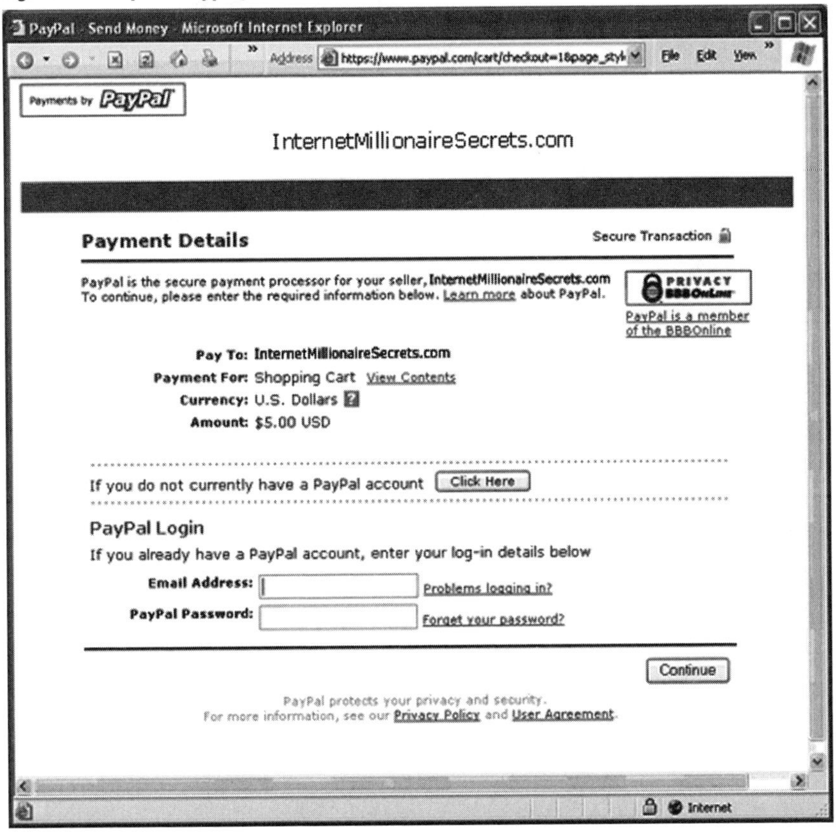

Despite this drawback, the PayPal system is an excellent way to get started, and it is free for low-volume users.

2. *Mal's E-Commerce.* A very popular provider of basic e-commerce shopping cart services is Mal's E-commerce Limited. This young company, still run by Mal (Stewart) himself, powers thousands of e-commerce websites worldwide.

Mal's e-commerce is also cheap—in fact, the basic shopping cart is free. An upgrade to more complete services that will allow you to link to a payment processor to process credit card orders in real time will cost you only $8.00 a month, too.

My wife's online business, SweaterBabe.com, used a slightly customized version of Mal's shopping cart software to create the page shown in Figure 14–3. The result is a cost-effective but custom look for the central shopping-cart functionality.

Figure 14–3. SweaterBabe.com checkout screen.

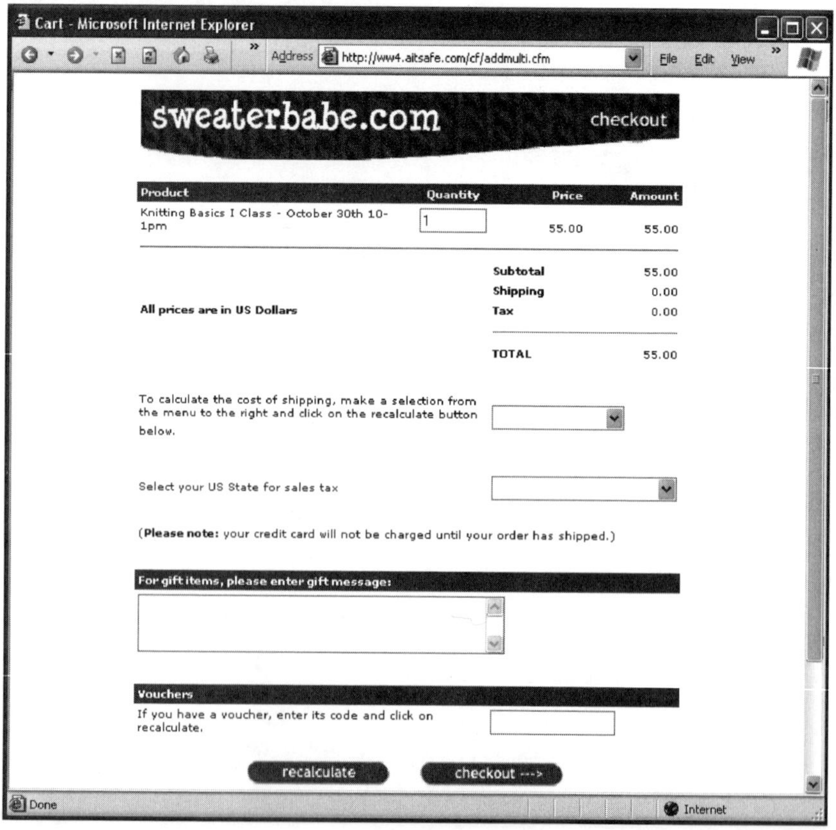

You should note, though, that the resulting URL that appears in the address bar in Figure 14–3 does not show "www.sweaterbabe.com," as a customer might expect to see. This is because the shopping cart is actually hosted by the Mal's central servers, not on the SweaterBabe.com site itself. Although this solution keeps the costs down, you should consider that it may scare off some security-concerned customers.

Unfortunately, the system is a bit technical. On the frequently asked questions (FAQs) page about his service, Mal says: "… I think it's fair to say that you do need at least a basic understanding [of HTML]. In particular you need to know how hyperlinks are constructed and how to create a form."

If you already have these programming skills, Mal's E-commerce can be a good solution. If not, you can try one of the easier-to-implement systems and revisit Mal's in the future if your needs warrant.

3. *Yahoo! Small Business.* Yahoo now claims to host one of every eight stores on the Internet. The company has successfully used its huge traffic base to attract users to its e-commerce services and also tried to make its storefront offerings easy to use.

If you are going to set up a more complicated store where you would like to be able to display multiple items in an easy-to-view format, the Yahoo solution is a fairly good one. The "help" documentation is not very good, but the service's tools can be figured out without too much trouble by trial and error.

Yahoo allows a fair amount of customization. The heart of the Yahoo shopping cart is the module in the center of the screen labeled "Your Shopping Cart," as shown in Figure 14–4. While this module is not changeable, you can see that KitchenKapers.com has modified all of the surrounding graphics and text to create a pleasant and consistent look.

Another nice feature of the Yahoo! Store packages is that they can display to the customer the image of each item in the shopping cart at checkout.

Unfortunately, Yahoo! Stores for small businesses are rather expensive. As of this writing, basic storefront technology starts at $39.95 a month, a midlevel business solution jumps quickly to $99.95 a month, and a full-fledged online store is $299.95 a month. In addition to these monthly fees, Yahoo also charges a small percentage of every sale. These are pretty high costs compared to many other providers in the market today.

It's a good bet that Yahoo will continue to improve its services as time goes on, however, so it may be worth it to invest in building your store with Yahoo's e-commerce solutions if you are confident that your future growth can absorb its expenses.

Figure 14–4. KitchenKapers.com checkout screen.

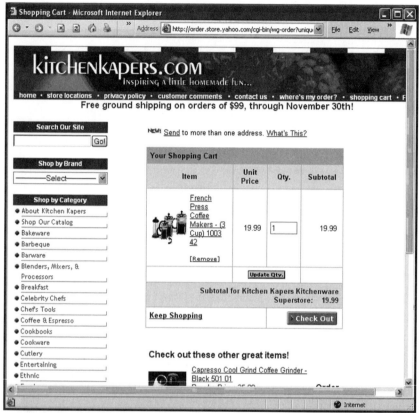

4. *Custom Shopping Cart Solutions.* Of course, you can also commission a custom system to accommodate the shopping needs of your new e-business. However, I would caution against this approach.

There is absolutely no need to build a new shopping system from scratch these days. Don't be convinced otherwise by technical salespeople. Even the most complicated multimedia, cross-platform, multicurrency systems can be built from prepackaged software modules at bargain prices. You will most likely be better off "renting" a simple system from an application service provider (ASP) provider such as those I've discussed in Chapter 9.

INTERNET MILLIONAIRE SECRET:
Digital Delivery

Another exciting capability of the Internet is that it can help you sell products that are delivered digitally. This means that you don't have to ship a physical object but can instead e-mail or offer the product by download to the customer. This saves a huge amount of cost, administrative hassle, and customer service expense.

Digital delivery is only possible with products that are text- or information-based, such as books, music, or software. Microsoft Word, Adobe PDF, MP3, or other file formats that contain the products transfer quickly and easily via the Internet, so all you need is a way to manage the downloads and charge the customers for their purchases.

While many companies are tackling some aspect of digital delivery, the best one that I have found so far is called PayLoadz. While its competitors often specialize only in the sale of e-books or music, this company offers the secure sale and downloadable delivery of digital files of all sorts. By uploading your files to Payloadz's secure servers and installing the basic shopping-cart buttons on your website, you can offer your digital goods for sale securely without having to manually send each customer file purchased and manually process the transaction. PayLoadz integrates all of these functions into one helpful service that offers free trials and then starts at just $15 per month for premium service.

Be sure to check them out if your business is going to offer digital downloads (and visit InternetMillionaireSecrets.com for my latest download service recommendations, too).

Critical Questions for an E-Commerce Vendor

Here are the questions you should ask an e-commerce provider before you entrust your new business to it. Although no two services are exactly alike, there is an increasing amount of standardization across websites, and these fundamental principles will apply to any vendor in this space.

▲ How will I receive orders from the system? By e-mail, fax, or another delivery method?

▲ Is the order information processed automatically? And how quickly?

▲ Are customer records retained by the system? If so, for how long?

▲ Do payments automatically process upon purchase or do they require manual attention?

▲ What parts of a transaction does the system generate automatically? For example:

Customer order confirmations

Shipping confirmations

Order tracking confirmations

Sales tax calculations

Shipping costs calculations

▲ Does the system provide order tracking?

▲ Are there easy reports to determine best sellers and profit margins?

▲ Will the system allow you to set discounts and coupons?

▲ How easy is the system to implement?

▲ How easy do customers find the checkout process?

▲ What technical support is available?

▲ Is the system compatible with the systems my hosting company is already using for my website?

▲ How secure is the system and the customer data?

▲ How easy is it to provide refunds to customers?

▲ What are the policies and fees incurred by chargebacks?

▲ What is the fee structure? What is the breakdown of up-front fees versus monthly fees versus usage charges (percent of sales)?

▲ What is the contract length?

▲ Is the system scaleable? That is, will the system be able to grow if I get more traffic?

▲ Are there uptime guarantees? Whose problem is it if the system goes down and my sales are delayed or stopped?

▲ What about transferability? How easy would it be if I need to move my store and customer data to another system?

▲ How does the system handle sales tax for different states?

▲ Do you need a business bank account?

▲ Does your business need to be incorporated?

▲ Can the provider give references from other satisfied customers with needs similar to yours?

Although this is a rather long list of questions, you can see that most of them can be answered with a little online research.

For example, by reviewing the shopping carts of the provider's existing customers, you can get an idea of how easy it is to use. The Internet makes this easy—you can simply visit their websites and try some sample transactions yourself.

The more technical questions can usually be answered by reviewing the website of the provider (especially the Frequently Asked Questions [FAQ] section) or asking the company's salespeople or technical support staff to give you additional data. Lastly, you can contact customer references by e-mail to make certain that all the claims that the provider is making are reliable.

15 THE EBAY PHENOMENON

OF COURSE, EBAY is the clear leader in incubating aspiring e-businesses and providing online selling services to entrepreneurs worldwide. Meg Whitman, eBay's CEO, said in a speech in June 2006 that more than 1.3 million people now make all or part of their livelihood selling on eBay. And a July 21, 2005 study conducted by eBay reported that U.S.-based eBay members sold more than $10.6 billion of merchandise during the first six months of 2005 alone, according to the same eBay survey.

Is eBay Right for Your New E-Business?

Given all of eBay's features and the wide reach of its network, I'm sure that you're asking this very question.

Although many good books have been written about eBay, most of them focus on telling you "how" to use eBay, not helping you to decide if it's the right solution for your business. As this book demonstrates, there are many types of e-businesses and even more e-business vendors for you to choose from. Here is my summary of eBay's strengths and weaknesses as a store provider for entrepreneurs. It's my hope that this material will help you evaluate eBay's "fit" for your new venture.

eBay Strengths

▲ *High Traffic.* The very high traffic that eBay receives can help you quickly get your products in front of a lot of people by listing them in an eBay auction or in an eBay store. Because eBay's huge audience naturally uses its search capabilities to locate products in both its auction and store networks, it's much easier for shoppers to find you and your products on eBay than on the general Internet. This can be a crucial advantage to a startup business that has yet to build any brand recognition or customer base.

▲ *Ease of Use.* Setting up your first auction sale on eBay is a quick and easy process. No knowledge of HTML or other computer code is needed to get your goods included. There are also no startup or recurring fees associated with opening a "Seller" account on eBay auctions (unlike eBay stores, which I'll discuss later in this chapter).

▲ *Unique Items Marketplace.* Although eBay's original story—that the company was started because the founder wanted to help his wife sell her collection of Pez candy dispensers online—was a fabrication for publicity purposes, it remains true that eBay is a great marketplace for unique and collectible items.

The depth and breadth of eBay's huge audience means that you can probably find a willing buyer for almost anything that you'd like to sell. The size of this audience for eBay auctions may also mean that your grandmother's hat collection or a collectible Star Wars toy will get better attention and command better prices on eBay than at any local garage sale or flea market.

Listing and posting each item using the eBay auction posting system is cumbersome, but it can be worth your time given the huge audience that may see it. Because a larger audience usually yields more bidders and higher sale prices, sale of unique items on eBay can bring better profit that can more than recompense you for your time and eBay's many small listings-related fees.

▲ *Commodity Items Marketplace.* On the other hand, eBay is also great for buying and selling commodity items such as batteries, socks, used books, name-brand appliances, or other easy-to-recognize items. Here you can save listing time by simply copying your previous auction descriptions and reposting them. Customer service is also minimized because the known nature of your goods minimizes questions.

(You may have noticed that I've left out semi-unique items of which you have multiple but not mass quantities to sell. This category is the basis of many e-businesses, but these items are a pain to sell on eBay because of the difficulties and expense of listings, relistings, customer service, and auction administration. This is why I generally recommend starting your own website using templates instead of starting out on eBay.)

EBAY POWERSELLER:
DAVID YASKULKAS, BLUEBERRY BOUTIQUE

David Yaskulkas got started on eBay in the fall of 2002 from his home in Massachusetts. After the birth of their twin boys, his wife was interested in finding a way to generate some part-time income without leaving their house. The story of how they turned to eBay is both inspiring and instructive because the Blueberry Boutique they started is now the number-one seller of men's shirts and ties on eBay and has grown into a million-dollar e-business. Here is how Yaskulkas describes his e-business experience:

Q: What does Blueberry Boutique sell?

Yaskulkas: We offer luxury apparel and accessories with designs from Armani to Zegna at 40 percent to 80 percent below retail, including shirts, ties, sunglasses, jewelry, and organic apparel.

Q: Is this a successful business for you?

Yaskulkas: Thankfully yes. In our first year, we grew to Platinum PowerSeller status on eBay, meaning sales of at least $25,000 per month with a top customer service rating.

Previously, I was chief marketing officer for a national nonprofit, and within six months of starting this online business, I came on full-time. We've grown to six employees selling on our own web-site—blueberryboutique.net—and through other online marketplaces such as Amazon, Overstock, Shopzilla, Yahoo! Shopping, and more, in addition to eBay.

Q: How and why did you get started on eBay?

Yaskulkas: When our boys were small, my wife Debbie was looking for part-time work that wouldn't require leaving the house. She decided to try to sell a few things out of our closet on eBay.

Q: Was eBay an obvious choice for you?

Yaskulkas: Well, we were already enthusiastic eBay shoppers. Besides, I had people-to-people selling in my blood because my parents had a very successful flea market business, and I had worked with them part-time and summers. I suppose eBay is the twenty-first century version of those 1970s and 1980s flea markets that were so great for buyers and sellers alike.

Q: Were you nervous about becoming an eBay seller?

Yaskulkas: We knew that we could start selling slowly and test things. It was important not to risk too much capital. Our "big risk" was buying a $200 digital camera to take pictures of the things we planned to sell online. If our plan didn't work, we could return the camera within thirty days and get our investment back. I'm happy to say we never returned that camera.

Q: Was it difficult to get started on eBay?

Yaskulkas: No, we used inexpensive listing tools available directly from eBay. But you need more sophisticated third-party tools and partners in order to scale. We now use ChannelAdvisor marketplace management software, a leading certified eBay solutions provider.

Q: Would you recommend becoming an eBay seller to others?

Yaskulkas: Yes, eBay has a very important place in the e-tail universe. The barrier to entry is very small, and there's a huge audience. Margins are very tight and fees can be high, but the fees are analogous to what a brick-and-mortar store would pay to be in the right location in the right shopping mall.

Q: How about e-business in general? Do you think aspiring entrepreneurs still have a chance today to build new e-businesses?

Yaskulkas: Absolutely. There are incredible opportunities still out there, many of which we can't even conceive of yet. Entrepreneurs who don't participate in e-commerce will fall by the wayside. You don't need to be a pure e-commerce play like Blueberry Boutique, but every new business needs to be investing in e-commerce in whatever way is appropriate for it. Every retailer especially needs to examine every distribution channel it has available; it will see that the highest growth rates are in e-commerce.

I would say that you're better off if you're not selling products in a mature category, though. We now have 4,000 competitors in ties, for example. It's much easier if you focus on new products and services that others are not yet offering.

Q: What would be your top money-saving tips for new entrepreneurs?

Yaskulkas: I would very much emphasize preserving the capital you have until you have thoroughly tested your plans and products. It's extraordinarily easy to get started and test a new business on eBay, and you should do that before investing heavily.

Q: What do you think is the number-one reason for the success of Blueberry Boutique?

Yaskulkas: We take care of our customers. We don't go to sleep at night with one dollar in our pockets that is from an unhappy customer. Because eBay is so large and often faceless, we feel we need to go the extra mile in customer service. We offer 100 percent unconditional guarantees, easy returns, and even have a $25,000 surety bond in place from buySAFE/Liberty Mutual to protect our customers. We support important charities with our auctions.

We also carefully reinforce our brand every chance we get so that customers will remember they purchased from Blueberry, not just from eBay. These factors help us earn more than twice the average repeat business ratio on eBay.

Q: Any closing remarks?

Yaskulkas: Our family is very thankful for the opportunities that eBay has helped provide. It's extraordinary to work from home and be with our children. Our marketing and strategic philanthropy consulting work has been extremely rewarding, and our experience with groups like the Professional eBay Sellers Alliance has sharpened our expertise and broadened our relationships—all growing out of our eBay success.

Q: Is there an Internet Millionaire Secret you can share with readers?

Yaskulkas: I can unhesitatingly tell your readers that they should follow their dreams as well. If they're squarely focused on adding value to customers, trying to give back to the community along the way, and of course working really hard, they'll be very successful on eBay.

eBay Auctions vs. eBay Stores

The majority of eBay's traffic and business is in the online auction business that made the company famous. The introduction of this bid-driven marketplace for goods of all sorts has created a huge and successful worldwide user community. Many members of this community will freely admit being "addicted" to the excitement of hunting down and bidding on items on eBay.

However, many buyers also find the auction nature of the traditional eBay purchasing process frustrating. They don't want to wait three days, four hours, and twenty-seven minutes until an auction closes to determine if they actually purchased a product or not.

The limited-time auction format also poses frustrations for sellers. For sales of multiple items or larger lots of inventory, they find that they must relist products constantly after each auction ends. Although this tedious task can be automated somewhat with special eBay Power Tools software, the software generally involves a large up-front fee and/or a recurring monthly fee, plus each relisting also incurs fees that can add up quickly.

AUCTION DEFAULTS AND FRAUD

The other major complaint about online auctions is that many buyers default on their promised bids.

Although eBay has done a pretty good job of quantifying trustworthiness with the little stars that users receive for each successful transaction on the network (see Figure 15–1), there are still many transactions that fall apart because of buyer default or fraud.

In Figure 15–1, for example, you can interpret that the user who's identified as "millions05" has received positive feedback on thirty-one successful transactions. It is not uncommon to see experienced eBay buyers and sellers who may have thousands of transactions to their credit. Each additional level of positive feedback that's accumulated leads to a different color star associated with that level. You can also click on the underlined name and number to reach a page displaying all the feedback (both positive and negative) that an individual user has received over time. Referencing these transaction numbers, stars, and feedback reviews can help you determine with whom you may (or may not) want to do business on eBay.

Because the auction format depends on bidding among multiple shoppers over periods of hours or days, auctions lack the immediacy of an instant purchase. A buyer may have changed her mind about or even forgotten her obligation by the time it comes to paying the amount she promised when she won the auction.

Figure 15–1. eBay user ID showing the number of successful transactions and positive feedback rating.

millions05 (31 ☆)

Additionally, there are so many new users constantly entering the eBay marketplace that many of them simply don't recognize the obligation they have to pay for items that they have won through bidding online. Sellers on eBay can, of course, relist items for which payment is not received, but only after attempts to contact the auction's high bidder have failed. (Attempts to contact bidders can be frustrating and time-consuming for sellers, but are required in order to prevent further customer service issues.)

Relisting can also be expensive. After a failed auction, eBay will refund the majority of its per-listing fees (including the insertion and final value percentage-of-sale amount fees). However, it requires the seller to wait at least one week after pursuing resolution with the auction's high bidder first, and then still does not refund many of the smaller marketing and formatting fees that it charges.

EBAY REACTS TO USER FRUSTRATION

Frustration with these aspects of both the buying and selling experience led eBay to make two major modifications of its original auction system: a "Buy It Now" option and eBay stores.

▲ *Buy It Now.* The addition of the "Buy It Now" option relieved a lot of buyer frustration because, as the name suggests, it allows shoppers to complete and confirm purchases at a predetermined price instantly. For shoppers used to traditional in-store retailing that offers posted prices on a cash-and-carry basis, this option is preferable to having to compete in an auction process that can extend over days. Experts estimate that 30 percent to 35 percent of eBay's sales are now transacted in nonauction formats.

▲ *Fixed-Price eBay Stores.* To help attract more sellers to its services, eBay also introduced eBay stores, online stores where an entrepreneur can sell products at fixed prices (rather than individual items in competitive auctions). They also allow store owners to post multiple units of the same item so they don't have to constantly relist items in the auctions.

These stores are reasonably easy to use and gain the benefit of eBay's large traffic, but they are rather expensive, too. Depending on their size and features, eBay stores currently cost $15.95, $49.95, or $299.95 per month, plus a minimum charge of 5.25 percent of the final value of each item sold through the store, plus a number of other smaller fees depending on your marketing approach and the price of the items you sell. From time to time eBay changes these fees (usually raising them, of course); in addition, several more percentage-based charges may be added on for each sale for item listing, highlighting, and promotion.

The basic eBay store is still a reasonable deal, especially if you are already a fan of eBay. It includes only five pages of display and limits your outgoing e-mail newsletters to 5,000 recipients per month, but the store templates are easy to use. They are specifically designed to get a new user online and selling as quickly as possible.

Higher-priced eBay store packages include more pages, greater e-mail newsletter mailing capability, and better technical support. You would have to decide if these upgrades are worth it for your business.

eBay Weaknesses

However, both eBay auctions and its stores still suffer from some major weaknesses. So, although eBay is clearly the leader in the auction space, these factors are significant contributors to the ongoing need for stand-alone e-commerce stores such as I am describing in this book.

BARGAIN HUNTERS AND SELLING COMPETITION

From a seller's perspective, eBay's biggest weakness is that its audience is primarily bargain hunters. They have come to eBay looking for a deal and are often willing to work through week-long auction processes to get them. Additionally, the search features on eBay make it easy for shoppers to price-compare your goods instantly. This is bad news if you are a seller because it drives down your profit margins.

Similarly, the very size of the eBay marketplace means lots of competition. If you are selling unique items, this can be good and drive your sales prices upward, but if your goods are at all common, you will be faced with many other sellers offering similar goods at low margins.

YOUR BRANDING: LOST ON EBAY

Another problem that I have with eBay from an entrepreneur's point of view is that it limits your ability to display and develop your brand. This is especially true in the auctions, where the eBay branding and logos overwhelm any material you put up (and links to your website are actually prohibited in many cases). The eBay stores allow more customization but still require at least a minor eBay logo and toolbar across the top of every page of your store.

David Yaskulkas, the CEO of eBay PowerSeller Blueberry Boutique (interviewed earlier in this chapter), recognizes this issue and recommends paying special attention to your graphics when selling on eBay to counteract it. As he says, "If you don't reinforce your brand with great graphics, your customers will only remember buying from eBay, not from you."

As a new business owner, the best way to guarantee your profit margins is to develop a strong, positive brand image and relationship with your customers. Unfortunately, eBay makes it difficult to do that, so you need to spend extra time and attention on counteracting the problem.

INTERNET MILLIONAIRE SECRET:
A New, Local eBay

Although eBay takes advantage of the Internet's global nature to facilitate among parties worldwide, most of these deals are then completed by the seller shipping something to the buyer.

But what if you want to sell something too difficult to ship? Or if you are selling a service that only appeals in a local area? A lot of transactions take place in purely local markets. Maybe the e-business model you're hoping to pursue targets local customers, too.

Buying a used dining room set or an overstocked plasma TV doesn't always makes sense on eBay because shipping costs can be huge. Similarly, the services of a local gardener, babysitter, or masseuse don't require shipping at all, but can only be delivered in a local area. In both cases, many customers would prefer to drive to a nearby location to receive the item or service today instead of waiting for the mail to bring it to them.

LiveDeal.com is an eBay type e-commerce site that solves these dilemmas for both buyers and sellers. Founded in 2003, the company quickly attracted users nationwide for the services it makes available to all 70,000 zip codes in the United States. The company's mission is to bring the best e-commerce tools to entrepreneurs interested in reaching local markets.

Becoming a seller on LiveDeal.com is similar to the easy process pioneered by eBay. (In fact, the founders of LiveDeal.com are former eBay executives). Best of all, selling individual items and even creating a store on LiveDeal.com is free.

The service that LiveDeal.com offers is a combination of eBay's self-service marketplace plus the online classified-ads approach of CraigsList.org (Be sure to read Chapter 16 for an explanation of Craig's List if you are not already aware of it). You can post items to sell from your garage (like you would on eBay) but target only the audience in your local town (like a classified ad in your local paper). LiveDeal.com is thus a hugely helpful opportunity for entrepreneurs looking to clean out their garages of items too big to ship easily (e.g., furniture, refrigerators) or to sell location-restricted services or goods or real estate. In fact, Rajesh Navar, the CEO of the company, told me that one of the company's most popular selling categories is pets! I visited LiveDeal.com and quickly confirmed that there were currently thirteen golden retrievers for sale, believe it or not.

Another big difference from eBay is that listing items for sale or even setting up a store is free (except for car sales). Although this policy may change in the future, Navar tells me that the free policy is a key part of LiveDeal's current strategy, so you can probably count on it for a while.

This is not to say that LiveDeal.com is a nonprofit company, though. Like eBay, it charges fees for highlighted listings, multiple-item photos, and other promotional upgrades, as well as a percentage based on the final sales price of your transactions. Because it only charges based on successful sales, though, costs are purely performance-based, which is an excellent option for cash-strapped new entrepreneurs.

LiveDeal.com's approach has been very successful. It attracts more than a million unique visitors each month, has mediated hundreds of millions of dollars worth of transactions, and has listed over $1 billion worth of goods/services for sale. This explosive growth is due to the appeal of this unique, hybrid online marketplace service, which is used by more than 1 million buyers and sellers monthly.

With no cost for listings and a rapidly growing community of buyers and sellers in almost every part of the United States, LiveDeal.com sounds like an excellent option for you if you are considering the sale of goods or services that your parent's generation would have listed in the classifieds section of your local paper. A phrase I suggested to Navar that summarizes the potential of LiveDeal.com's appeal to aspiring entrepreneurs is "empowering local entrepreneurship." Not a bad corporate motto, huh?

If you're considering focusing on a local or regional target market for your new business, LiveDeal.com may be a good service for your needs.

eBay: Love It or Leave It?

Although eBay has many positives, the combination of its bargain-hunting audience, competitive markets, and poor branding capabilities largely force sellers into competing on price. This is obviously undesirable and is compounded by the relatively high costs of eBay's selling services.

You'll *love* eBay if:

▲ You like participating in or running auctions.

▲ You are selling unique items that deserve special listing and customer service because they are likely to offer good profit margins.

▲ You want to start or test e-commerce business ideas quickly and inexpensively in a high-traffic environment.

As a seller, you may be disappointed that:

▲ eBay can be expensive (in either the auction or eBay store format).

▲ eBay requires a fair amount of customer service because of the complexities of auctions.

▲ The bargain-hunting customers and many competing sellers that eBay attracts force your prices down.

▲ eBay prefers to promote and build its own brand more than yours.

Despite these weaknesses, many e-business owners still choose to operate stores on eBay. My guess is that they have built their businesses specifically around the auction model or with systems or products that fit well with eBay's services and audience.

Sellers on eBay probably also justify its weaknesses and expense the same way that real-world merchants justify paying high rent to have their stores in high-traffic areas: location, location, location!

16 DEVELOPING KILLER CONTENT ON A STARTUP BUDGET

THE WAY YOU present your e-business to the world is the key to its success. It is important that your website looks professional and credible so that customers will trust the products you are selling. Ideally, your site's content will also be interesting and unique enough that they appreciate your brand and remember to shop with you again.

You need to develop two types of content to make this happen: a "Hollywood pitch" and website copy.

The Hollywood Pitch

It's important to have a clear idea of what your business does and what it offers to its customers—both for your own thinking but also because friends, family, customers, and even potential investors are all going to ask you, "So what does your new business do?"

The best way I have found to encapsulate your new business concept is to use what I call the "Hollywood pitch technique." You identify the basic elements of your business and compare them to familiar, existing concepts or previous successes in a pseudo-mathematical equation.

In Hollywood, new movie and TV program ideas are often pitched this way because it uses already existing success stories to give listeners a quick, positive impression of what you are proposing. Boiling down your business idea to this quick summary will also help you focus on what is important and unique about your business.

For example, the hit TV show *American Idol* might have originally been pitched in Hollywood as "an updated *Star Search* with *Hollywood Squares*-style celebrity judges and cell phone voting." Similarly, the Austin Powers movies might have been pitched as "1970s James Bond meets Inspector Clouseau to save the world!"

Drawing on these examples, our model entrepreneur from Chapter 6, Webster, might say that his new business offering information about Classic Cadillacs is "KellyBlueBook.com plus ConsumerReports.com plus the Yellow Pages focused on Classic Cadillac owners."

Figuring out the key concepts and buzzwords for your e-business will also help you write effective copy for your website and construct effective "meta tags" to help your search engine rankings. (Don't worry—I'll explain what that means in Chapter 20!)

Now, ask yourself: How can you summarize your new business using this Hollywood pitch approach?

Copywriting for Your E-Business

Even if you're selling commodity products like batteries or socks, you'll need accurate and persuasive website product descriptions to convince your audience to purchase from you.

If you are offering more unique items or services, your website needs to communicate the value of your goods in a concise and compelling manner.

If you're embarking on a more information-intensive or publishing-related venture, your copy will essentially be your product, so it is even more critical to your success.

In all cases, the Internet can once again help you deliver compelling written materials cost-effectively, even if you are not a good writer (or speller) yourself. Don't underestimate the importance of well-written copy because it is more important than you may think. You'll need good and regularly updated copy for:

▲ Website pages

▲ Product descriptions

▲ E-mail newsletters

▲ Customer service documentation

▲ Advertisements

▲ Business correspondence

If you are a good writer, you can probably fulfill your e-business's content creation needs yourself. There are two basic situations, however, that may warrant your getting some writing help:

▲ You are not a particularly good or fast writer (or at least you don't enjoy it).

▲ You are too busy to do a good job at writing the copy your business needs.

INTERNET MILLIONAIRE SECRET:
Freelance Copywriters

As usual, the Internet can help you solve your problem. (By now you knew I was going to say that, didn't you?) There are thousands of experienced writers available who would be happy to contribute to your site's content needs on a project basis. You can find good writers looking for work by going online and posting a small ad (usually for free) to ask for help with your specific writing needs. Try these resources to start (also be sure to check InternetMillionaireSecrets.com for my latest recommendations and deals on freelance copywriting services):

 ▲ ***Websites for local high schools, community colleges, and universities.** Students are always looking for part-time work. Student writers may also want to help with your writing assignments just to gain professional experience.*

 ▲ ***Craig's List.** This international classified-ads website takes postings for just about anything (and I mean anything!). The site has a* *huge audience and you'll definitely get responses for any reason-able offer. (Details on Craig's List are at the end of this chapter.)*

▲ ***Elance.*** *This online marketplace can be used to solicit multiple bids on larger projects from a wide variety of freelance contractors. The basic-level service (simply posting an ad) is free to use; if you want to use the Elance website to handle invoicing and billing for the writing services you buy (advanced service) there's a charge of 6.75 to 8.75 percent of the project fee depending on the project budget size. In either case, you can use the service to identify cost-effective freelance help.*

Regardless of how you recruit your part-timers, be sure to be specific in your ads about the length of the written pieces you need and the style (e.g., product descriptions, advertisements, informational articles, website promotional copy, etc.), as well as your deadlines and offered compensation.

You'll soon find that finding and hiring freelancers is a great, cost-effective way to increase your productivity. This strategy also will work well for graphic artists, Web designers, photographers, customer service staff, and even salespeople.

Outsourcing via Craig's List

While it's not as much of a secret as it used to be, if you don't know about CraigsList.org, you should check it out.

Craig Newmark started his now-famous list in 1995 simply as a way to help his friends in the San Francisco area keep up on local events. His timing was excellent, and the rapidly growing Internet audience appreciated the free classified-ad style listings the site provided. People told their friends, who told their friends, and traffic exploded. Today, Craig's List is active in dozens of major cities on five continents, and eBay recently invested to purchase a minority stake in the company, too.

As a small business owner, you should care about Craig's List because it is a great resource to find inexpensive help to grow your business. While much of the site is occupied with personal ads, buying and selling of used household items, roommate searches, and chitchat, there are great business resources there, too.

I would direct your attention to the section called "Gigs," which can be a gold mine of resources for an entrepreneur on a limited budget. Gigs are simply postings of help-wanted ads. You can post ads for help in areas where you might need it to grow your business. Because the jobs are usually short-term and project-based, you will be able to avoid hiring full-time employees and also pay discounted rates to the contractors you engage who value their flexibility, are unemployed, or who live in lower-cost areas.

Computer Gigs is the most useful category for finding e-business help, although Writing Gigs, Creative Gigs, and Labor Gigs may all have application as you grow your operations. If you post an ad looking for Web design, copywriting, or research assistance, you'll quickly receive dozens of e-mail responses. If you are clear in your ad about what you need and what you're willing to pay, you'll be able to quickly find inexpensive part-time help for almost anything.

This advice is true even if you don't live in a metropolitan area covered by Craig's List, as long as you're in need of services where the results can be delivered electronically via some type of digital file that can be sent to you by e-mail or FTP or downloaded from a Web page. Copywriting, design, and research services all qualify.

As one of my entrepreneur friends says: "Don't think you can do it all. In a small business if you insist on doing everything yourself, you're going to run out of hours in the day and your business will suffer."

Some of the research for this book was even conducted with help from Craig's List. My posting for research help generated a response from a young man named Jason who lives in rural Alabama. (Even though he doesn't live in a metro area covered by Craig's List, he is smart enough to look in the Los Angeles Computer Gigs postings for work that he could do remotely in his spare time. You can try the same in reverse if you live in an area not yet covered by Craig's List.) Doing this research myself would have been an inefficient use of time, but Jason was more than happy to find the facts and figures that I requested for the $8/hour that I offered (which goes a lot further in Alabama than in Los Angeles, too!).

Best of all, most postings on Craig's List are free, so what do you have to lose?

REALITY CHECKS BEFORE INVESTING REAL TIME AND MONEY

IF YOU'VE COME this far in the book, you are almost ready to begin launching a new business. Congratulations!

However, before you go beyond the small price you paid for the book and begin spending real money, I'd like to spend a few pages helping to ensure that your new million-dollar business idea really has the potential you believe it does.

To do this, I'm going to offer you a checklist of tough questions to consider, as well as some basic financial analysis tools.

"Million-Dollar Idea" Reality Checks

Once you have run your ICICLE analysis and begun applying it to your chosen target markets, you should see specific business opportunities emerging. Each of these opportunities should offer a million-dollar business potential that is also well suited to your personality.

To thoroughly examine the e-business ideas remaining in your Millionaire Idea Journal and help you determine which are the real winners, here are some questions to ask yourself about each one.

Due Diligence Questions

In the financial world, before an acquisition or investment is made there's a process called "due diligence." Here is my list of due diligence questions for your e-business:

- ▲ What is the Hollywood Pitch for your new e-business?

- ▲ Can you clearly explain what value you will be adding to the marketplace by offering this improvement, product, service, or information?

- ▲ Is there real demand or need for your offering, or is your idea more driven by the fact that it "would be cool" for you to create it?

- ▲ Does your target market want your product/service enough to pay for it? If not, can you give it away for free in hopes of attracting enough audience traffic to make money through advertising instead?

- ▲ Is there any history of people paying for similar products or services?

- ▲ Can you name some companies that do similar things successfully today?

- ▲ Is your target audience online where you can most easily reach them, or will you need to pay for costly real-world advertising and promotions?

- ▲ How large is the potential customer audience?

- ▲ Will the audience or advertisers pay enough to make the venture profitable?

- ▲ Who are the competitors?

- ▲ How will you be different?

▲ How much money and time can you afford to invest in the venture?

▲ How long can you sustain that level of involvement?

▲ What is the minimum time commitment you'll need to make to get the business to succeed?

▲ What is the minimum amount of revenue that you would need for this business to support you?

▲ If the business were to go really well, what is the most money that you think you could make?

Due Diligence Financial Analysis

In addition to the investigative part of a due diligence process, a good investor will always also run financial calculations to determine the potential value of a business. Such valuations are a whole specialty themselves that is beyond the scope of this book, but I can offer you some basic financial exercises to help.

Don't worry—this will be easier than you think and very valuable! I spell these calculations all out for you in the next sections. The reality check that some simple calculations offer can save you a world of pain if you discover that you may have overestimated the financial potential of your new business.

BASIC FINANCIAL CALCULATIONS

The most important question to answer when starting a business is, "How much money can I make?" Gross profit margin is the important first step in that calculation. Here's how you can calculate it:

Selling Price for 1 Unit of Good or Service – Your Cost of 1 Unit of Good or Service = Gross Profit in Dollars

So, if you used this equation by filling in numbers appropriate to your actual costs and prices, you might get a result as follows:

$ 50.00	Selling Price for 1 Unit of Good or Service
– $ 35.00	Cost of 1 Unit of Good or Service
$ 15.00	Gross Profit Margin in Dollars

Gross Profit Margin (Expressed as a Percentage). Additionally, you could calculate your gross profit margin as a percentage by dividing gross profit margin in dollars by the revenue of one unit, like this:

$15.00 / $50.00 = 30%

Gross profit margin is a useful way to calculate and compare the profitability of different products and businesses that have different costs, prices, and sales volumes. It can also be a good way to price products (e.g., "I must make at least 15 percent in order for this endeavor to be worth my time").

CALCULATING PROFITABILITY

The next appropriate financial analysis question is to calculate how profitable the business will be once you succeed in getting some sales volume. In this calculation, we'll assume that over a one-month period you were going to sell 1,000 units of your goods or services, as follows:

Basic Profit Calculation for One-Month Sales of 1,000 Units

$ 50,000	Selling Price of 1,000 Units of Goods or Services
– $ 35,000	Cost of 1,000 Units of Goods or Services
$ 15,000	Gross Profit

Now let's also account for the overhead costs associated with running your business. Overhead usually includes expenses such as telephone calls, Internet access, paper and toner for your printer, and other recurring costs. Let's say that these expenses add up to $1,000 per month. We could then revise our previous calculation to get a more precise profit number, as follows:

$ 50,000	Selling Price of 1,000 Units of Goods or Services
– $ 35,000	Cost of 1,000 Units of Goods or Services
$ 15,000	Gross Profit

then:

$ 15,000	Gross Profit
– $ 1,000	Monthly Overhead Costs
$ 14,000	Net Profit

or:

$14,000 / $50,000 = 28% (Net profit margin expressed as a percentage)

These basic calculations suggest that you would be left with $14,000 of profit at the end of our sample month. You would want to use this 28 percent margin to pay yourself, pay taxes, and invest in more inventory, etc.

To figure the potential profits for your proposed business, you can substitute your own prices, costs, and sales volume numbers into these equations and calculate for yourself. That's the best way of determining whether you are likely to make enough money from your new business to support yourself.

There would also normally be marketing, personnel, depreciation, and other costs included in these calculations. I have omitted them here for the sake of simplicity, and because many of these expenses are minimized or may be eliminated altogether in many e-businesses through effective use of this book's strategies. If these are significant factors in your new business plan, subtract those costs from your gross margin also to get a more accurate picture of the potential of your business.

REINING IN OVERHEAD EXPENSES

As you can see from these calculations, keeping your expenses down is the second most important factor in business success (ranked second only to finding a product/service you can sell at a profit).

Watch out! With the enthusiasm that often accompanies the start of a new business, it is easy to get caught up in shopping and overinvest in new equipment, cell phones, conference passes, personnel, office space, etc. Falling into this trap can drain your capital and saddle you with recurring payments for services and goods that you may not really need. It can also eliminate your profits, so please be careful!

PAYING YOURSELF

You should also examine the profit remaining for you at the end of what you forecast would be a typical month. If you divide that profit amount by the number of hours you spend earning it, are you making a living wage?

If not, can you expect growth in your business that will increase your sales volume or allow you to raise prices enough to make more money for yourself?

Many entrepreneurs go into debt when starting new businesses because they underestimate the difficulty, costs, or timeline associated with launching a new venture. Applying the calculations and being realistic about your sales potential can help prevent this mistake. These calculations are also important to do to see if you can make back enough money to repay whatever one-time startup costs you incurred when setting up the business (which I also left out of the previous equations to keep them simple).

Seeking Support

To do such calculations correctly, most business people will use a Microsoft software program called Excel. This spreadsheet program is widely available (in fact, it or similar spreadsheet software may already be installed on your PC) and can make calculating and updating such figures quick and easy.

Of course, you can also use software like Quickbooks or hire an accountant to manage your finances. Asking your accountant to help you set up software to calculate your profit margins, as I have in the previous example, would be an excellent first step.

One of my favorite maxims is: "Have faith in your new business, but also be sure to run the numbers!" Please heed this advice. It's not the most fun part of starting a new business, but it is more than worth the effort.

18 AN ACTION PLAN FOR YOUR MILLION-DOLLAR E-BUSINESS

BY NOW YOU'VE learned enough about building a million-dollar online business to be dangerous! Resist your urge to charge ahead, however, and organize your thoughts and plans so that you can be as effective as possible.

No one can do everything at once, so it's important to write down and prioritize the many tasks it will require to get your new business up and running. Developing a personalized action plan will help you to take advantage of all the information that I've shared with you so far.

Although it may sound challenging, developing an action plan does not have to be hard. It simply means writing down all the steps you can think of that will need to be taken to reach your goals. Then you put the tasks in order.

How to Create Your Own Action Plan

To develop an action plan customized to your business, you should start with complete research of your target market, growth of that market, your proposed suppliers, your potential competitors, and your profit potential.

Here is an outline of the types of questions that you should ask yourself as you develop your new business.

"TARGET MARKET" STATISTICS

What statistics can you collect about your intended audience? These numbers can help you quantify how big an opportunity you are targeting. They can also be useful in convincing partners and advertisers (or spouses!) that you are pursuing a valid opportunity. Statistics can also be used very effectively on your website and in your marketing materials to prove the need for your services.

Surf the Web to find as many articles as you can about your targeted consumers. Free e-mail newsletters from trade groups in your chosen field are another good source for statistics. Then analyze the information you've collected about your targeted consumers in terms of the following questions:

▲ Are their numbers growing or shrinking?

▲ Are they spending more or less than previously?

▲ What other products or services go well together with the ones you are going to offer?

SUPPLIERS

Use the search engines to find appropriate suppliers for your business. Do you need goods that you are going to resell or just services to help you run your business? The Internet can offer you tons of information on both with just a few clicks.

Make a list of your key needs and spend some time using Google to locate them. Pay particular attention to the "Sponsored Links" results that show businesses catering to needs related to the words you searched upon. Checking their websites or contacting those suppliers by e-mail for current pricing can quickly help you understand the fundamental costs of your new venture.

COMPETITORS

Similarly, you should examine closely what your competitors are doing, including their pricing and service guarantees. Think broadly about keywords you can use to locate these competitors when searching so that you find as many as possible.

Although you may not want to alert competitors to your new business, it can be valuable to sign up for their free e-mail newsletters. These subscriptions will help you keep track of their activities automatically by simply reading the e-mails that they send you.

FINANCIAL ANALYSIS

Once you have accumulated credible pricing and market information, you should revisit your financial analysis. Run the equations that I shared with you in Chapter 17 to make sure that you have a reasonable expectation of turning a profit.

By now you have doubtless thought even more about the challenges and opportunities of your new business. Use the equations to help prove your case to yourself!

BEWARE OF ANALYSIS PARALYSIS

While this sort of "reality check" research is extremely important to do before you start building a business, I also want to warn you to avoid analysis paralysis. Many entrepreneurs love independent, analytical work and spend a lot of time surfing the Web; making lists of suppliers, competitors, or pricing; or using spreadsheets to crunch numbers. These are valuable activities, but only to a point! I frequently need to remind such entrepreneurs that they have started a new business to make money, not to conduct research studies or build the perfect financial business model.

It is easy to fall into the analysis paralysis trap because you can control the work yourself. Launching a new business requires stepping outside your usual comfort zone to offer a product or service to strangers. That sort of activity intimidates most people, and conducting endless research and analysis can be a shield against the fear of failure.

The easiest way to guard against this tendency is simply to be aware of it. Watch your daily routine and measure your progress against goals and timelines you set for yourself. If you find analytical tasks taking longer than you expected, check yourself for analysis paralysis and get moving again!

> The point of all this research is to give you as much knowledge as possible as early in the business formation process as possible. The more you know, the better decisions you can make. Making better-informed decisions will also help you save money because you will make fewer mistakes!

Implementing an E-Business Action Plan

Here is a sample action plan that you can customize to develop an implementation plan for your new business.

Sample Action Plan

1. Decide on a target market.

2. Research and price suppliers for products/services in demand by that target market.

3. Decide on the product or service to be offered.

4. Investigate production, fulfillment, or other issues specific to your products.

5. Work out roles, obligations, and agreement with partners or staff.

6. Brainstorm company names and URLs.

7. Research and register URLs appropriate to your new company's activity or products.

8. Set up company e-mail accounts for yourself, plus separate e-mail accounts for customer service and any partners or staff.

9. Create or commission a logo and graphics to use when customizing your website template.

10. Consider whether incorporation, copyright/trademark registrations, insurance, business licenses, DBAs, bank accounts, or other administrative issues need attention.

11. Diagram the website for the business on paper.

12. Apply for a credit card merchant account, if appropriate.

13. Write the copy for each page of your new site; prepare your copy using Microsoft Word so it will be ready for easy cutting and pasting into the website template.

14. Build out your website using a design template.

15. Create a privacy policy (following the tips from Part 5 of this book, Legal Issues and Administration).

16. Build out an online store to showcase products/services for sale.

17. Develop an inexpensive plan to test your new business online.

18. Set up an account with an e-mail marketing list-management service.

19. Create banner ads for use on Microsoft's Banner Network or elsewhere.

20. Have friends review and test your website and online store.

21. "Soft launch" the site to the public to do free testing and receive feedback.

22. Begin marketing!

SETTING PRIORITIES

Don't prioritize your tasks by what's the most fun or easiest to do. When building your new e-business you should always first take care of those issues that (a) take the longest to pay off (so that they can progress without you while you focus on shorter-term goals) and (b) enable other people to do their work.

Issues that take the longest to pay off. Although it may be more entertaining to sit around and come up with names for your new business, it's more important to contact suppliers to determine if you can source your products affordably. Here's why.

Although both tasks are important, coming up with names is something you can do by yourself at any time of the day or night or on weekends, whereas obtaining pricing information from suppliers is only going to happen when those suppliers get around to it and only between 9:00 a.m. and 5:00 p.m. on weekdays. *Start first with the job that will take the longest to complete.*

Issues that enable other people to do their work. You should pay special attention to ensuring that other people's efforts are able to proceed by getting them whatever they need from you to move forward. For example, if your partner or assistant is building your website but you are supposed to be creating or sourcing the logo for him to use, be sure to get that logo completed so you don't slow him down.

Once you have your partners fully supplied, then you can return to work that you can complete solo. The alternative is to have able-bodied people waiting for each other. That is a poor and expensive use of time and money.

SETTING TARGET DATES

The next step for implementing an action plan successfully is to assign names and dates to each task.

The names assigned should be those people who are responsible for completing the task. Ideally, each task will be assigned to just one person. That person should have the authority to make decisions and motivate others as needed to get the job done without having a lot of meetings about it. (Of course, if you are working alone, this should be a quick decision!)

Next, the timeline for completion of your action plan should be determined. *Each task should have its own deadline.*

Be sure to consider the way that different tasks and people are dependent upon the completion of other tasks when picking your target dates. You may need to rearrange the task list to accommodate these dependencies. Be sure to consult with any other team members to see that they agree with the dates you select, especially if you have assigned the tasks to be their responsibility!

Be as aggressive as you can be in assigning target completion dates to your tasks, but also don't be so aggressive as to be unrealistic. You don't want to discourage yourself by quickly falling behind simply because you were unrealistic with your planning.

Make allowances for vacations, weekends, and holidays in giving people time to get back to you with information you may need. Remember, the launch of your new business may be the biggest thing in your life, but the rest of the world is not likely to rearrange its priorities just to help out!

DRAFTING YOUR OWN ACTION PLAN

Create a draft action plan in your Millionaire Idea Journal following these five steps:

1. Write down all the tasks that you see as critical to getting your business started. Feel free to borrow from the sample action plan to get started.

2. Organize the tasks in priority order, reflecting both those tasks that will take the longest to bear results and those that other people need you to finish before they can complete their work.

3. Review the list for missing steps or out-of-order priorities.

4. If you are working with others, assign a person's name to each task to show that it is his or her responsibility.

5. Assign target completion dates to each task.

Once you have this list completed, you should review it weekly. A weekly review will give you an opportunity to update your plan with new ideas and delete completed tasks so that you can stay on track.

BUILDING YOUR WEBSITE

Design templates make the process of building a website very easy. You can type directly into the online editor that such services provide to you and never have to learn any HTML programming.

INTERNET MILLIONAIRE WEBSITE-BUILDING SECRET

Once you have decided on a URL for your new e-business, you'll find it easiest to purchase the domain name from the same company that will host your site (probably the one with the best website design templates, if you're following my advice). Consolidating these purchases with one vendor will also help you get the best deal.

What you need to know is that it will take one to three business days for the new website to become available online to the public. It may even take that long for you to have behind-the-scenes access to start constructing your website pages. You need to allow this time for the new domain name registration and hosting information to propagate out to all the millions of Web servers on the Internet so they will recognize and display the new site you are building. By doing so, your new site will be immediately available online worldwide as soon as you finish it.

So, if you expect to start building the pages for your website this weekend or one evening after work, be sure to register your domain name and initiate the site configuration process to the Web a couple of days in advance. You don't want to find yourself twiddling your thumbs just when you hoped to get started!

Here's the process I recommend to get your website up and running as quickly as possible:

▲ *Prepare your branding.* Decide on your brand name. Is it the same as your URL or different? How are you going to refer to your business when you write about it or make a logo? Then also decide on a slogan: What catchphrase will make your customers remember your business?

▲ *Diagram your site.* What are the sections of your website? Your own website navigation scheme should obviously reflect the priorities of your business's customers; however, typical websites start with just five to ten pages of basic information, including:

Home page with general information or welcome copy explaining your business

Products or services pages

Store or online shopping pages

"About the company" pages

Contact or customer service pages

▲ *Write website copy.* Start a document in Microsoft Word for each of the sections of your website. Write the copy that each page needs to be effective. Although it's tempting to type your website information directly into the templates online, it's a better idea to write it up beforehand in Microsoft Word. The document created will be easier for you to edit and it will also create a backup copy of your work for reference.

▲ *Create an identifying footer.* Every page of your website should have copyright, ownership, contact, and legal information at the bottom. You can type up a simple notice, like the following, and use the template system to install in on the bottom of each page:

© YourMillionDollarBusiness.com—All Rights Reserved. Click Here to Contact Us.

You probably also want to include a link to your privacy policy if you are collecting e-mail addresses or customer information through your site. (More details on privacy policies are available in Part 5, Legal Issues and Administration.) Of course, there are thousands of variations on these basic themes.

▲ *Build the site.* Once you have these pieces in place, you can then go online and assemble your website fairly quickly by simply cutting and pasting the copy you've already prepared into the website template you've chosen. This strategy may sound simplistic, but it works. By following this basic plan (and making allowances for any customization needed for your business's specific product display, advertising, or data collection needs), you can get a professional-looking website up and running in a very short time. In fact, following this process, I have built fully functional e-commerce websites in an afternoon using only Microsoft Word and an Internet browser!

19 TESTING YOUR NEW BUSINESS

HOW CAN YOU be sure that your new million-dollar business can actually generate a million dollars for you? One good way to be certain is to thoroughly research and test your business before investing real money in promoting it.

Unlike in the real world, you can start a business online with very little capital. You don't need to lease a store, invest in inventory, buy displays, invest in equipment, or install new phone lines. Instead, you can test your new business very cost-effectively by simply putting up a website to see how customers react. Sometimes online entrepreneurs don't even have the products for which they are taking orders until they first prove the demand for such products by receiving their initial orders from customers.

How Much Should You Commit?

You should invest as *little* as is required to test your business model. I recommend spending *the least money,* spending *the least time,* and making *the least number of long-term commitments* as possible to get the business launched.

Why? Years of experience and my research results have consistently shown that entrepreneurs often change direction soon after they launch their new businesses! They learn so much in the early stages of their business about what is easy, what is difficult, what competitors are doing, what others have tried, etc., and all of this information can change a business model quickly.

This risk of change may sound frightening, but it is for the better because it means that you have learned enough about your new business to make some necessary changes, and those changes helped to keep you from investing too heavily in areas that are now not so necessary or attractive to you.

INTERNET MILLIONAIRE SECRET:
Minimize Commitments

One way to save yourself money when launching your business is to stay flexible by avoiding long-term commitments, especially early on. When your business is young, you need to be open to learning from your mistakes. Don't overcommit yourself, or your limited resources, until you're sure that you're on the right track.

For example, when starting a new business, it is tempting to choose a name and logo as your first step. Although that is a fine place to start, once they've settled on a name and logo, many entrepreneurs want to order 1,000 or 5,000 business cards! Because they can save a few dollars on the volume purchase, they think this purchase is justified.

This is not a good idea because within a few weeks or months (long before anyone could give away 5,000 business cards), new business owners often learn enough about their new market and business to decide that their names or logos aren't as appropriate as they originally thought.

My practical advice: Don't try to save money by buying in bulk or signing up for seemingly cheaper long-term contracts at first. Your business is too new to know precisely where you are going to end up. Order business cards only in quantities of 250 at a time and, as much as possible, limit your contracts to month-by-month arrangements.

Live-Testing Phased Plan

If your research and analysis confirms the business potential of the new e-business, it's time to launch your website. Follow the guidelines and plans I've shared with you in order to get your products and services out on the Internet so other people can see them.

The phases of the testing plan I recommend here can last as little as a few days or run for weeks or months while you incorporate feedback received from the tests. It's up to you to run the testing process appropriate for your business, but I am certain that you don't want to spend time and energy and money promoting a website that has not been thoroughly tested.

Why? Because testing is designed to uncover problems. If you don't allow sufficient time for quality testing your site, you could find that your marketing efforts will be wasted.

Premature marketing can bring floods of people to your new site just when you are busy fixing a critical broken piece of it uncovered during testing earlier that day. Finding a broken or unappealing website is one sure way to lose the business of people who were potentially your best customers.

BETA TESTING

Before publicly announcing your new business, start by having friends and family members visit the site to offer suggestions. In the software business, this phase where friends help test the product is called a "beta test."

During the beta testing, try to encourage your testers to offer detailed reviews of what they like or don't like, rather than simple "it's nice" type comments. You can elicit better feedback by telling them that you are going to invest a lot of time and money growing this business, so you'd appreciate their honest feedback up-front so you can avoid wasted effort.

If all goes well with your friends and family review, it's time to start promoting the business to the general public.

SOFT LAUNCH

After your beta test is complete (and presumably has gone well), don't try to promote your new online business like Hollywood does its movies. You don't want everyone showing up on the same Friday evening for the premiere. Instead, you want to attract just a few real customers to make sure that all of your systems are working and that the website is attractive to people who don't know you at all.

This next phase of testing with a live audience is called a "soft launch." It means that the website is up and running and is "live" to take orders, but still has not been fully promoted to the public, just in case something goes wrong.

This is the phase when you can start doing some marketing to get the word out about your new business. Banner exchanges, link exchanges, and e-mails to a broader group of acquaintances are good examples of ways to draw a small amount of traffic that can be useful during the soft launch test. (These marketing tools will be explained in Part 4 of the book.) Feedback from this expanded group will allow you to polish the site further so that it is really ready to shine when you officially launch it for business.

DRAFTING YOUR TESTING PLAN

1. Develop a first draft of your testing plan using the guidelines established in this chapter.

2. Create a list of friends and family members who can serve as "beta testers" for you.

3. Assign tentative deadlines for each phase of testing.

4. Consult with your partners or suppliers to make sure you can meet those deadlines.

5. Initiate your beta test and revise the website according to feedback received.

6. Initiate your soft launch and revise according to feedback received.

7. Launch!

LAUNCH!

Once the soft launch has successfully been completed, you are ready to go live with a full launch of your new e-commerce business. This is when you play all of your best marketing and promotions cards to get as many people to start visiting your new business as possible. Congratulations!

> **DON'T BE AFRAID TO LAUNCH**
>
> If you have built a good website and the feedback from your testing is positive, launch it. I know that it can be scary to "take the plunge" and publicly commit to a new business that everyone can see, but you need to launch it if you are ever going to make money! The website (or the e-mail newsletter or the ads or whatever) may not be perfect, but they probably never will be.
>
> One of the great advantages of the Internet is that it is easy and cheap to update. Take advantage of this strength and get your business launched as soon as it is sufficiently tested. You can "tweak" it forever, but *making money should be your top priority,* not perfectionism.

Marketing Your Business

Once you've conducted enough testing to be confident about the launch of your new business, it's time to start marketing it to a wider audience so you can attract more customers.

Marketing is basically defined as those things you do to attract customers to your new business. Whereas traditional businesses depend on billboards, newspaper ads, TV or radio spots, and word-of-mouth, the Internet offers you a wide array of new techniques that you can use in addition to those traditional methods. Some of them are surprisingly effective and affordable, too.

The Internet's ability to help you reach so many people so inexpensively is one of the primary reasons I recommend using it to build your million-dollar business. In Part 4, I'm going to introduce you to the proven marketing strategies that have helped many people build successful online businesses.

PART FOUR

INTERNET MARKETING SECRETS
FOR YOUR E-BUSINESS

20 "NO BUDGET" MARKETING SECRETS

THE TRADITIONAL "big company" way of planning a marketing campaign is to first decide how much money you have to spend and then figure out ways to spend it. Although I'll discuss good places to spend marketing money if you have it, I'm going to continue to assume that you are reading this book because you want to become a millionaire, not because you already are one!

Consequently, I'm going to first focus on the many ways that you can use the World Wide Web and e-mail to advertise your business inexpensively or even for free.

Even if you had a multimillion-dollar marketing budget, it can take weeks or months to set up the advertising programs that big companies use. Traditional advertising is too slow to rely on in today's wired economy. I know that you want to move fast, and so do your customers. Therefore, I'm also going to introduce you to techniques that you can start using today.

Free Marketing Resources

LINK EXCHANGES

The cheapest and simplest way to promote your website is to exchange links with other websites. This is done by simply e-mailing or calling other site owners and offering to place links to their website on yours if they will do the same.

This sort of activity used to be mostly for fun, but link exchanges have become increasingly important to small e-business owners because of their importance in determining their sites' rankings in search engine listings.

Search engines try to deliver the best websites in each category to any query that they receive from visitors to their sites. A common way for the search engine to try to determine the most relevant and popular sites is to count the number of links to that site from other related sites.

If your site about hot dogs has 100 other hot dog–related sites linking to it (perhaps from suppliers of hot dog buns and condiments and so on), then many search engines will presume that your site is more valuable and relevant to people searching on the term "hot dogs" than a similar site with only five or ten links to it. A highly linked site will probably receive a high "page rank" and be seen by more users of the search engine who conduct hot dog–related searches. Since more highly ranked search results means more visitors to your site and more business, link exchanges can be very helpful to growing your e-business.

It's important that the links be from related sites, however, and ideally from highly trafficked ones as well. For example, one link from the hot dog section of AOL or a top hot dog manufacturer's site would be more helpful to your site's traffic than dozens of links from unrelated sites about jewelry, travel, patio furniture, or online dating.

BANNER EXCHANGES

Another free marketing technology is to join a banner ad exchange service. In this case you create a banner advertisement graphic and submit it to the service. You then install the service's banner ad code on your website by copying and pasting the code into your website template just as if you were using Microsoft Word. Then, every time your website displays two ads from the service, the banner exchange will track those exposures and cause your banner to be shown once on the site of another online business using the same service.

These services are usually free because the operator makes money by selling the extra advertising impressions generated by requiring you to show two ads for every one of yours they display. (The ratio of ads displayed can vary among services, but the principle holds true regardless.)

The original leader in the banner exchange market is now owned by Microsoft Corp. and is simply called Banner Network. The service is available for free through Microsoft's Small Business Center website.

You can also find other banner exchange services such as e-bannerx.com and Click4Click.com by searching on the term "banner exchange" in your favorite search engine.

SEARCH ENGINE PLACEMENT

Unless you have an already established brand name, most people will find your e-business site through search engines like Yahoo and Google. Getting your website listed so that it shows up prominently in search results can bring you lots of customers.

There is a complicated art and science to helping websites position themselves for high search-engine results ranking. It can be worth the time to learn these techniques because of the huge amounts of traffic that search engines funnel to their top-ranked sites.

There is also an ever-changing landscape of services and opportunities because of the intense competition among the search engine companies, but here are my current recommendations for developing your own search engine strategy.

▲ *Free Google and Yahoo Submission.* The simplest way to get started with search engine placement is to submit your URL directly to the top search engines. Both Google and Yahoo provide this service for free currently, although the links are well hidden. Yahoo, in particular, does not encourage it or guarantee results, because it is trying to build fee-based businesses instead. Both companies are increasing their sales of their own advertising programs, too. This means that by the time you do find the free URL submission pages, you will also have been hit with distracting offers to advertise with the search engines using their pay-for-performance programs: Google AdWords and Yahoo! Site Match.

Nevertheless, you should fish around on the sites of the top search engines to see if you can find these links in order to submit your website listing. It should also be noted that there are many, many software programs and services that automate the submission of a website's URL to search engines and website directories. Often these services are even included in the hosting packages you'll need for your website.

INTERNET MILLIONAIRE SECRET:

The Free Listings Directory Behind Google

Most search engines compile their databases of website information using automated software programs called "robots" or "spiders" that "crawl" across the Web cataloging all the sites that they find. Unlike those automated services, the free DMOZ Open Directory Project (ODP) is compiled by human beings who visit, review, and manually add entries on every website in the directory. While this practice seems a bit old-fashioned, its noncommercial nature offers the opportunity for entrepreneurs like you to submit your website's listing to the ODP for free.

What's even more important is that many other search engines rely on the ODP listings to build their own search directories. The Open Directory powers the core directory services for many of the Web's largest and most popular search engines and portals, including Google, Netscape Search, AOL Search, Lycos, HotBot, DirectHit, and hundreds of others. So, if your website is included in the ODP, it will often soon start showing up in the search results of many other search engines all across the Web.

▲ *ODP Submission Technique.* The Open Directory Project (ODP) is a worldwide directory of websites built by thousands of human volunteers over many years. You must visit DMOZ.org to request inclusion of your new website in its listings.

As the instructions there will tell you, it's important to find precisely the right category (out of thousands of them) in which to submit the URL and description of your site. Choosing the proper category is important to help ensure that the ODP's results remain accurate, but also to help your site show up as soon as possible. Since you are dealing with unpaid volunteer human editors, submitting your site in the wrong category can cause them to pass your submission along to another editor, where your request will then enter at the end of the long queue of similar requests.

INTERNET MILLIONAIRE SECRET:
Become an ODP Volunteer Editor

Although many e-business professionals complain about their search engine rankings, few realize that they can directly influence the listing process by volunteering to become an Open Directory Project category editor.

By agreeing to help evaluate and manage the listings in categories related to your e-business, you can help ensure that your website is properly presented in the ODP results (and therefore in many other more famous search engines as well). Of course, you must also agree to fairly administer the listings of other sites in your category (which will probably include competitors).

Basic Search Engine Optimization Techniques

Search engine companies closely guard the methods that they use to find and rank the websites included in their search indices. While these technologies remain trade secrets in many cases, it's clear that the mission of search engines is to deliver results relevant to the surfer's query.

As a result, the search engine companies will necessarily continue to try to deliver as their most popular search engine results the most helpful, easy-to-read, information-rich websites that are well-visited and linked to by other relevant sites. Regardless of which particular search engine you try to optimize your site to attract, it's clear that several key factors will continue to be important when designing your site to attract search engine traffic.

MAKE YOUR WEBSITE SEARCH-ENGINE FRIENDLY

There are four categories of search engine content on your site that you should be certain to optimize. The first three of these are called *meta tags.* The information about your site contained in meta tags is not obvious to the user but is descriptive in nature —hence the name "meta." A meta tag does not appear visually on your website's pages but is instead hidden in the HTML code that tells the browser program how to present your site to a visitor. All website templates today include easy ways to access meta tag code, so updating these fields in plain English, as explained next, is not as difficult as it may sound.

The fourth category of search engine content is written introductory copy that you should place on the top of your home page regardless of the design you otherwise want to implement.

Here are further details on each of the four categories of search engine information:

1. *Meta Tag One: TITLE.* The title of your home page and other key pages should contain the most searched-upon keywords relating to the topic and customers of your site. Users see this information appear along the top line of the browser window, and it is the first thing that many search engines check for when registering your site.

2. *Meta Tag Two: KEYWORDS.* These words should also be the most searched-upon words and phrases for your site's specialty. In this case, however, you can usually include up to approximately 256 characters and run them all together, separated just by commas with no spaces. This allows you to fit more words and also makes it as easy as possible for the search engine spiders to read them.

3. *Meta Tag Three: DESCRIPTION.* The last meta tag often indexed by search engines is an approximately 200-character field that allows you to write several short, keyword-rich sentences describing in plain English what your site and products are about. Again, you should make sure that these sentences are full of your best keywords so that the search engines will show this description of your site in search results relating to that topic when searched by customers.

4. *Site Summary.* In addition to cataloging a site's meta tags, many search engines also scan the first few visible lines or paragraphs of a website's visible text to get a more in-depth understanding of its content. Consequently, you should write two or three short sentences to put at the top of your home page that summarize your site's (or that page's) offerings. Like the Description meta tag, these sentences should also be full of keywords. The "Hollywood pitch" for your business (discussed earlier in Chapter 16) will be useful here in identifying your site's most important concepts and keywords.

These first few lines of copy on your home page are so important that some search engines ignore meta tags entirely and borrow the Site Summary wholesale to display as part of their search results.

Although the degree to which search engines rely on these four fields varies widely, they are so easy to complete that you should spend enough time to be certain that you have optimized the words included in each one. *The best words are those that your potential customers are most likely to use when searching for services/products like yours.* By taking care to research the most appropriate keywords and include them in your new site's meta tags and home page Site Summary, you will have greatly improved your site's chances of receiving accurate and highly ranked search engine results.

INTERNET MILLIONAIRE SECRET:
Free Search Engine Optimization Research
Here's an easy and clever way to help you pick the best keywords to use when filling in your meta tags and writing your site summary:

Visit the websites of competitors! Once there, if you click on the Microsoft Internet Explorer browser menu at the top of your screen where it says "View," you can scroll down to click on an option called "Source." The document that this point-and-click action calls up for you is the underlying HTML code of your competitor's site. If you look closely at it, near the top you'll usually see the meta tags that they use spelled out in plain English.

If that competitor is successful, you may want to consider using similar keywords yourself—or figure out different ones to tackle in order to differentiate yourself.

Create Quality Content

Of course, the best way to gain good search engine rankings is to produce high-quality content that users find valuable. Regardless of how each search engine company develops and tweaks the search algorithms that it uses to stock its database of websites, all search engines are striving to find and rank highly the best content in each topic area.

Offering accurate, helpful content will naturally lead other sites to link to you, and for word-of-mouth to spread about your business. The search engines will eventually pick up on this quality content and traffic to help propel your site toward the top of their search results.

Search engine optimization services make a business out of making this seem more complicated than it is, and their tips and tricks can often help improve a site's ranking at least temporarily, but the page ranking of a well-designed site with good content should eventually rise toward the top naturally. (Of course, if you want immediate gratification, you can use one of the pay-per-performance advertising techniques—we'll soon discuss in Chapter 22—to pay for a number-one ranking right away.)

Submit Your Listing Sooner Rather than Later

One of the first tasks to complete once you have decided on a business, product, and URL is the launch of a basic website optimized to help your site quickly get listed in popular search engines.

Because it can take weeks and often months for a new site to be indexed and included in the major search engines, you should put up and submit to the search engines an introductory site with the basic information they require for indexing as soon as you can. This basic information simply includes the four key categories of search engine information described in the Search Engine Optimization section above.

Although it is tempting to wait until your whole site is perfect and ready for formal launch, you want it to show up in the search engines as soon as possible so you can start attracting visitors and business. Don't delay the potential arrival of new customers who would find your site through search engines. Start by nailing down initial versions of your site's title, meta description, keywords, and some summary introduction copy, then post a simple if minimalist version of your site and submit it! Then you can update the site (and the meta tags) with a more polished version later, when you are also ready to start promoting it.

WHAT ABOUT PROFESSIONAL SEARCH ENGINE OPTIMIZATION SERVICES?

There are many services on the Web that offer to help you submit and optimize your website to get high rankings on search engine results. These services go beyond the "no budget" efforts we've discussed so far because you pay experts to help you.

The effectiveness of these services is also controversial. Obviously, the service providers insist that they are very helpful, but I have heard users complain that they received little for their money. Additionally, the technologies of some of these services border on spam, so some are deliberately blocked out by the search engines as soon as they figure out what is happening. This can get your site deleted from a search engine's database entirely. Ouch!

My recommendation is to learn as much as you can yourself to improve your search engine rankings first. Then, if you feel that you could use additional help, you will be better educated to research the current providers online and pick one to try.

SUBSCRIBE TO SEARCH ENGINE NEWSLETTERS

There are also a number of free e-mail newsletters to which you can subscribe to learn about the latest in search engine marketing. I recommend ClickZ's Search Engine Watch newsletter, for example. Visit Internet MillionaireSecrets.com for links to this and other free e-mail newsletters.

21 SMALL BUDGET MARKETING SECRETS

ONCE YOU HAVE proved your new business model by generating some revenues, you should consider spending additional money to promote your business. Most million-dollar businesses online use a combination of free marketing tactics (covered in Chapter 20) and the paid services we'll cover now.

E-Mail Newsletter Marketing

Staying in touch with your audience via e-mail is a required skill in the modern world of online marketing. One of the best things about the Internet is that you can send newsletters by e-mail basically for free.

My number-one recommendation for new e-business owners is to start collecting e-mail addresses from your audience as soon as you can. Preferably, you will start this e-mail collection at the same time that you launch your first introductory site for submission to the search engines.

You can even encourage people to share their e-mail addresses with you by offering incentives such as free downloads or prizes.

I believe that e-mail addresses are worth this effort. E-mail marketing is the most cost-effective way to keep in touch with your customers. It is also the most effective way to retain those customers or visitors who have already expressed interest in your site and services. Although they may not have made a purchase on their first visit, if you can get an e-mail address, then you can keep in touch with them until they do. Since acquiring new customers is the most difficult and expensive project that any new business faces, it should be among your top priorities to retain those you've already converted. E-mail is your best solution to this challenge.

Collecting E-Mail Addresses

The easiest and cheapest way to collect e-mail addresses is to add a simple "mailto" link to your website. (The website template programs I recommend can help you do this easily.) Then write copy for the site that encourages people to e-mail you with their e-mail addresses so you can build a list of these potential customers.

E-Mail Newsletter Management Services

Even though you can manage a list of e-mail addresses and send out mass mailings to them yourself, once your list grows, you will want to consider acquiring your own mailing-list management software or engaging an application service provider (ASP) offering services in this area.

Installing and managing e-mail software is a task that's best left to technically inclined folks. If you are one, doing it yourself can save you some money. However, my research has consistently found that entrepreneurs are better off focusing their energies on business issues than technical ones. That's why I recommend using an ASP service for e-mail management as well.

These services basically act as a database for your list of e-mail addresses. They manage the e-mail addresses plus other information that you collect about your audience, such as names, street addresses, gender, zip codes, etc.

The better services also provide nice-looking HTML e-mail newsletter templates that you can use to send out your marketing communications. You should be able to customize the look of these templates to include your logo and to match the look of your website. (This is another example of ASP services helping you to run your Internet-based business without your having to know HTML or other programming languages.)

HOW TO CHOOSE AN E-MAIL SERVICE PROVIDER

Like all of the website and related services we're discussing, there are many providers of e-mail address list management and mass e-mailing services. Finding the best one for you will depend on several fundamental decision factors, most of which revolve around ease of use for you:

- ▲ *List Size vs. Pricing.* Most e-mail services base their prices on the size of your list or mailings. So how big do you expect your list of e-mail addresses to be?

- ▲ *E-Mail Collection.* How easy does the service provider's system make it for you to collect e-mail addresses from visitors to your site?

- ▲ *Sign-Up Customization.* How easily can you customize the e-mail sign-up process?

- ▲ *Design Customization.* Does the service offer a variety of design templates that you can use to quickly and easily produce professional-looking e-mailings?

- ▲ *Reports.* Will the service provide detailed reporting on your mailings, their clickthrough rates, and unsubscribe/bounce/forwarding rates?

- ▲ *Unsubscribing.* How easy is it for recipients of your e-mails to unsubscribe? (This consideration is legally important to avoid being accused of being—or worse, sued as—a spammer!)

- ▲ *Importing.* How easily can you add or update your subscriber database?

- ▲ *Exporting.* How easily can you export the data if you want to back it up or use it elsewhere?

E-MAIL MANAGEMENT RECOMMENDATION

Although there are many e-mail management companies trying to compete for your business, my top choice for e-mail management services is Constant Contact. This ASP company provides the easiest-to-use website and the best-looking templates that I have seen so far. Competitors such as bCentral's ListBuilder offer similar services, but it is not nearly as easy to use or to produce professional-looking e-newsletters. Both also offer free trials to start.

For an example of how to use e-mail marketing to build your e-business, read on to learn about a surprisingly successful e-business that exclusively sells parrot toys.

E-MAIL MARKETING ENTREPRENEUR:
KIT MANCHESTER, BIRDSJUSTWANNAHAVEFUN.COM

Kit Manchester has built a fascinating niche business catering to the very specific needs of pet parrots and their owners. Even more specifically, her BirdsJustWannaHaveFun.com website sells what she calls "foraging and enrichment toys" specifically designed for these large bird pets.

Kit has had great success using e-mail marketing to increase her sales, so we discussed her business in order to share some of her hard-earned expertise with you.

An executive at a healthcare company that went out of business in 2000, Kit interviewed for similar positions with other companies but was not excited by any of them. Around the same time, she and her husband had purchased a pet parrot that would change her life.

When she went shopping for toys for her new pet, she was disappointed in the prices, quality, and creativity of the toys available for large birds. She found that although there are lots of customers for smaller bird toys, most pet stores don't stock the specialized toys that large birds need because there's not enough turnover in these products to make them profitable.

Recognizing this market inefficiency as a business opportunity, Kit hired a Web designer to build a site to sell the bird toys she had started making herself for her own bird.

Trying to build a business focused exclusively on selling parrot toys was a bold step, but Kit saw the need in the marketplace from her own experience. Her first products were simple, high-quality, safety-tested parts for parrot toys that allowed people to make their own bird toys. Then she gradually evolved her focus and began selling finished foraging and enrichment toys. A local avian veterinarian also validated the need for her specialized toys, especially for parrots with behavioral problems.

Kit recognized that choosing a niche market to focus on was important. As she puts it: "Anyone who has a small business and tries to compete with Wal-Mart is not going to be in business for very long." She thought that by offering a product line unavailable elsewhere, she would have a better shot at profitability.

Today, Kit has proved the worth of her approach. BirdsJustWanna HaveFun.com now has five employees, plus a bookkeeper. It has taken over the whole top floor of Kit's home, plus two bays of her three-car garage. The website has a national reputation among parrot enthusiasts and is starting to gain an international reputation as well.

According to Kit, e-mail marketing has been "very, very valuable" to the growth of her e-business. "Pretty much 100 percent of our business is online, so it's been critical to our success to keep in touch with my customers by e-mail. E-mail newsletters keep us in customers' minds, even if they don't make a purchase right away," she says.

BirdsJustWannaHaveFun.com uses an ASP e-mail management service to administrate this important aspect of its business. Kit chose the Constant Contact service to manage her subscribers and send out two types of newsletters: a monthly information newsletter designed to educate her audience (without pushing products), and a weekly sales edition that more specifically shares information about products and promotions.

Her two-pronged e-newsletter strategy is useful to note—most people would not think to send out a newsletter that doesn't push products for sale. Kit continues to do so because her sales growth supports her theory that "you have to give to get." By spending the time to write and share objective, original articles that inform her audience of parrot lovers about various parrot-related issues, she builds her brand and establishes credibility in her customers' minds for later purchases, even if they don't buy immediately.

E-mail management is a service that any entrepreneur can start in-house simply using Microsoft Outlook. So why did Kit choose to use an

ASP like Constant Contact instead of e-mailing customers directly herself? She gives two good reasons.

First is that the antispam filters that many Internet service providers and users have on their e-mail accounts today are set to block e-mail from unrecognized senders. This would greatly reduce the effectiveness (the "open rate") of any e-mail she sent, so she sees paying for a well-recognized outside service as insurance that's well worth it.

Second, using an e-mail service provides lots of statistics to help track the effectiveness and value of her newsletters. For example, from the service provider's system, Kit knows that an average of only 2.3 percent of her e-mails bounce, versus 15 percent to 20 percent (or higher) for many other e-mailers, especially those who try to send out mass e-mails themselves. She can also tell that her e-mails average 21.8 percent clickthrough from readers, compared to only 8.9 percent across other businesses.

She also values the fact that she effectively has a technical team working for her to maintain her e-mail system and to constantly improve the products to make them easier to use and more effective.

Kit points out that the newsletters have been helpful in planning the growth of her business. For example, from the responses to the newsletters, she can tell quickly which products are going to be popular and adjust her inventory accordingly.

The reports provided by the system also help her see that most of her customers spend most of their time online on the weekends. Knowing that helps her time her newsletters to come out at the right time to reach the audience members when they are most likely to be shopping. She can then also make other decisions accordingly—for example, making sure she's fully staffed on Mondays, which is when she needs to do the most order processing and shipping because of the weekend's orders.

As a former corporate executive and retired Air Force veteran, Kit has been most surprised at how much she likes being an entrepreneur. She sees the daily variety of challenges as constant learning opportunities. She recommends e-business to aspiring entrepreneurs like you because that's the direction she sees customers moving. "When you go into a physical store," she says, "often the employees—if you can even find someone to help you—don't even know the products; they just want to show you what they have in stock. Shopping online is so much more time-efficient that it's now the way that many people want to buy."

INTERNET MILLIONAIRE SECRET

Consistent publishing of a quality e-mail newsletter is the most important marketing technique that I recommend. You simply cannot lose by consistently reminding your customers of your e-business with a respectful and informative newsletter. Although it is sometimes challenging to find the time to maintain a regular publishing schedule, the e-businesses that do always benefit substantially.

In addition to demonstrating the potential importance of e-mail marketing for your e-business, BirdsJustWannaHaveFun.com also shows how picking a good niche market offers a path to success that likely would not have been sustainable in traditional retailing.

By identifying a niche that was being poorly served and serving it well instead, Kit Manchester (and her feathered friends) are now at the top of the pecking order in online sale of toys for parrots.

REAL BUDGET MARKETING SECRETS

TRADITIONAL BUSINESS advertising techniques are very limited in their effectiveness and accountability. With broadcast, print, or outdoor advertising, business owners can never be certain how well they work. This problem is summed up in the old joke about advertising: "I know half of my advertising works, I just don't know which half."

Luckily, the Internet has once again improved upon traditional business methods to help you build a cost-effective e-business. In addition to traditional-style display advertisements using banner graphics on website pages, new advertising tactics unique to the Internet include pay-per-click and affiliate advertising programs.

These new strategies are a huge improvement over traditional methods because they are both trackable and cost-effective—and if you're an advertiser, they allow you to pay only *after* you are certain that a customer is interested in your product!

Additionally, small advertisers (like you) who could never afford TV or billboard ads can use these new techniques at whatever budget level they can afford to get started and grow their ad budgets purely from profits generated by their previous successful advertising.

Pay-Per-Performance Keyword Advertising

Pay-for-performance marketing is a very popular strategy. This is a type of online advertising where you (as the advertiser) only pay the website (the publisher) if and when a visitor to the publisher's site clicks on your ad and visits your website. In many cases, the ad only costs you money if the visitor goes beyond just clicking on the ad and completes a further action, such as signing up for a newsletter, asking for more information, or making a purchase.

Many pay-per-performance advertisements are provided by search engine companies such as Google or Yahoo through keyword advertising programs. The advertiser (you) picks keywords that are relevant to your business. Then when a visitor conducts a search using those keywords, their search results will also include your ads because they were triggered by a search using the keywords you chose.

For example, if you are selling auto parts, you might choose keywords like *muffler, tire,* and *carburetor.* Then when a potential customer searches on one of those words on Google, your ad for mufflers would appear next to the natural (free) search results. *However, you would not pay anything for that ad to appear on the page unless the surfer clicked on it to visit your website.* This cost can range from as little as ten cents to several dollars per click, depending on the competition for your keywords.

It can be expensive to attract site visitors this way, but because each of them is prequalified for interest in exactly what you are selling, the conversion rate for sales can be much higher so that the advertising truly more than pays for itself.

Keywords can also be used to help match site pages with appropriate advertising without the visitor even having conducted a search. For example, if someone surfing online visits a website that is participating in a keyword content-matching advertising program and then lands on a page on that site that contains your keywords, the advertising program will display advertisements there that are relevant to those

keywords just like in the auto parts example, but without the user having conducted a search first.

As a website owner, you can use these keyword and pay-for-performance
advertising strategies both as an advertiser and as a publisher. As an advertiser, you can use them to incentivize the search engines and other site
publishers to post your ad on pages displaying relevant content. You
would then pay the website publishing the ads for each clickthrough or
other action you designate.

Similarly, you can use the programs as a publisher to make money by
showing advertisements from other advertisers on your website. To make
any real money requires some significant traffic, but if you grow your traffic to those levels, the pennies can add up!

To sign up for a pay-per-performance advertising program you can visit
Google's AdWords service or Yahoo's advertising services; many other
providers online have similar services, too. To find the best deals, visit
InternetMillionaireSecrets.com for my latest recommendations in this rapidly growing market.

PAY-PER-PERFORMANCE ADVERTISING ENTREPRENEUR: RAY ALLEN, AMERICANMEADOWS.COM

A real-world example of a million-dollar e-business built largely through
the use of pay-per-performance marketing techniques is American
Meadows.com. Ray Allen, the founder, started his company's website in
2000 to sell wildflower seeds to gardeners. While wildflower gardening
may sound like a niche interest, it is an example of a widely popular
hobby specialty that the Internet can be used to exploit very profitably.

With experience from the advertising industry and a previous wildflower seed-catalog business, Ray recognized the value in pay-per-click
advertising early on. By buying keywords that display advertisements
related to specific flower species and writing compelling advertising copy
to attract attention, he has used pay-per-performance advertising to consistently (and cost-effectively) attract new customers and build
AmericanMeadows.com into a profitable e-business.

Although many entrepreneurs are frightened of paying for advertising
when their businesses are still young, Ray recommends using pay-per-
click strategies because they allow you to only pay for performance. In his
case, he often pays over $1.00 per click to attract each visitor, but because

his average sale is $72.00, he can afford to buy many "clicks" and still make money with every order placed.

Pay-per-click (PPC) ads can be dangerous if poorly managed, however. In Ray's first experiments with the new ad medium, he spent more than $500 in one night and received zero orders! Of course, this experience quickly taught him to be more careful setting limits on his advertising system budgets and in choosing the keywords he wanted to purchase.

With a little testing (at low-budget amounts), Ray could quickly see which keywords were the best at converting visitors into purchasers by using the free reporting tools in the AdWords website. For example, he found that buying the keyword term *gardening* caused his text ads to show up many times because so many people search on that general term. However, since only a percentage of these "gardening" searches are likely to lead to a purchase of wildflower seeds, Ray learned to narrow his keyword purchase targets considerably. In many cases, he has to pay more for targeted keyword ads, but he can be confident that those purchases are worth the cost because they more often deliver visitors who convert into purchasers on his website.

The use of pay-per-performance keyword advertising has been the primary driver of AmericanMeadows.com's traffic and revenue growth. The site has grown to 400,000 unique visitors/day and millions of dollars in annual sales. The company is also able to offer more than four times as many seed types for sale than it had ever been able to profitably include in its print catalogs.

Even better, according to Ray, is that the business is much more profitable than his previous catalog-sales-based seed business. When the money that he traditionally spent on printing and mailing print catalogs to customers nationwide was spent instead on a website promoted by PPC ads, AmericanMeadows.com was able to reduce its retail prices over 50 percent—while still providing the same quality products and maintaining the same or better profit margins, too.

Ray emphasizes the importance of writing appealing advertising copy and paying close attention to what competitors are doing to ensure the continued appeal of your PPC ads. For example, many of American Meadows.com's competitors rarely, if ever, update their keywords or ad text, while he takes advantage of seasonal trends and holidays to regularly improve his ads.

He believes that entrepreneurs without real-world stores often have a competitive advantage in the keyword advertising space because their exclusive online focus allows them to devote more time to PPC strategies. In Ray's case his online only team has used the pay-per-performance tools so effectively that he can now live in Florida because he only needs to spend three to four weeks a year in Vermont, where his original wild-flower seed farm was based!

Ray sees pay-per-performance advertising as nothing less than a revolution benefiting entrepreneurs: "With the Internet anybody can get national or even international reach that no small business has ever had before," he says. "Pay-per-performance advertising then lets entrepreneurs self-finance the growth of their businesses to potentially unlimited levels because they can simply grow their ad budgets out of their own revenues."

INTERNET MILLIONAIRE SECRET

Ray Allen's experience highlights how new entrepreneurs can start with almost nothing and tap pay-per-performance advertising to expand their reach and prove the viability of their products or services with less risk than ever before.

Although many of the "pay as you go" spending strategies recommended in this book can help an entrepreneur effectively manage limited capital, pay-per-click (PPC) advertising offers an even better "pay only as you grow" approach because you don't have to pay for the ads until after a customer has already demonstrated interest in your product by clicking on your ad.

Almost no startup capital is needed to begin attracting customers using pay-per-performance advertising. With the purchase of just a few keywords, even you can be a global competitor tomorrow with a number-one search engine display for your products or services that is sure to attract customers.

Affiliate Program Advertising

Another form of pay-for-performance marketing is called an affiliate program. Although we discussed affiliate programs in Chapter 4, that discussion was focused on using such services as a publisher so that you could make money by displaying affiliate advertisements on your website in order to earn commissions from sales generated by your users clicking on the ads.

As an advertiser, you are on the opposite side of the fence in using the services of an affiliate program—you want to recruit other website owners (publishers) to post your ads on their websites. These publishers will promote your products by taking those ads and running them on their own sites in exchange for a commission on the sales they send your way from the advertising they display on your behalf.

Similar to the keyword advertising strategy discussed previously, when these publishers choose to post your ads, you only have to pay them after visitors perform your desired action. Typical actions required from affiliate visitors before you have to pay the publisher website are a clickthrough to visit your site, sign up for a newsletter, or make a purchase. When the visitor completes that action, the affiliate program tracking software will automatically note the activity and pay the affiliate from your account the commission amount that you have designated for that action.

For example, you post an ad about your auto parts website with an affiliate program. Another website owner (the "publisher," in affiliate speak) then signs up to be an affiliate of yours. That company's webmaster posts your ad on its site. You designate that you will pay that affiliate publisher ten cents for each visitor to your website that it sends via your ad and $5.00 for each purchase that those visitors make. Then, whenever surfers to the publisher's website click on your advertisement, your affiliate program account will be debited ten cents (plus a commission to the affiliate program of about 30 percent). If the customer then makes a purchase of your auto parts, your affiliate program account will be debited $5.00 (again plus a commission to the affiliate program service) to the credit of the publisher website that sent you the new customer.

I like affiliate programs very much. They allow you to engage website owners worldwide to promote your product on a very time- and cost-efficient basis.

AFFILIATE PROGRAM RECOMMENDATIONS

The biggest company in the affiliate program business is Commission Junction. This company is good at what it does, but is quite expensive for startup advertisers ($3,000 setup + $3,000 commission deposit just to get started, plus $500/month minimum billings). It also charges a commission of 30 percent on top of every ad bounty paid. This means that a commission owed to one of your affiliates of $10.00 would end up costing you $13.00 after Commission Junction adds its fees.

There are many affiliate program companies available. Alternatives include LinkShare, ClickXchange, and clixGalore, for example. These networks generally offer less effective but more affordable, smaller-scale affiliate tracking and promotions programs. Setup and monthly fees are often lower and they have less reach than Commission Junction, but given the large price difference, they may be appropriate for your business, especially when starting out or testing.

Additionally, some website shopping cart systems (like the upgraded levels of Yahoo! Stores) include their own affiliate program software. Because it's included in the service, such included services can be a cost-effective way to launch an affiliate program.

As you would expect, however, doing it yourself is more work. Whereas Commission Junction has a huge network of affiliates already established for you to reach, and it also tracks and pays all commissions generated, starting your own affiliate program leaves those administrative tasks in your lap.

AFFILIATE PROGRAM ADVERTISER ENTREPRENEURS: LIZ GAZER, RUGMAN.COM

Liz Gazer is an expert at exploiting affiliate program advertising to build sales for Rugman.com. A family-owned business that has been selling Persian area rugs for three generations, the company's then-president Aslan Mirkalami recognized the opportunity to expand its business to e-commerce in 1998.

Today, the company is a profitable leader in the online rug trade and employs more than twenty people. In fact, online sales through Rugman.com have replaced the company's offline business entirely and it no longer has a real-world showroom or store at all. Given that high-quality handmade area rugs are a very tactile and visual product, the business's ability to recruit customers online who cannot touch the merchandise before purchase is even more impressive.

Liz helps Rugman.com recruit, retain, and incentivize affiliate publishers to promote the company's carpets through their websites. She manages almost 3,000 of these affiliates on a day-to-day basis, each of which is busy promoting Rugman.com's products for her on a commission-only basis through Commission Junction.

Individual affiliate publishers receive a percentage of each sale that they deliver to the Rugman.com site. More important, because of these incentives, the affiliates spend lots of their own time and energy finding creative and customer-friendly ways to build Rugman.com's sales.

Although managing several thousand affiliates worldwide is a big enough job to require a full-time specialist and a significant budget, you can start smaller and gradually build your affiliate sales force and budget. As Liz points out, Rugman.com is happy to pay for whatever sales are generated by its affiliate team because it only pays out money *after* the affiliate has delivered a proven sale.

Liz recommends affiliate marketing to anyone looking to build a business online. She says:

> It's expensive to build a new brand online today, but affiliate marketing can help you gain exposure for your products in areas you could never afford to reach through traditional ads. With traditional advertising, you can't verify that your sales were directly related to a particular ad. With affiliate marketing the online tracking technology is so wonderful that you can track the effectiveness of every advertisement placed. What's not to like about not paying for an ad until after you know it has generated a sale?

INTERNET MILLIONAIRE SECRET

Investing in an affiliate marketing program can be a cost-effective way to promote your new e-business. Commission Junction and other providers essentially provide you access to a worldwide sales force of commission-only salespeople, each with their own website audience. These affiliates can bring both sales and credibility to a new product or brand you are launching.

If you provide compelling sales commission incentives through such affiliate relationships, you can quickly have thousands of websites around the world actively marketing your products. Even better, you don't have to pay any of these folks until they actually bring you sales, so you can grow your marketing budget and reach purely out of profits generated by previous affiliate sales!

HOW TO CHOOSE AN AFFILIATE PROGRAM

Important questions to ask of an affiliate-program provider include:

▲ How do you recruit affiliates to join my program?

▲ How wide is your existing network of affiliates already?

▲ How many other advertisers do you represent?

▲ What are the startup fees, monthly minimum charges, and commission-based fees that you charge?

▲ What kind of reporting and tracking do you provide?

▲ How does your service guard against abuse of its system by unscrupulous publishers (click fraud)?

▲ Can I export and transfer my affiliate network to another provider if I am not happy with your service?

▲ What kind of results are companies similar to mine experiencing using your system?

▲ What kinds of commissions or other sales incentives do you recommend that I provide to recruit and retain affiliates?

COPYRIGHT, TRADEMARK, AND INCORPORATION CHOICES

ALTHOUGH THIS BOOK is no substitute for professional legal advice, I'd like to introduce to you several of the legal issues you should be aware of when starting your new business, including incorporation, trademarks, and copyrights. You're welcome to use this information as general guidelines, but please be sure to consult an attorney about the specifics of your own situation before taking action.

Legal Filing Services

Many businesses have sprung up to help new business owners like you trademark their names, incorporate their companies, and file copyrights. While trademark, incorporation, and copyright filings are legitimate and valuable tools, they may not be necessary for an early-stage business like yours.

Don't let the advertising of these form preparation and filing companies scare you. Each one of these legal issues has its own set of expenses and benefits that you should weigh individually as your business grows.

You can own and operate a legal and successful million-dollar business for years without using any of these services.

Choosing a Name for Your Business

Naming your business is an important task, and you're probably already thinking about it. Whether you incorporate or operate as a partnership or sole proprietorship, it can still be helpful to have a company name that is different from your given name. A company name can help establish your credibility with potential customers and also begins the marketing process by suggesting what your company offers to anyone who hears or reads your company's name.

For example, a discount sock retailer owned and operated by a woman named Julie Gordon might simply bill customers and accept payments as "Julie Gordon." This is a common practice among individuals who work alone and are unincorporated ("sole proprietors"). While that is legal, it misses an opportunity to brand Julie's business with a more descriptive name that will help people understand what she does as soon as they hear or read her company name.

Instead, I would suggest she file a "doing business as" (DBA) fictitious name statement with her local city or county clerk's office to establish a brand name for her venture. This filing will allow her to open bank accounts and receive payments in the name of that business instead of just in her own name. (Such filings and the required newspaper publication of the resulting notice can usually be completed for $25 to $50.) Julie might then choose to call her business Julie's Discount Socks or even Sock-o-Rama if she wanted to be more playful.

Though it is tempting to be clever or cute with the name you choose for your business, my experience suggests that simple and descriptive names are better. In addition to making it easy to recall your company name, a simple and descriptive name will lessen customer service difficulties from customers who don't understand why a credit card charge from "Julie Gordon" appears on the credit card statement when they probably would remember a purchase appearing from JuliesDiscount Socks.com.

TRADEMARK ISSUES

Given the global reach of the Internet, you must be more careful about potential trademark issues than entrepreneurs needed to be in previous years. For example, ten years ago a business like Julie's Discount Socks would probably only have reached customers in a local or regional area. Consequently, there would have been little problem of confusion or competition from other businesses with similar names (e.g., Jim's Discount Socks, Julie's Discount Shoes, Discount Socks by Julie, etc.) located in other towns, other states, or other countries.

Today, however, when you put up a website you can instantly reach into and compete in local markets all over the world. That's why you should do your best to come up with a unique identifying name for your business to avoid confusing customers. If customers are confused by similarities between the name of your business and competitors' company names, that can lead to trademark infringement lawsuits from those competitors.

Although filing a federal trademark registration is a good idea if you have a major investment in your brand or business name, it can be expensive. You should consult an attorney about the specifics of your situation, but you can probably wait until you have gotten your business started. That way you'll know whether it is worthwhile hiring attorneys to help you with a proper federal trademark filing before incurring the expense.

In the meantime, your business name (if it is different enough from previously existing competitors) will probably be automatically protected by "common law trademark" rules. In most states, these laws will apply to your business name as soon as you start publicizing it for business to the general public. (It is a good idea to keep dated copies of your original marketing materials from your initial launch in case your business start date ever becomes an issue.)

DOMAIN NAMES

A domain name is the part of a World Wide Web address that comes after "www" and before the .com or .net extension. Like your business name, it is to your advantage for both marketing and legal (i.e., trademark-related) reasons to choose a unique and easily memorable domain name for your online business. (See Chapter 10 for my recommendations on how to select a domain name.)

The best domain names are easily remembered, and shorter is better, too. For example, I would recommend "DiscountSocks.com" over "Julie GordonsDiscountSockorama.com." Most Internet browsers accept up to twenty-nine characters in a domain name, but that is far more than most consumers want to type in or even remember.

The most common and popular domain names for businesses in the United States currently are .com names. As the Internet continues to grow, however, I expect that .net, .info, .biz, .org, .us, and other available domain name extensions will also grow in popularity. If you can find a good, descriptive, and unique domain name for your business, be sure to check if similar names are already taken by competitors using the other extensions.

INCORPORATION

The basic business structure for an unincorporated individual is a sole proprietorship. If you start a business in your own name, using your own Social Security number, and have no partners, you are automatically a sole proprietor.

If you work with others and agree to share revenues, costs, and risks, then you can easily create a partnership. In both of these cases if something goes wrong, you and your partners can be sued personally for any resulting damages.

Corporations are legal structures designed to protect you (and any co-owners) from this liability. A corporation is essentially a fictional person to which you contribute the appropriate assets to run the business. It should have its own bank accounts and tax identification number, which are different from yours. The point of a corporation is that it is separate from you in case somebody decides to sue you for reasons relating to your business. This protection is called a "corporate shield" or "corporate veil," and it can protect you and your assets (such as your house) from being lost in a lawsuit brought by unsatisfied customers.

Is incorporating a good idea? Yes, absolutely. The question for you is "when"?

Incorporating costs hundreds, often thousands, of dollars. Even if you are the sole owner, a corporation also requires separate bank accounts, record keeping, and tax reporting every year for as long as it exists—all of which can be a hassle and expensive.

As an early-stage entrepreneur, you should evaluate the risks of your new business. Are the products or services you are selling likely to lead to lawsuits against you? For example, selling medical devices that people depend on for their health is more risky than publishing a newsletter about movies; one carries the risk of personal injury from the product, the other doesn't.

If you are in a business with a low probability of being sued, or you don't have any assets worth protecting, you can probably wait longer to file for incorporation than entrepreneurs in higher-risk businesses with more to lose.

This is not legal advice, so please consult an attorney and a tax adviser for more information on these topics specific to your situation.

COPYRIGHTS

Like incorporating services, there are many vendors trying to scare business owners into filing federal copyright registrations. My perspective on these services is similar to the incorporation services just discussed: Filing federal copyright registrations is definitely a good idea, but only worth the time and expense if you have something worth protecting.

The United States joined the Berne Convention (an international copyright treaty) and in 1989 passed laws that caused the automatic copyrighting of any work that is put into a fixed medium of expression (i.e., written down). This means that you do not have to file any papers or even put the copyright symbol (©) on a work to have it be copyrighted in the United States. However, filing federal copyright papers will increase the damages you can win in court if you prove another person infringed (i.e., illegally copied) your works.

So, as with trademarks and incorporation, if you have some works that are especially valuable, they are probably worth the effort on your part to apply for a federal copyright registration. However, given that your business is new, you probably have not written your most valuable works yet. So once again, you can probably wait until you are confident that your business is successful enough to be worth protecting.

Again, please consult an attorney for more information on these topics and advice on your specific situation.

INTERNET MILLIONAIRE SECRET:
Privacy Policy Legal Work for Free!

Privacy policies are more important than ever due to congressional action that has attempted to reduce the flood of spam e-mail that we all receive. The law requires that you post a clear explanation of what you will and will not do with the e-mail addresses and other personal infor-mation that visitors to your website may choose to offer you.

While drafting a privacy policy that's in compliance with federal law is normally a job for a lawyer, the Internet once again comes to your res-cue: Simply go to your favorite search engine and type in "privacy pol-icy." The search results will offer you links to hundreds (probably thousands) of professionally written privacy policies in use across the Web. Find a few of them posted on websites in your field. By mixing, matching, and adapting the provisions in these examples to meet the requirements and policies of your own e-business, you can quickly cre-ate a template for your own site's privacy policy.

Of course, I still recommend that you use this resulting draft only to educate yourself and to discuss with your attorney, not to actually post it. Rapid changes in online law necessitate some professional consul-tation on this matter, but with a rough draft already in hand you will potentially save hundreds of dollars of billable attorney time.

BANK ACCOUNTS

Regardless of whether you incorporate, it is a good idea to set up separate bank accounts for your new business so that you can manage your expenses and revenues more carefully. It will also prepare the way for you to grow the business most easily.

As mentioned previously, it is also a good idea to complete a DBA fic-titious business-name statement. Most banks will require one if you want to accept payments in any name other than your own. A DBA simply says something to the effect of "I, Jim Brown, am going to be operating a busi-ness called Fantastic Photographs." Filing and publishing such a DBA statement will then allow Jim to open a bank account under the name "Fantastic Photographs" and accept payments in that name.

CREDIT RATINGS

When the business is new, it will most likely operate on your credit rating. If you have good credit, this will be easy. When starting a cor-poration, you will want to file for a separate Employer Identification Number (EIN) issued by the Internal Revenue Service.

Although this separate number will be linked to your credit to start, if you are prudent with the new company's business activities, it can grow to have its own credit rating in addition to yours. You can facilitate this process by opening trade accounts with your local suppliers that can act as trade references for you later.

Getting a credit card in the name of the company is a good way to begin your new company's credit history. If you apply for a credit card processing merchant account (to accept online payments), this credit rating will be important as well.

WARNING: DON'T GET DISTRACTED BY ADMINISTRATION

When starting a new business, it's easy to get distracted by all these administrative duties. Such registrations, formalities, and legal details are proper and should be pursued, but they also represent a very real danger of distraction. I have seen many entrepreneurs spend more time on administration than on their new businesses, or spend a lot of money organizing a business that has not yet been tested, or both!

In the early stages of starting a new business, it is critical that you put your time, money, energy, and creativity into the business, not into paperwork. Until you've shown that the business is worth all the time and expense of making the filings, you should concentrate on making money.

In the best case, your business takes off first and you can file the appropriate papers later (or hire someone else to do it). In the worst case, the business is not as successful and you change it significantly or even shut it down. Then the time and money you've spent on administration has been wasted. You might also be saddled with recurring filing and fee obligations every quarter or year until you go through another series of paperwork obstacles to shut down the business.

While I completely recommend that you respect all the legal and administrative requirements of your local and federal authorities, until your business is making real money, they are not likely to care about your business anyway. Your job is to build a business first—don't get distracted by the small sense of accomplishment you can gain by conquering bureaucracy. Spending all of your time on filing forms and paying fees is no way to build your million-dollar business!

If you are the type of person who can get bogged down easily in paperwork, "LESS PLANNING, MORE DOING!" should be your strategy in starting your new e-business.

24 PARTNERS

SHOULD YOU SHARE YOUR MILLION-DOLLAR IDEA?

ONE OF THE first questions any entrepreneur with a new business idea asks herself is, "Can I do this alone?"

Every entrepreneur is challenged to get a lot done in a short period of time with limited resources. Whereas being your own boss has tremendous appeal, entrepreneurs have to be careful that they don't bite off more than they can chew. Sharing your business ownership with partners may help you run farther and faster than you could alone.

Benefits of Partnership

Partners can bring a lot of value to your new venture. There are both business and personal reasons why you may want to share your burdens with a partner. These include:

▲ Additional brains, hands, and energy to develop your business

▲ Additional relationships and financial resources

▲ Companionship

Negatives of Partnership

Of course, these positives can be outweighed by negatives if things don't go well. Some of the downsides to having a partner can include:

▲ Decision-making and coordination delays

▲ Financial pressure from having to support two owners

▲ Distraction from business due to personal conflicts

▲ Potential creation of a competitor

In short, sharing the risk with a trusted friend can help to greatly increase your capabilities and reach, but in order to gain these extra resources, you need to be ready to spend some time on management issues and share the rewards as well.

The decision about whether to share your new business with a partner is one that only you can make. I generally recommend it because the companionship you provide each other can be critical in staying motivated, especially during the demanding early days of the business before any revenue has begun arriving.

How to Partner

If you decide to partner, I have advice on how to go about it. Although everyone loves the idea of doing deals "on a handshake," there are so many important issues in starting a new business that I strongly recommend reviewing two key points—trust and documentation—before inviting another person into your operation.

DO YOU TRUST THIS PERSON?

Before any other considerations, you must trust the person you are considering as a potential partner. If you have any concerns about another person's honesty or integrity in dealing with you, you should not involve that person in your business.

DID YOU PUT THE DETAILS IN WRITING?

Second, I strongly recommend writing down the details of your relationship. It doesn't have to be a fancy legal document, but you should record up-front the basic expectations you both have, including:

▲ Who owns the business?

▲ Who is contributing money and how will it be repaid?

▲ Who gets paid, and how much and how often?

▲ Who pays the costs?

▲ Who keeps the profits?

▲ How will you make important decisions about hiring people, leasing office space, and buying equipment or furniture?

▲ Who has final say in decisions if there is disagreement?

▲ Whose credit rating can the business draw upon if necessary?

▲ Who has signing authority on the company's bank accounts?

▲ What happens if one partner decides to cut back on her time commitment or end her involvement with the business? Or what happens if one partner dies unexpectedly?

It is far better to discuss and settle these issues early in the development of your business rather than later when the business has grown to have assets, customers, and revenue that greatly increase the stakes. Discussing them in detail will also help both you and your partner clarify expectations for the venture and avoid misunderstandings later.

I understand that these are delicate topics, especially if you're partnering with a friend or family member. Sensitivity is recommended to help you to approach these topics in a friendly manner, but it is not a good excuse to delay resolving them. Even the best of relationships can falter during hard times, such as after an illness or a bad decision. Even the most basic written agreements can help you, your partner, and your business make it through these situations.

Alternatives to Equal Partnership

Though the natural inclination of most people is to split things fifty-fifty with their partners, you should know that there are many other ways to structure a business relationship. You should consult an attorney for more information, but a few words here about legal structures may be helpful.

In most states, a simple agreement between two or more individuals to start and operate a business results in a partnership being legally formed. This can be true even if the agreement was simply a conversation and never written down. If you want to avoid this default setting in the law, it is important to write down the details of whatever agreement you and your partner(s) decide upon.

Alternatives to partnerships include corporations, limited and general partnerships, limited liability companies, and many other variations. Each of these legal structures is designed to meet the needs of certain kinds of businesses, often because their founders want specific control over the ownership, profit allocation, and decision making for the company.

If, for example, you want to own 70 percent of your company and split the remaining 30 percent between two other partners, you should consult an attorney to talk about becoming incorporated or forming a limited liability company. It's not as complicated as it may sound and can help ensure that all partners are clear about their stake in the venture, thus avoiding complications later.

EARN-OUTS

It is also possible to grant ownership in a company to partners, but only when they achieve certain goals. For example, your cousin Fred says he can help your new business by bringing you $50,000 worth of sales from people he knows. Of course this sounds great, but you don't want to give Fred half of your company unless those sales actually materialize.

With the help of an attorney, you can craft a deal with Fred that rewards him with 50 percent ownership of the company only after that revenue arrives. You can even make his ownership proportional to the success of his sales efforts, so that if he only brings in $30,000, Fred gets only 30 percent ownership instead of the 50 percent. Since Fred had to "earn" his share, this approach is called an "earn-out."

VESTING

Similarly, you can grant Fred 50 percent ownership of the company, but only if he works full-time with you for a certain period of time. In this case, you might grant Fred part ownership only after he's done two years of successful work for the company. This process is called "vesting" and can be attached to any sort of timeline or milestones that make sense.

Like the earn-out, vesting can also be proportional. So, if Fred does great work for one year but leaves in year two for another job, the contract could provide for Fred to receive the 25 percent of company ownership that had "vested" in his one year of work with you, but he'd lose the rest on his departure from the company.

Consult an attorney for more details on employment agreements and corporate structure, but rest assured that you can probably arrange almost anything that is appropriate to protect you and your business.

BEFORE PARTNERING, CAREFULLY THINK IT OVER

1. In your situation and considering the needs and potential of your new business, would "two heads be better than one"?

2. Make a list in your Millionaire Idea Journal of people whom you trust and respect and may be available to help you.

3. Give consideration to exactly what skills or resources each of them would bring to your new business.

4. Evaluate whether any of them have important skills or resources that could make a big difference for your new company.

5. Consider how much time they have available to help you, their need for current income, their work history, and any other factors that may affect their ability to help you or their trustworthiness.

Internet Millionaire Secret: Venture Capital Is Dead

No discussion of partnering would be complete with mention of investors. The good news is that you don't need venture capital anymore.

More specifically, one of the most surprising aspects of the e-business revolution is that the declining costs of Internet services (and the infrastructure to deliver those services) mean that you no longer need millions of dollars in venture capital (VC) to start a successful e-business. Raising money from friends, family, or "angels" is still common when starting a new e-business, but even that is not necessary unless you plan to launch a complex, highly technical new service or invest up-front in significant inventory, office space, or personnel.

I have worked for and with companies backed by tens of millions of dollars from the top venture capital firms in the world, so I know both sides of the startup story. Although venture capitalists can add a lot of value, I can also guarantee you that today, you no longer need the backing of a Kleiner Perkins, Goldman Sachs, or Idealab to get your own successful e-business started.

Did you happen to notice that this book profiles dozens of successful e-business entrepreneurs and only one of them took investment from venture capitalists to get started (and that was ten years ago when e-commerce systems were still highly technical and expensive)?

In many cases, the entrepreneurs profiled in this book tried to obtain venture capital money but were turned down or even ignored by VC firms because their ideas were "too small." Instead, the lower costs and risks of starting e-businesses today let these entrepreneurs gradually ramp up their efforts. Working from home part-time is a great way to build a side business or expand a hobby that can grow into a profitable full-time occupation.

By tapping the services of ASPs (as recommended throughout this book), you can emulate these success stories by accessing the equivalent software tools, PCs and servers, bandwidth, audience reach, customer service support, and distribution systems of a multimillion-dollar, VC-backed dot-com for just dollars per month, and without giving up any equity ownership in your new company, either.

The relative ease with which anybody with a good idea can start a new e-business is such a powerful trend that I predict that many venture capital firms are soon going to have to reevaluate their operating strategies. Most VCs prefer to invest $3 million to $5 million at a time (if they invest at all in early-stage companies), but that is far more than most e-businesses today need to get started. Capitalizing on all the opportunities in "microbusinesses" created by entrepreneurs like you is a major opportunity for venture capitalists, but increasingly they are going to need you more than you need them!

My advice to you is to start your own e-business today following the many cost-effective strategies detailed in this book. Even if you want to raise money for expansion later, you'll get a much better deal if you approach potential investors with a functioning online business than just with an idea and a smile.

25 CONGRATULATIONS!

AFTER READING this whole book, I know that now you have the tools to identify and evaluate new e-business opportunities like never before. I hope that you'll put this education to good use by building your own e-commerce business and making yourself a million dollars.

As you set forth on this exciting journey, I have some last words of encouragement for you.

New Businesses Are Being Born All the Time

You may think that you don't have much chance to build your own million-dollar e-business because everything has been invented already or because there's already too much competition.

My research and history both prove that this is wrong! Every generation has benefited from improvements in products, processes, or communications in ways that their parents and grandparents never could have foreseen. With all the new opportunities presented by the Internet revolution, you are in a unique place of opportunity. Never before has it been so easy to make incremental improvements in existing items and market them worldwide so inexpensively.

Originality Is Not Required

In fact, you don't even have to be original or invent a new thing. Most products are actually simply improvements on previously existing products. The million-dollar businesses that they created were just waiting for the first entrepreneur to recognize the opportunities that they offered.

Most businesses simply take existing technologies and business models and copy or improve them to create new successes. Think about it! Products that we all take for granted today have been the basis of so many fortunes and companies. Every product you use started small—probably with just one person.

For example, you know all of these brand names, don't you?

BRAND	IMPROVEMENT MODEL
La-Z-Boy	Chairs, but more comfortable!
Levi's Jeans	Trousers, but more durable!
TiVo	VCR recording, but better!
Nike	Athletic shoes, but better fitting and cooler looking!
eBay	Garage sales, but on a 24/7, worldwide basis!
FedEx	Package delivery, but faster!
Jelly Belly	Jelly beans, but with more unique and tasty flavors!

Most people thought that the products these businesses sell were already "good enough." But they were wrong!

Each one of these multimillion-dollar success stories is based simply on improving a previously existing product. If you refuse to be satisfied with "good enough," you have the chance to build a million-dollar e-business, too. The best news is that you're reading this book, which proves that you already are ready to roll. Drawing on the exercises in this book, you should have identified business areas of your own where you have both interest and competitive advantages. By focusing on one of your key target markets, you have an opportunity to invent or improve or popularize your chosen products on a global scale.

Only <u>You</u> Can Make You a Millionaire

The ability to turn millionaire *potential* into millionaire *fact* is yours. I'm limited to sharing written advice with you, but the actual work has to be done by you.

With my background in e-business, and the additional advice drawn from interviews and surveys with hundreds of successful e-business entrepreneurs, this book offers you the most comprehensive package of Internet Millionaire Secrets available anywhere. There are no vague strategies for "envisioning abundance" or tapping the "power of positive thinking." Instead, I wrote this book to help you develop a practical, specific action plan for building your own millionaire e-business.

As David Bach, the best-selling financial planning author, says about his own book in *Start Late, Finish Rich:*

> Books don't change people's lives. People change their own lives. The fact that you are reading this book right now is no coincidence. There are literally millions of books out there right now that you could be reading. This one ended up in your hands for a reason. The reason is that you are ready to make a change.[1]

In the same way, I believe that you have taken the first big step on the road to building your own successful e-business by reading my book. If you have gotten this far, you have demonstrated your dedication to your new mission. By now, you know more about building new Internet businesses than 99 percent of the people on earth!

I've shown you, in detail, how the costs of starting a new business have dropped significantly as the Internet has grown. Don't be one of the millions of Americans who just dream about being your own boss. With the many Internet Millionaire Secrets I've shared with you in this book, you know that "insufficient financial resources" is no longer an excuse for delaying your destiny.

Have Faith in Yourself

The cornerstone of any entrepreneur's success is faith. To build your own business into a million-dollar success story, you must believe in your ability to offer a superior product or service to your audience. You have faith in your friends, your family, your religion—why not have faith in yourself for a change, too?

You've probably spent years, maybe even decades, getting up each morning to go to work for someone else. You've proved that you have the work ethic to make things happen. Now it's your turn. If you have faith in yourself and develop a strong action plan (following the principles outlined in this book), you can put one foot in front of the other and execute that plan, just like you've been executing the plans of other people for so long.

The only thing stopping you from doing it is simply going out and doing it.

Acknowledge Your Doubts

Doubt is the opposite of faith. Whereas you might expect me to instruct you to ignore your doubts, I actually suggest the opposite. It's important to embrace your doubts and give them careful consideration. They might be trying to tell you something valuable.

I recognize that no one can have 100 percent faith all of the time. That is a state of grace (or ignorance!) that humans rarely attain. By recognizing your doubts and giving them their appropriate consideration, you can more easily compartmentalize them and move on. If you are just worrying for no purpose, try to redirect your energies back into something more positive—like work.

"Keep your eyes on the prize" and remember the goals you have set for yourself and your new business. Envision how implementing your action plan could improve your life by generating an extra $1,000 a month. How about with an extra $10,000 or $100,000 a month?

As Robert Kiyosaki says in his bestseller *Rich Dad's Cash Flow Quadrant:* "You can always quit. So why quit now?"

Recognize Your Cycles

My research has consistently shown that motivation comes in cycles. You should pay attention to your own work cycles to take advantage of them when they are up, and back off when they're down. For example, perhaps you should save sales calls or important negotiations for midweek afternoons, when you know you're generally rested and enthusiastic, while taking care of less critical administration on Monday mornings when you're generally wishing you were still at the beach. *In other words, why try to work a corporate-style schedule when you no longer work for a corporation?*

Other cycles to be aware of are cycles of doubt about your business. For me, these moments usually come at night or first thing in the morning. Experience has taught me, however, that these episodes of doubt come regularly, almost regardless of what's going on in my businesses. They are just the natural product of a creative mind considering all the possibilities.

Don't be surprised that you, too, will have regular episodes of doubt about your new direction. If you can recognize a pattern as to when these moments occur, work to fill those time slots in your schedule with motivating or even distracting activities, such as business lunches, sales calls, or even breaks to read a book or surf the Web for a few minutes. You should also share these doubts with those you trust and try to be positive about incorporating the feedback that other people provide to you.

It's okay not to have faith 100 percent of the time. Learn to recognize your cycles of positivity and of doubt, and adjust your work schedule and project plans to match them. That way you can get the most done without torturing yourself with doubt during your downtimes.

Calm Your Fears

Fear is the big brother of doubt. Like doubt, fear is okay in measured doses, but you should never let it run your life or your business.

If you are afraid that you may not have the education, contacts, investment capital, or personal fortitude to continue, I hope that this book has helped you to see that none of those things are the keys to building a million-dollar business. Instead, entrepreneurial success is about finding good ideas and having the courage to get out of bed each morning to do the hard work of implementing them, step by step.

This book has taught you about many cutting-edge tools and strategies for building new businesses. To calm your fears, I hope you'll recognize that this knowledge gives you competitive advantages not even taught at the Harvard Business School.

Remember: It was the so-called experts who built the *Titanic*, but amateurs who built Noah's Ark.

Value Your Mistakes

In my experience, fear of mistakes is a much larger factor in business than most people will admit. This is because the financial stakes in business can be so much higher than most other daily decisions.

My answer to this worry is that mistakes are to be expected as a normal part of business. Each mistake you make brings you one step closer to finding the solution you need to get to the next level. Mistakes can also save you money by helping to uncover correct solutions before you invest heavily in inappropriate strategies or people. The secret to Internet Riches is not just to make as few mistakes as possible, but also to keep the damage from those mistakes to a minimum.

The more mistakes you make the better off you can be—provided you are also sure to learn from each mistake that is made. (Even better is if you are smart enough to learn from the mistakes that you see others make.)

It's easy to get caught up in placing blame or regretting bad decisions, but those reactions are not nearly as productive as figuring out what went wrong and how you can do better next time. Recognizing that mistakes can be valuable, and doing your best to benefit from them, will give you much greater peace of mind—and you'll sleep better, too.

Know When to Change Direction

One of the biggest mistakes that entrepreneurs make is not recognizing when it's time to change direction. Falling in love with their own dreams, many new entrepreneurs work so hard that they stop listening to the outside world. You need to keep your ears open, and don't be afraid to change your plans.

Just as smaller mistakes can benefit you, having the courage to admit a mistake and redirect, rename, move, or change your new business as soon as you recognize the need will get you to your million-dollar goal that much faster.

Get Going!

Now you've gained decades of business experience, education, and expertise by reading this book. It's time for you to get going and launch your new e-business.

As you know, all of my recommended strategies deliberately minimize the amount of cash investment you need to make. Anyone can afford to get started with my amazing $25-a-month website budget. You can even do it at night or on the side while keeping your current job.

Why not get started and at least test the million-dollar e-business ideas I've helped you generate? You can refer to each of the appropriate chapters for financial, planning, and technical tools that will make it as easy as possible for you. The only thing stopping you now is taking the first step.

If you have a good idea, the sooner that you act on it, the better. More than 85 million domain names have now been registered, and according to VeriSign, Inc. (one of the companies that manages Internet domains), 8.5 million new domain names were registered in the third quarter of 2005 alone. E-commerce is a bit like real estate, where the best locations go first. So, if you have a business idea or juicy target market that others have not yet uncovered, you would be wise to stake it out as soon as possible.

Start Acting Like a CEO! You Are in Charge! Congratulations!

Remember, for every famous billion-dollar business, from Ford Motor Company to eBay, there are many more new, small, million-dollar businesses that are less famous but still very lucrative. And most of those businesses have been started just in the last five years by a single individual, like you, who had a dream about becoming a millionaire. It's my hope that the e-business secrets and opportunities that this book has shared with you will help make your dream e-business come true. Because you're in charge now, please visit the website at InternetMillionaireSecrets.com to leave me feedback. I'd love to hear what you think of this book and receive your suggestions for improvement.

Notes

1. David Bach, *Start Late, Finish Rich,* New York, Broadway Books, 2005, p. 9.

INDEX OF E-BUSINESS ENTREPRENEURS AND SERVICES

Internet Riches contains discussion of dozens of successful e-business entrepreneurs and service providers, including:

AmericanMeadows.com

ArtFairCalendar.com

Bathboats.com

BillOReilly.com

BirdsJustWannaHaveFun.com

BlueberryBoutique.net

Bookslut.com

CafePress.com

CommissionJunction.com

ConstantContact.com

CooksIllustrated.com

Craigslist.org

DigitalMediaWire.com

DrudgeReport.com

eBay.com

FARK.com

GoDaddy.com

Google.com

InternetMillionaireDomains.com

InternetMillionaireSecrets.com

InventiveParent.com

iPowerWeb.com

LiminalInstitute.org

LiveDeal.com

MobileTracker.net

NormDarwish.com

Rugman.com

ScoobyMods.com

Seyberts.com

Sittercity.com

SweaterBabe.com

TheTshirtNexus.com

TrafficMatt.com

WeddingChannel.com

APPENDIX B

INTERNET RESEARCH SKILLS

Another amazing benefit of the World Wide Web is the instant access it provides to information. As a new business owner, you should take advantage of online search engines like Google and Yahoo to learn about your new market, products, and competitors. Search engines are a critical weapon in today's business arsenal because they can provide so much information for so little cost.

If you are not already familiar with how to use a search engine, here are some tips for beginners, as well as more sophisticated tips for advanced users.

First, *think broadly.*

To start your research you should be general with your concepts and words. This is the key to successfully finding what you want using a search engine. Don't get fixed on a particular phrase or an overly specific description of the information you are seeking because that will limit the results you get back from the search engine. You are more likely to find worthwhile results if you first try several alternative names and phrases for the subject of your search in order to identify the most important key terms unique to that topic.

For example, in a search for the best suppliers of rubber bands, you might start by searching on RUBBER BANDS, but you should also try RUBBER BAND or just OFFICE SUPPLIES. Similarly, instead of CLASSIC CADILLACS, perhaps ANTIQUE CADILLACS would be a useful search. These variations can be important because the information on the Web was put there by different people from all over the world, so their local phrases, slang, and even spelling might not match yours exactly. Using synonyms to explore broadly at first will help you learn the key terms specific to your area of research; knowing those terms will later help you narrow your search to find precisely what you're after.

Being more specific is your goal ultimately, but it only helps after you've identified the appropriate unique words and phrases needed to locate pages focused on your desired information. For example, searching on FLEETWOOD, SEDAN DE VILLE, or ELDORADO (all models of Cadillacs) from the start would quickly help you find more specific information on Cadillacs, but it would also narrow the search, possibly eliminating related information about other models like the Calais, Escalade, or Seville that may have been useful to you.

Even searching on common misspellings sometimes is useful, especially for difficult words like *accessibility* or when searching on people's names that have common variations, like Jim versus James or Johnson versus Johansson, and so on.

GOOGLE/YAHOO RESEARCH SKILL SPECIFICS

If you visit www.Google.com or www.Yahoo.com, you will see a blank box into which you can type your question. Click on the "Search" button and you will quickly get pages of results relating to your chosen topic.

The problem with search engines is that they are more about quantity than quality. Typing in general or nonspecific questions can easily return thousands or even millions of results. That many results essentially makes the search engine unusable.

By learning a few tricks, you can quickly improve your results. This is because most all search engines are built using the rules of "Boolean logic," which allows for search strings that can help you search more effectively. Here are some examples.

SEARCH TYPE AND EXAMPLE

AND. Wherever you have a blank space in a search query, a search engine interprets that space as the word *and*. So typing in CLASSIC CADILLAC will make the search engine look for pages that have both the word *classic* and the word *Cadillac* on any part of that page, even if they are not connected. Typing in CLASSIC CADILLAC to Google, you will get more than 2 million results from pages that contain those two words.

QUOTES. Typing your phrases in between quotation marks will force the search engine to look not just for the individual word, but for the words together and in the order you specify. So, if you type in "CLASSIC CADILLAC" (adding the quote marks), your search is narrowed down to a more helpful 120,000 results. A good start, but still too broad to be useful.

OR. Continuing the search, you could add the words REPAIR or MECHANIC to the query if you want to find someone qualified to fix a Classic Cadillac. You could type the query like this: "CLASSIC CADILLAC" REPAIR OR MECHANIC. This tells the search engine to look for pages that contain the phrase *Classic Cadillac* and also the word *repair* or the word *mechanic*. The OR search reduces the results down to about 11,600.

MINUS. Adding the minus sign (–) will tell the search engine not to include results with whatever term you place after the minus sign. For example, a query of "CLASSIC CADILLAC" REPAIR OR MECHANIC-DEALER would subtract any results that included the word *dealer* from your search. (It is important that there be a space in front of the minus sign but not after it.) This search technique trims our results down to about 600.

You can continue this process to narrow down your results until you find the information for which you are looking. Learning to identify the appropriate keywords is not hard; it just takes a little practice.

These tips will work on almost any search engine, so if Google is not your favorite, feel free to try them elsewhere, too.

SPONSORED RESULTS

Some search engine results are placed there by advertisers instead of being natural products of the search engine's search process. In practical terms, they are usually the results that appear across the top and/or side of a search results page under a heading that says something like "Sponsored Result" or "Advertisement" or "Sponsored Site."

Although it is annoying to be constantly barraged by advertising on the Web when you are a consumer, this type of advertisement can be very helpful to you as a business owner. It can help you locate suppliers and determine who your competitors are.

Supplier Searches. Finding reliable, affordable sources for your products or services is one of the foundations upon which any successful business rests. Whether you are following an Efficiency Millionaire, Product Millionaire, or Niche Millionaire strategy, you are going to be dependent on someone, somewhere for the goods, information, services, or technology that enables you to sell to your target market.

Using Google or the other search engines is a great way to find the best suppliers for you. By typing in keywords relevant to your needs, you can quickly locate firms offering such goods from all over the world.

With a few more clicks of the mouse, you can probably also e-mail these suppliers or visit their websites to obtain pricing and delivery information. The days of being dependent on local suppliers are over.

The Sponsored Sites section of search engine results is a particularly good place to look for potential vendors and partners. If a firm is advertising in these places, it is a pretty good indication that the company is familiar with e-commerce, will have a website to provide you with key information easily, and is more likely to do business online and by e-mail 24/7—all of which can make your life easier than it might be working with suppliers who still insist on phone calls or faxes during normal business hours.

Competitor Searches. Similar to locating suppliers, search engines are very powerful tools for learning about and keeping track of your competitors. By typing in keywords relevant to your product, niche, or target market, you will be able to call up listings of companies offering similar services.

You will find many competitors already listed in the Sponsored Sites section of the search engines. As with potential suppliers, this means that they probably have websites where you can learn about their services and pricing with just a few clicks of your mouse.

How can you find out how big a business your competitors are operating? It can be difficult to judge how successful a competitor is by looking at its website.

As I have shown you in this book, a good-looking site can be easily built without necessarily having a big business behind it. So here are two additional tricks I recommend for analyzing your competition: reverse link searches and Alexa.com searches.

▲ *Reverse Links*. One useful way to evaluate the popularity of a competitor's website is to learn how many other sites link to it. While this sounds like it would be complicated, it is actually quite easy. Visit Google.com and type link:www.thecompetitorsdomainname.com in the search box. Believe it or not, this easy trick will produce a list of every website listed in the Google database that links to your competitor's site.

▲ *Alexa.com*. This free website review and tracking service is owned by Amazon.com. You can visit Alexa.com and type your competitor's URL in the search box at the top. Click on Web Search and it will give you an extensive review and traffic analysis of the competitor's website (assuming it has enough traffic to be ranked).

If these techniques show few links or little traffic to your competitor's site, they may not be as big a threat as you imagined. Pretty handy, eh?

SO WHAT?

Why all this interest in search engines, you ask? Because information is a competitive advantage. If you know how to find higher-quality suppliers with lower prices, keep up with the news relevant to your target market, and efficiently monitor your competitors, your million-dollar business will be stronger and more profitable.

GLOSSARY OF E-BUSINESS TERMS

To help you navigate the complicated and often technical world of e-business, I've written this "plain English" glossary of 100+ e-business terms, buzzwords, and phrases.

Affiliate: A website publisher that has agreed to display commission-generating affiliate advertisements on its websites. The affiliate displays these ads in hopes of earning a commission or "bounty" from the advertiser when its users perform the action specified by the advertiser, such as clicking on an ad or making a purchase. Such commission-based advertisements are generally provided through affiliate-ad brokering services or directly from the advertiser.

Affiliate program: An affiliate program offers an online advertiser the ability to embed tracking codes in its website advertisements in order to track the users who click on its ads and make purchases. The advertiser then shares these ads with website publishers (often through an affiliate-program brokering service such as Commission Junction), who post them on their websites. Once posted on the publishers' websites the affiliate earns a commission ("bounty") each time one of its users performs an action specified by the advertiser and tracked by the affiliate program software. These actions usually include clicking on an ad to visit the advertisers' websites or make purchases there. *See also* Affiliate.

Angel: An investor in early-stage companies who generally invests more money on more serious financial terms than a friend or family member, but less money (and on less stringent terms) than a venture capital firm.

ASP: Application service provider. An ASP provides access to software through the Internet, often for a monthly fee. Contrast this with traditional software providers who sell a program package that users install and host on their own computers for a one-time purchase price or recurring license fee.

Autoresponder: An e-mail utility that can be configured to automatically send a prewritten e-mail response to any e-mail received, often an acknowledgment of receipt or thank-you note.

B2B: Short for "business to business." Refers to a business activity that targets other businesses as its customers (instead of targeting consumers).

B2C: Short for "business to consumer." Refers to a business activity that targets retail consumers as its customers (instead of targeting other businesses).

Bandwidth: The amount of data that can be transmitted through a network connection. Dial-up connections offer low bandwidth and are consequently slow, while cable modems offer high bandwidth and can consequently transmit data more quickly.

Banner: A website advertisement that's usually rectangular in shape.

Beta test: A testing phase late in the development of a new software or Internet-based product where a number of users are invited to use the new application in exchange for their feedback on improvements needed before the product's release to the public.

Blacklist: In the Internet world, a blacklist is most often a list of e-mail senders who have been marked as spammers. Once posted on a blacklist, the e-mail sent from the offending domain servers will be refused delivery by other systems adhering to the blacklist.

Blog: Short for "weblog." A blog is a regularly updated commentary by an amateur or professional writer posted on the Web. Topics covered by "bloggers" include any subject imaginable, and the entries are usually formatted to post the most recent entry first.

Bounty: In e-business, a bounty is most often a commission-type payment given to a website publisher by an advertiser when the publisher's audience members perform an action specified by the advertiser, such as clicking on an advertisement or making a purchase.

Browser: The software program that you use to view the Internet. Usually Microsoft Internet Explorer, Mozilla, Firefox, Opera, or similar programs.

Business model: The process by which a business makes money. Simple examples include the retail sale of goods or services or publishing of content in order to attract advertising dollars.

Button: A website advertisement that's usually smaller than a banner.

Chargeback: The refund of a customer's purchase price (plus processing fees) for credit card purchases.

Competitive advantage: The advantage(s) that a person or business has relative to the competition. Examples include unique products, bigger marketing budgets, strong distribution, or experienced management. *See also* USP (unique selling proposition).

Content: An e-business word collectively encompassing information, pictures, video, music, commentary, or other human-generated creative works. Although an impersonal term, content is helpful shorthand when needing to distinguish a website's information or entertainment offerings from its technical services or merchandise products.

Conversion rate: The rate at which a website's visitors take an action desired by the business owners, such as converting themselves into paying customers by buying something. Usually expressed as a percentage, as in "14 percent of the 210,000 website visitors converted into newsletter subscribers, and 3.5 percent into purchasers."

Cookie: A small computer file that many websites place on the hard drives of users who visit their sites in order to track the user's activity and provide an improved user experience.

CPA: Certified public accountant in traditional business but "cost per action" in the context of e-business. This is a type of advertising where the advertiser only pays a small fee for every online user who takes a specified action, such as buying an item on the advertiser's website or filling out a form asking for more information. *See also* CPC.

CPC: "Cost per click." A type of CPA (cost-per-action) advertising where the advertiser pays a small fee (usually less than $1.00) to the website publisher or advertising service every time a website visitor "clicks" on a specified advertisement.

CPM: "Cost per thousand" (where M is from the Roman number for 1,000). CPM is the traditional way of charging for advertising, where an advertiser pays simply based on the number of people who view an advertisement. A banner ad on a website might command a $5 CPM, meaning that the advertiser will pay the website publisher $5 for every 1,000 impressions delivered (i.e., people who view it).

Craig's List: An extremely popular online network that offers free classified advertisements in dozens of major cities worldwide. The phenomenal growth of this service threatens traditional newspapers' advertising business and also offers a great resource for entrepreneurs to locate resources inexpensively.

Digital: Digital is a buzzword used to describe any information delivered via a computer-based system. The underlying structure of any information on a computer is composed of binary digital code (either ones or zeros, which are digits). Practically speaking, the process of measuring everything through tiny bits of computerized information is contrasted with analog media or information produced through more physical means, such as scraping a needle across a vinyl record to create sound or unwinding springs slowly to move clock hands to track time. The Industrial Age was based largely on analog technology; the Information Age's tools are digital.

Discount rate: This is not a discount of any sort from the entrepreneur's point of view, but a fee charged by a credit card processor for accepting a credit card payment. Usually 2 percent to 5 percent is automatically deducted from the monies received from the customer's payment.

Disintermediation: The removal of an intermediary. For example, e-business has disintermediated many middlemen because it can allow the consumer to deal directly with manufacturers, instead of having to purchase goods from intermediary distributors.

Domain: The domain is the central part of any website address before the ending suffix. It is also known as a URL, or universal resource locator. In the Web address InternetMillionaireSecrets.com, the "InternetMillionaireSecrets" part is the domain. Adding ".com" to it creates a complete domain name.

Domain forwarding: A setting on a domain name's Web servers that can automatically forward a website visitor from one domain to another. For example, if a surfer types in the domain "www.InternetMillionaireSecrets.net," she will automatically be forwarded to "www.InternetMillionaireSecrets.com."

Domain locking: "Locking" a domain means to configure a setting with the domain registrar service (from which you purchased your domain name) so that it is "locked" and cannot be transferred to another registrar or owner without confirmation from you.

Domain masking: Masking is when the same domain name that the user typed in still appears in the browser's address bar, even though the site being displayed is actually located at a different URL (usually because the domain has been forwarded). *See also* Domain forwarding.

Domain registrar: A service that licenses domain names and often also offers ancillary services, such as domain forwarding, website hosting, e-mail, etc.

Double opt-in: Most e-mail newsletters simply require a new subscriber to input her e-mail address into an online form in order to start receiving the publication. A double opt-in list (as the name implies) requires an additional confirmation from the new subscriber, such as response to a confirming e-mail sent out after the initial e-mail subscription request is received.

Drop shipper: A service that ships out products upon the receipt of orders from third parties. Practically speaking, this means an e-business owner may advertise and collect orders for a product she does not own or ever take possession of because the orders will be supplied and fulfilled by a drop shipper.

EIN: Employer Identification Number. A tax identification number that is assigned to businesses in the United States by the Internal Revenue Service (IRS). The business equivalent of a Social Security number.

Enterprise: A big business. Commonly seen in the phrase "enterprise software," meaning software designed to serve the needs of corporate customers.

Exit strategy: A strategy for concluding an activity and taking profits. Usually in reference to how a startup company hopes to sell itself or go public to cash in on successful growth.

Flash: A software program from Macromedia used for authoring web-based graphic experiences and websites. Often appears as animation or cartoons.

FTP: File transfer protocol. A method of transmitting files across the Internet. Often used to update website pages by "FTPing" files from the creator's computer to the computer server that hosts the website.

Fulfillment: The packaging and shipping of goods from a warehouse to a customer. In e-business, fulfillment is usually in response to customer orders generated by a website. It is often accompanied by related services such as returns processing, customer service, warehouse storage, and gift-wrapping.

GIF: Graphic image file. A type of image file format commonly used on websites because it limits the colors in an image to 256, which reduces the file size and allows for quick downloading. (GIF is pronounced with a hard "g," like the word *gift*, without the "t.")

Gross profit: A business's sales minus its cost of goods, but without deductions for personnel and overhead costs.

Guestbook: Web page software that allows visitors to a site to type in their names and comments to display to future visitors.

GUI: A graphical user interface (pronounced "gooey"). It is the design of the display that you see when using a computer, online or offline. It refers to the shapes, colors, and arrangement of the objects displayed on a PC screen. Most GUIs today use clickable icons to represent files and documents.

Hosting: A website is composed of files of documents and computer code. These files reside on a computer connected to the Internet, called a server, that is said to "host" them and thereby offer access to that website to online users.

HTML: Hypertext markup language. The basic computer language or code in which most Web pages have traditionally been written. In its simplest form, HTML consists of plain English (in English-speaking countries) augmented by "tags" that instruct the computer browser program how to display the text to a reader (by adding bolds, underlines, colors, and spacing). *See also* XML.

IAB: Internet Advertising Bureau. The IAB sets standards for advertising banners and buttons so that consistent sizes are used across the Web. These standards enable advertisers to more easily create and deploy the same advertisements across multiple sites.

IE: The Internet Explorer browser software program produced by Microsoft Corporation. It is the leading Internet browser.

Impression: A single viewing of a Web page or advertisement by a single person.

IPO: Initial public offering. When a privately owned company sells its stock to the public for the first time.

ISP: Internet service provider. A company that sells access to the Internet as a service. Well-known ISPs include Earthlink and AOL, as well as telephone companies selling digital subscriber line (DSL) service and cable companies selling cable modem connectivity.

Java: A computer language often used for Web-based applications because it is very good at transferring data across networks.

Javascript: A programming language most often used to add interactive features to website pages.

JPG: A file format for images originally developed by the Joint Photographic Expert Group (JPEG), it greatly compresses the file size of images commonly used on Web pages in order to offer graphics that are quickly downloaded.

Keyword: A word or phrase important to a subject or Web page relating to that subject. Keywords are used to help search engines identify the content on a page in order to index it appropriately so that Web searchers can locate it. Keywords are also used in pay-per-click advertising services, such as Google AdWords, that offer website owners the opportunity to bid on keywords relevant to their sites in order to have their advertisements displayed when a potential customer searches on or visits a website relating to the keyword.

Leverage: As with a physical lever, the concept of leverage in business is that disproportionately greater impact or reach can be obtained through use of a specialized tool or technique. In e-business, the inexpensive worldwide reach of the Internet offers greater leverage to a small business owner than was cost-effectively available to Industrial Age small businesses that were limited to local marketing.

LLC: Limited liability company. A type of company that combines the legal and tax structures of a traditional corporation with those of a partnership.

LLP: Limited liability partnership. A corporation-type business usually reserved for licensed professionals such as doctors and lawyers.

Merchant account: An account with a financial institution; needed for a business to accept credit card payments.

Meta tags: Descriptive words and phrases about a Web page's contents that a page owner can include in that page's code, but which remain invisible to the casual user. Traditionally used by search engines to categorize a website's content for indexing in the search engine's database.

Mobile: Wireless or cell phone related.

Monetize: To start making money from an idea, audience, service, or product.

Moore's Law: Most simply put, the concept that computing power will continue to advance rapidly and be accompanied by continued decreases in price. See also Chapter 2 of this book for more details on this "law" created by Gordon Moore, cofounder of Intel Corporation in 1965.

Nav bar: Short for "navigation bar." This is the line of menu options and icons that usually runs across the top of a Web page and/or browser. Clicking on it allows access to different functions and content offered by the program or website.

Navigation: A website's navigation is verbal shorthand for its arrangement of icons and menu choices that enable a user to "navigate" its services by pointing, clicking, and/or typing commands. *See also* Nav bar.

Newbie: A user new to the Internet.

Noozle: An e-mail newsletter.

Opt-in: Permission. When a user enters her e-mail address to request subscription to an e-mail newsletter or similar service, she is said to have "opted in."

Overhead: Common business term referring to the costs of running a business that are not directly related to production of its goods or services. Examples usually include office space and telephone lines.

Page rank: A number representing popularity and content relevance assigned by the Google search engine to each Web page in its database of websites. Page ranks generally start at zero for less popular pages and climb to 9 or 10 for the most trafficked sites on the Web.

Parse: Geek speak for breaking a subject or item down into small component pieces.

Payment gateway: See Payment processor.

Payment processor: A financial services company that specializes in obtaining authorizations for credit card purchases. An intermediary between the customer's credit card company and your e-business's merchant account, the payment processor receives requests for credit from the customer's transaction and verifies that the customer's credit card account approves such transactions so that your e-business's credit card merchant account can then receive the funds.

PDF: Portable Document Format. A document format (like Microsoft Word or WordPerfect) that allows you to create documents that preserve their formatting regardless of the user's system configuration and that cannot be readily modified by the recipient. Created by Adobe Systems, PDFs are widely used for e-books and other documents that are distributed online when their authors do not want them modified.

Phishing: A fraudulent activity characterized by sending out e-mails that pretend to be from a financial institution or other trusted account provider in hopes of tricking recipients into clicking on links in the e-mail or visiting fraudulent websites to disclose valuable personal information.

Pixel: The smallest unit of display on a computer monitor. Each very small dot of light and color on your PC screen is one pixel.

Podcasting: The digital distribution of recordings, usually via the Internet. To create a podcast, a radio show or similar audio program is recorded and then offered for distribution on a Web page so that interested listeners can download it to their PCs or mobile media players for listening later, after the show has concluded its normal broadcast time.

Pop-under: A type of online advertisement that appears on your computer screen when visiting a Web page but is not visible until you close the current browser window. The page you visit triggers the ad to appear but only "under" the active window. *See also* Pop-up.

Pop-up: An online advertisement that "pops up" when you visit a Web page; it creates a new browser window containing an ad.

Portal: A broad term generally used to mean a content-rich website that contains a lot of information or functionality. Yahoo is an example of a general portal, while some others are more focused, such as iVillage.com, a portal providing content targeting women.

Productize: To create a new salable product out of preexisting information, services, or goods.

Profit margin: The amount of profit remaining after all of a business's costs are deducted from its revenues. Usually expressed as a percentage.

QA: Quality assurance. The process of painstakingly reviewing all the information and links on a website to ensure that it is complete, fully functional, and accurate.

ROS: Run of site. An advertising term referring to advertisements that are placed randomly on any appropriate area of a website as opposed to being placed in a specific section like a sponsorship.

RSS: Really simple syndication. A software protocol that helps online publishers of information syndicate (i.e., automatically share) their information with other websites on an automated basis. RSS "feeds" often use XML to allow headlines or even whole articles of information to automatically appear on other websites once made available by the originating website.

Search engine: A huge database of information derived from World Wide Web pages that a search engine company (such as Yahoo or Google) compiles and makes available to users interested in finding information online. Users enter keywords to query the database for related results.

Search engine optimization: The process of adjusting a website page's content, links, and meta tags in an attempt to influence the site's ranking in the database of a search engine. Often focused on determining appropriate keywords relevant to the site's content and ensuring that they are distributed in the site's content so that the targeted search engine will increase the ranking of the site for that search term. *See also* Meta tags.

Serial entrepreneur: A business person who has started multiple new businesses.

Server: A computer connected to the Internet that is specially designed to host websites and allow speedy access to their files via the Internet.

Shopping cart: Software that mimics the use of a shopping cart in the real world by allowing online shoppers to choose and hold items for purchase and complete the purchase process by making payment.

Soft launch: The launch of a website (or other product) that is done without accompanying publicity. Usually a soft launch allows customer testing and feedback without media attention in case bugs are discovered by the users.

Sole proprietor: An unincorporated individual who owns her own business without partners.

Spam: Unwanted commercial e-mail. It should be noted that not all unsolicited e-mail is considered spam by users if the commercial offer is targeted enough to be interesting to the recipient.

Sponsored links: Commonly seen on search engines and increasingly on content websites, sponsored links are advertisements for websites that are usually automatically generated to appear depending on the search results or content of the page displayed. The links displayed are often determined based on keyword choices bid upon by advertisers.

Spyware: Pernicious software programs that "spy" on a user's computer activities in order to collect data on usage, passwords, account numbers, or similarly valuable information in order to share it with the spyware's distributor. Spyware is often installed accidentally by users when downloading other programs that do not disclose its inclusion in the download, or by clicking on links in unsolicited e-mails.

Streaming: See Streaming media.

Streaming media: Audio or video content that is delivered to a user's PC in approximately real time. It is contrasted with downloading media, wherein a user clicks to download a piece of media and must download the entire file and save it to the PC hard drive before it can be played.

UI: User interface. The PC screen presented to the user that offers a software program or website's services for selection, usually by pointing and clicking using a mouse or by typing text commands.

Upgrade: To purchase or install a newer, improved version of a product or service.

Upsell: To offer a customer additional products, services, or options in an attempt to increase her order. The classic upsell is the McDonald's cashier's well-known refrain, "Would you like fries with that?"

USP: Unique selling proposition. The characteristics that any entrepreneurial business should look for in its products or services that distinguish them from competitors'. Similar to a competitive advantage but specific to the company's product/service. *See also* Competitive advantage.

VC: Venture capitalist. A financial firm that specializes in investing money in early-stage companies, usually in exchange for equity and management participation.

Virtual community: An online user group that shares common interests and communicates primarily through Internet tools such as e-mail, message boards, or chat rooms, as opposed to real-world face-to-face interactions.

Webcast: The transmission of audio or video content through the Web. Similar to a closed-circuit radio or TV broadcast but only available to Internet users.

Webmaster: A job title referring to the person who is in charge of a website's technical operations.

WHOIS: An Internet service that lists the owners of domain names.

WYSIWYG: "What You See is What You Get." A term used to describe various graphic or website-building programs that show the results of a user's input exactly as they will appear once published on a website. This is in contrast to other programs that only display work in computer code or in truncated versions of the expected output.

XML: Extensible markup language. One of the languages used to create Web pages. It offers greater flexibility and power for development of interactive features than HTML, the original markup language of most website pages.

ACKNOWLEDGMENTS

The amount of personal investment it takes to write a book, especially a first book, is tremendous. For me, decades of personal experience and education accumulated until one day (with nudges from Bill O'Reilly, David Bach, and some other friends) I realized that I had something to say. The process of turning my opinions and experience into a nationally published volume has been a long one, but it has been a uniquely American journey.

Second only to my lovely wife, I would like to acknowledge the unique culture of the United States of America that allows an individual like me the freedom to pursue the life I want to live. Although it's rarely celebrated in our media and hardly taught in our schools, I remain convinced that entrepreneurship is the defining competitive advantage and achievement of American culture. Not everything our country does is appreciated by other countries or even by our own citizens, but it is in America that a boy like me from the inner city, with no connections or capital, has the best chance to rise to financial success, influence, and even fame based solely on his own hard work and talents. Our Founding Fathers and many generations of soldiers, immigrants, hardworking people, and especially entrepreneurs have built an unprecedented opportunity structure into our society that I am irrevocably appreciative of being allowed to participate in.

This book, as well as much of the progress in the rest of my life since I met her, would not have been possible without the continuing and loving support of my wonderful wife Katherine. Thank you so much for always being there for me and keeping the faith through our journey together. We still have many miles to go together and I look forward to sharing them all with you.

I also have to mention my lovely daughters—who, although not exactly contributors to the book-writing effort, shared their love in their own baby way, which has also been a tremendous inspiration.

Thank you to my mother, my father, and my brother for their ongoing support and encouragement of all my new initiatives since my earliest days. Mom—thanks especially for your time in reviewing the manuscript so many times, and to both my parents for continuing to lead by example in demonstrating how to reinvent yourself and succeed, both personally and professionally. To Carroll, Don, Agnes, and Norm, thank you for laying the foundations for this success.

Thank you Ti-ta and Shun-jong for adopting me and sharing your entrepreneurial spirit. As role models, you inspire me and my family daily.

Special thanks to Bill O'Reilly, whose initial recommendation that I examine business opportunities in publishing sparked the creative fire that led to this book. His team, including Makeda Wubneh, David Tabacoff, George Hiltzik, Jon Leibner, and Carole Cooper, are the best in the broadcasting business.

Thanks also to the many other smart, motivated, creative, and supportive friends and associates who have helped me along the way:

- ▲ Dr. Chuck Greenwood, whose friendship introduced me to self-help business books.

- ▲ David Bach, whose success continues to inspire me and whose much-appreciated assistance helped get me into publishing.

- ▲ Larry King—I enjoyed our work together and appreciate the confidence you placed in me.

- ▲ Glenn Beck—It was a pleasure working together to once again prove the potential of e-commerce.

I would also like to thank several great authors whose work helped inspire me to write this book:

- ▲ Robert Kiyosaki—Your books are amazing and your real-life success has served as a role model to me, both personally and professionally.

- ▲ Seth Godin—The practical information, concise writing style, and innovative marketing of your books have all inspired me.

- ▲ T. Harv Ecker—Listening to your tapes helped empower me to write this book.

- ▲ Thomas J. Stanley, Ph.D.—Thank you for your Millionaire Next Door series. It should be required reading in schools nationwide.

Thanks to Tammy Cabot for being so helpful in introducing me to the publishing world and to Kris Puopolo for encouraging my first efforts.

Thanks to Steve Mettler and Senad Prusac for your ongoing enthusiasm and support for my adventures. A shout out to my boys from East Quad—Ron Will, Ted Tsao, Alex Garbuio, and Paul Norton. Thanks for your friendship and the many, many good times together. To my brothers in arms, true fellow entrepreneurs, Eric Fedewa, Larry Lin, and Eric Young—thanks for the years of mutual encouragement.

Many thanks also to the hundreds of wonderful entrepreneurs who have shared their dreams with me over the years. I'm honored to have been included in helping you pursue your dreams.

Special thanks to the entrepreneurs who participated in The Liminal Institute surveys that form the underlying research for this book, and especially to those e-business success stories who participated in the one-on-one interviews. Thanks for sharing your stories with me. Together we are now able to inspire many more successes.

My deepest gratitude also goes out to my agents Shannon Miser-Marven and Jan Miller, who championed this book from its earliest drafts. Thank you both for validating and sharing my vision for a new kind of self-help business book and especially to Shannon for your continuing enthusiasm and support of my writing.

Last, thanks to Jacquie Flynn of AMACOM, who bought this manuscript and put so much into it; to Barry Richardson for his thoughtful and supportive editing; and to everyone else at AMACOM.

UPDATE TO PAPERBACK EDITION

Since it was first published in hardcover, *Internet Riches* has sold well beyond anyone's expectations. I'd again like to thank everyone at AMACOM for their important contributions to this ongoing (and still growing) worldwide sales success. This includes Kama Timbrell, Janet Rutledge, Andy Ambraziejus, Therese Mausser, Rosemary Carlough, Jim Bessent, Jenny Wesselman, Vera Sarkanj, and the many other fine folks at AMACOM.

And most of all, thanks to you, the readers worldwide, who have been so generous with your enthusiasm for my work.